Advance Praise for *Bernardin*

"Susan Blumberg-Kason has written a sparkling, revelatory biography of one of the twentieth-century's most influential women. This rich, deeply researched book brings to life the storied world of Bernardine Szold Fritz, celebrating her fierce independence and sharp wit as well as the movers and shakers she famously pulled into her orbit."

—Katie Gee Salisbury, author of *Not Your China Doll: The Wild and Shimmering Life of Anna May Wong*

"The incredible story of Bernadine Szold Fritz, who journeyed to Shanghai on a romantic whim and went on to swiftly conquer the world's most cosmopolitan city. Everyone who was anyone visiting Shanghai stopped in at Bernadine's, from Hollywood stars to European intellectuals and Mexican artists. Few other individuals did so much to forge Shanghai's unique east-west cultural mélange of the interwar years."

—Paul French, author of *New York Times* bestselling *Midnight in Peking: How the Murder of a Young Englishwoman Haunted the Last Days of Old China* and *City of Devils: A Shanghai Noir*

"*Bernardine's Shanghai Salon* offers an intriguing window into legendary 1930s Shanghai at its most glamorous and swashbuckling. The narrative revolves around a salon in the style of Gertrude Stein's and Alice Toklas's, which Bernadine had attended in Paris. Western celebrities including the likes of Charlie Chaplin and Claudette Colbert make appearances and mingle with iconic Shanghai characters such as Lin Yutang, Sir Victor Sassoon, Emily Hahn, Sinmay Zau, and Daisy Kwok. The author strikes the right note between historical substance and sometimes scandalous stories—just as the finest salon should!—bringing to life a who's who of globe-trotting literati during an unforgettable time."

—Claire Chao, author of *Remembering Shanghai: A Memoir of Socialites, Scholars and Scoundrels*

"This dazzling portrait of a woman in her prime and a cosmopolitan city at the very peak of its Golden Age deftly draws us into the heady whirl of 1930s Shanghai and the woman who connected it all. Bernardine Szold Fritz was a remarkable woman both ahead of her time and very much of it, and her Shanghai salon brought together some of the 20th century's major literary and cultural figures—yet until now, she has always been a minor character in histories of the period. With this book, Bernardine steps from behind the scenes, and takes her rightful place in the spotlight."

—Tina Kanagaratnam, co-founder of Historic Shanghai

"Susan Blumberg-Kason's picaresque narrative of 1930s Shanghai expatriate Bernardine Szold recalls a lost world of fascinating characters and histories. Populating Szold's Shanghai salon were an extraordinary mélange of Chinese and western intellectuals, journalists, artists, actors, dramatists, diplomats, restaurateurs, capitalists and idealists. Superb cameos of Charlie Chaplin, Anna May Wong, the Soong Sisters and many others will delight readers. This book is a must read for anyone interested in 1930s global literary and artistic society."

—Yunxiang Gao, author of *Arise, Africa! Roar, China!: Black and Chinese Citizens of the World in the Twentieth Century*

"*Bernardine's Shanghai Salon* is a heady, inspiring plunge into the creative hotbed that was 1930s Shanghai. With a tour guide's eye for captivating locations and a scholar's sensitivity to history and individual voice, Susan Blumberg-Kason honors the charismatic former journalist and Midwestern Jew who became a cultural doyenne in the 'Pearl of the Orient.'"

—Karen Fang, author of upcoming *Background Artist: The Life and Work of Tyrus Wong*

"Susan Blumberg-Kason's biography shines an important light upon Bernardine Szold Fritz, a mostly forgotten Jewish American writer who spent a lifetime bringing together the Chinese and Western arts communities. Drawing from a vast archive of letters, unpublished manuscripts, and news reports, Blumberg-Kason reveals the life of a woman who facilitated international friendships, organized galas, ballets, theatre productions, art exhibits, and poetry readings, all while navigating personal crises, medical dramas, and a not-quite-right fourth marriage. Kason delivers an intriguing tale of Old Shanghai, 1930s Chinese luminaries, cultural intrigue, and the power of friendship."

—Elizabeth Rynecki, author of *Chasing Portraits: A Great-Granddaughter's Quest for Her Lost Art Legacy*

"*Bernardine's Shanghai Salon* is a fascinating, deeply researched biography of the woman who made 1930s Shanghai a hub of modern culture. This book transports readers to a vibrant city where Bernardine befriends expatriates and local artists alike. Every notable figure who traveled through Shanghai seems to have visited her, from modernist painters to movie stars. After holding cultural events in her home, Bernardine established a theater company and produced large-scale performances of ballet and Peking

Opera. Behind her boundless curiosity and enthusiasm, though, Bernardine had complex relationships with her family. Blumberg-Kason handles Bernardine's difficult personal life with care in this vivid portrait."

—Sunny Stalter-Pace, author of *Imitation Artist: Gertrude Hoffmann's Life in Vaudeville and Dance*

BERNARDINE'S SHANGHAI SALON

THE STORY OF THE DOYENNE OF OLD CHINA

SUSAN BLUMBERG-KASON

Post Hill
PRESS

A POST HILL PRESS BOOK
ISBN: 979-8-88845-031-4
ISBN (eBook): 979-8-88845-032-1

Bernardine's Shanghai Salon:
The Story of the Doyenne of Old China
© 2023 by Susan Blumberg-Kason
All Rights Reserved

Cover design by Conroy Accord

Post Hill Press
New York • Nashville
posthillpress.com

Published in the United States of America
1 2 3 4 5 6 7 8 9 10

To Nancy Lilienthal and David Szanton

CONTENTS

AUTHOR'S NOTE

Chinese romanization, or the way of writing Chinese words in English, has undergone a number of different styles over the last century. This story takes place before the advent of pinyin, the romanization system developed in China in the 1950s and now used in many Chinese communities around the world and in academia. To stay true to the era of this story, I have mainly used the Wade-Giles style of romanization that was most prevalent when Bernardine lived in Shanghai. The Huangpu River in Shanghai today was spelled Whangpoo in Wade-Giles in the 1930s. And people like Zhang Xueliang, the Young Marshal, would have been known back then as Chang Hsueh-liang. I use yesteryear's Peking, Nanking, and Canton instead of today's Beijing, Nanjing, and Guangzhou.

Yet when I write about a Chinese province that is not quoted from a source in the 1930s, I use the pinyin for the ease of storytelling. So in describing a book by Rosa Rolanda, I include the Chekiang ham Rosa wrote about but write that Helene Chang's father had been governor of Zhejiang Province. Chekiang is the Wade-Giles while Zhejiang is the now-common pinyin.

To complicate matters, while Wade-Giles and pinyin are used for Mandarin, the Shanghai dialect employed a different romanization system. To stay true to the era and the place, I use the Shanghai dialect spelling for names like Sinmay Zau, because that is how he wrote his name, rather than Shao Xunmei in the pinyin.

There are other differences in romanization that don't align with Wade-Giles or pinyin. Bernardine's friends' clothing boutique is often spelled Tsingyi in memoirs and narratives, but the shop's advertisements list its name as Tsingi. I've chosen to use the spelling based on the shop's advertisements. I've also decided to use the way Bernardine spelled her friend Tong Ying's name in the correspondences from which I quote, even though her name was more commonly written as Tang Ying or Tang Ing.

In English, Emily Hahn went by the nickname Mickey. Other authors have referred to her as Mickey, but to avoid confusion I have chosen to keep her name as Emily, apart from when I quote from Bernardine's letters. I also refer to Bernardine's theater company as the International Arts Theatre, which is how they appeared in their own printed material. But the Shanghai press wrote "theater," so when I quote from newspaper articles, I stay true to their original spelling. The same issue occurs with the Chicago Little Theatre and other Little Theatres in the United States and in London. I use "theatre" except when quoting from an article that uses the American spelling of the word.

Finally, Bernardine never used a hyphen between her surnames, but other writers have sometimes stated her name as Szold-Fritz, which appears in a source or two in my bibliography. This stray hyphen seems to have first appeared in the credits of the 1981 film *Reds*.

PART I

BECOMING BERNARDINE

"I had something—something that appealed to distinguished people—I wasn't aware of it—I took it for granted that I would never know any except creative, exciting people— but I had an enthusiasm, a vitality, and even then I imagine, an exotic kind of personality that appealed to people."[1]
—Bernardine Szold Fritz

---

[1]   Sheila McHugh Simmons, "Bernardine Szold-Fritz" book proposal, page 10.

CHAPTER ONE

THE SLOW TRAIN TO
MANCHURIA, 1929

Bernardine Szold was certain she had just made the worst mistake of her life. Why had she ever agreed to marry Chester? She barely knew the man. Collapsed in her berth as her friends toasted her outside the train on the Gare du Nord platform, their champagne flutes raised high, Bernardine grumbled to herself, "My God, my God, whatever am I doing, whatever am I doing?"[2] The train started to pull away from the station, and Bernardine mustered up just enough energy to wave a final farewell to her friends.

"I might as well have been leaving for Mars for all I knew of what was ahead of me, and had I known, I should have clung still more tearfully to those who came to the train to see me off on the first lap of my journey," she recalled many years later. "It was all very comic, and very tragic."[3]

No sooner had the train left Paris did the conductor slide open the door of Bernardine's first-class compartment. There, next to the

---

[2]   Bernardine Szold Fritz, "The Trans-Siberian Railroad to Marriage in Dairen," unpublished manuscript, page 1.

[3]   Ibid.

conductor, stood a gaunt woman and two teary-eyed children. The conductor placed their suitcases against the wall while the children fell to their knees.

"Oh, lady, good, beautiful, wonderful lady," they cried. "Don't put us out, good lady, don't. Would you let us sleep outside on the floor, beautiful lady? We are going to see our daddy. Oh, please let us sleep in here. We will be good, lady."[4]

The conductor explained that this woman and her children had nowhere else to stay and that the second bed in Bernardine's compartment was the only free space on the train. They were headed to Moscow, where Bernardine would also disembark for a short layover before continuing on to northern China and her fiancé, Chester Fritz. The couple would wed in the Manchurian city of Dairen before heading south to Shanghai, Chester's home for the past decade, where they would start their married life together. Bernardine tried to protest when the children started to wail.

As much as Bernardine felt put out, she was a mother herself. Bernardine's daughter, Rosemary—from her first of four marriages—had turned fourteen earlier that year and was tucked away at a Swiss boarding school run by a protégé of Isadora Duncan. Many years had passed since Bernardine had lived full-time with her daughter; Rosemary's years of boarding began almost as soon as she was old enough to start school.

The conductor left, closing the door behind him. The woman and her two children remained silent but proceeded to stare at Bernardine as if she were the intruder, not them. Even as Bernardine resigned herself to sharing her berth with these three strangers, sleeping upright in a chair all night while they took the two beds, she still could not shake off the feeling that she had made a terrible mistake in leaving her expat life in Paris for the unknown in Shanghai, new husband and all. "For it was only then, for the first time that I realized how frightfully far off and utterly unknown China was."[5]

---

4   Bernardine Szold Fritz, "Across Siberia," unpublished manuscript, courtesy of Bernardine's family, page 3.
5   Ibid.

As the train crossed France into Germany—the woman and children silent but still staring—Bernardine tried to convince herself that she was indeed making the right choice in marrying Chester. She thought she'd found lasting love in her first two marriages, but both husbands turned out to be uninhibited philanderers. In her third marriage to New York literary agent Otto Liveright, she agreed to marriage only after Otto convinced her that love would naturally develop later. They ended up arguing more than they got along, so that marriage only lasted a couple years.

Despite these three failed marriages—all by the age of twenty-nine—Bernardine still felt optimistic about finding a devoted husband. She also believed it was more socially acceptable for her to marry than to live with a man without a legal commitment. Now that she was about to marry Chester, she certainly hoped she had found a lasting relationship.

Bernardine had briefly met Chester—a romantic adventurer just like herself—at a polo match in Shanghai just as she was concluding a fourteen-month, around-the-world trip with her friend, the American heiress Barbara Harrison. When the women returned to Paris after leaving China, Bernardine found dozens of telegrams from Chester, imploring her to return to Shanghai and marry him. He wrote that he had never met anyone like her and promised her a life of comfort and adventure.

At first, she didn't take Chester's telegrams seriously, figuring he was just acting on a silly infatuation. Yet as he continued to send them, Bernardine confided in her friends in Paris, including Barbara, the only person she knew who had met Chester. Her friends all advised Bernardine to give Chester a chance. Now thirty-three, she was almost twice the age she'd been when she first married and knew more of what she wanted in a marriage, they claimed. Also, she may regret not taking this opportunity to move to Shanghai, one of the most vibrant and cosmopolitan cities in the world. When Bernardine thought about the chance to live in Shanghai, coupled with Chester's professed love for her, she decided to accept his proposal.

A wildly successful investment broker from North Dakota, Chester had come out to Asia over a decade earlier and never left. He put work first, and in his free time, he was often found on a horse: showing off his prowess on the US polo team and Shanghai's fabled paper hunts, modeled after a fox hunt but without said fox. Chester wasn't shy when it came to women. But in 1929 when he turned thirty-seven, he hadn't connected with any in Shanghai on the same level as he had with Bernardine. He confided these feelings in a letter to his beloved aunt Kathrine back in North Dakota three weeks before his wedding, describing Bernardine as "a most fascinating lady, and I am in love with her not for what she has accomplished, or her family, but because of herself. As a conversationalist, she is brilliant, thus arises the mystery as to why she should be interested in me."[6]

***

Bernardine's de facto travel companions wore on her nerves until their train crossed Germany and entered Poland around midnight on the second day. In the town of Stettin, just inside the Polish border, Bernardine had just dozed off to sleep when the train stopped. A customs official walked through the cars, meticulously checking the passengers' papers. When he came to Bernardine, he flipped through her passport and found her Polish visa.

"This expired yesterday," he said, pointing to the visa.

Bernardine looked at him with wide eyes. Surely he had made a mistake. Before she had left Paris, she had gone to lengths to apply for visas not just for Poland but also the Soviet Union, Manchuria, Japan, and China—all good for the next three months. Chester had suggested they marry at the US consulate in Dairen, Manchuria, followed by a honeymoon across the Yellow Sea in Japan, so Bernardine thought she had boarded the train well prepared for her journey across and around Asia.

"Yesterday," he said again, waving her passport as if he couldn't wait to let go of it. "You need a new visa."

Dressed in her nightgown and robe, Bernardine could feel her blood pressure rise. She couldn't read the Polish writing on her visa

---

6   Chester Fritz and Dan Rylance, *Ever Westward to the Far East: The Story of Chester Fritz* (University of North Dakota: 1982), page 139.

and had no idea what it said. She thought back to Paris when she had applied for these visas. She was specifically told they would last through the summer until she finished her honeymoon and had settled into her new home in Shanghai.

Maybe the customs official would take pity on her because she was about to be married and her friends were waiting in Moscow to send her off. If she missed her train, she'd be a day late meeting those friends and her waiting fiancé in Manchuria. Surely the official wouldn't make her leave the train in the middle of the night. "I wept, I wailed, I stormed, I pleaded. I might as well have tried to bring tears from the Rock of Gibraltar."[7]

The Polish customs official shook his head and ordered her to stay the night in Stettin, instructing her to sort out her visa issues in the morning.

"I was thrown out of the train more or less in my nightgown," she recalled.[8]

And with that, the train carrying the mother and two young children rode off into the darkness toward Moscow, leaving Bernardine behind.

***

Bernardine spent the following day in Poland handing out bribes—five dollars here, ten there—while she raced from government department to government department, speaking in her best German. The Polish officials understood her since Stettin was just over the border from Germany. Bernardine didn't have a lot of money, but the government officials she visited refused to sign her visa paperwork without a kickback. Once she had completed the necessary forms and finally collected her coveted visa, Bernardine was able to board another train to Moscow that very evening. She had only lost one travel day and could still meet her friends in the Soviet capital.

---

[7]   Ibid., page 3.
[8]   Ibid., page 2.

Moscow in 1929 attracted people from all over the world interested in a new form of government: Communism. That included American artists like Maud Cabot, a friend of Bernardine's from Paris who exhibited with Jackson Pollock and Mark Rothko. The Soviet Union had only been in operation for seven years by the time Bernardine arrived in Moscow to catch the Trans-Siberian that would take her to China and Chester.

It seemed like ages since Bernardine had been able to confide in a friend or simply engage in a stimulating conversation. She hadn't spoken to anyone about her unexpected delay in Poland or the whimpering children in her compartment. So as soon as she arrived in Moscow, she unleashed two days' worth of stress and worry. She enjoyed a captive audience amongst her friends, including Cabot and her future husband, artist Patrick Morgan. They were a free-spirited group and felt the best way to lift Bernardine's mood would be to show her one of Moscow's most famous sights. "They suggested that we go straight out and stand in line to have a look at Lenin in his coffin."[9]

Bernardine loved her friends' sense of humor, and it seemed like the perfect antidote to the gravity of her stress from the train. Bernardine was also curious to see Lenin's tomb because she and Barbara Harrison had missed it on their way back to Paris half a year earlier. While the weather had been blustery cold back then, now on Bernardine's return in June, the temperatures were mild and more suitable for sightseeing. Plus, Lenin in death had been elevated to a cult of personality, something the world hadn't seen much of by the late 1920s.

But just as soon as the group headed out, the clouds opened and rain poured down so hard they found it difficult to continue on. So much for Lenin.

Her Moscow sojourn ended the next day, and Bernardine found herself back at a train station bidding another tearful goodbye to friends, reluctant to part from them. There were no more reasons to delay her journey to Manchuria. Chester was waiting, and she needed to face her trepidations head-on.

---

[9]   Bernardine Szold Fritz, "The Trans-Siberian Railroad to Marriage in Dairen," unpublished manuscript, page 4.

CHAPTER TWO

HONEYMOON IN MANCHURIA, 1929

Bernardine meant to stop for the night in Harbin on her train journey to Dairen, just before she would reunite with Chester. It had been two weeks since she had bid her friends goodbye in Paris, and she looked forward to resting up and showering in Harbin. But when her train arrived in this Manchurian city at seven o'clock in the morning instead of the planned four o'clock that afternoon, she checked in with the US consulate there and found a number of letters waiting for her.

They were all from Chester. As Bernardine opened and skimmed each, she sensed the urgency in his words. He couldn't wait to reunite with her and begin their married life together. "Please hurry," he wrote.[10] With such eager and impatient pleadings, Bernardine couldn't possibly stay a night in Harbin. All that worry about making the wrong decision suddenly seemed silly and juvenile. Yes, she would forego a restful evening in Harbin and instead board the night train to Dairen. She asked a staff member at the US consulate in Harbin to wire Chester of her new arrival time and promptly accepted early dinner plans with the

---

[10] Ibid.

US consul, a Mr. Hanson, at the Harbin Yacht Club. Bernardine's train would not leave until eleven that night.

The next morning, when her train reached the city of Changchun, Bernardine sent a wire to Chester on his boat, which he had had sailed up from Shanghai to Dairen, across the Yellow Sea from Korea. Chester had access to boats because he presided over the Yangtze Gorges Steamship Company. Bernardine telegrammed Chester: "Arriving tonights express instead of tomorrow meet me dearest Chester Fritz amconsulate Dairen arriving tonights express instead of tomorrow meet me dearest."

On the last leg of her trip, Bernardine felt numb with fatigue. She couldn't rest properly from Changchun to Dairen because the Japanese train did not contain sleeping berths.[11] Whatever sense of calmness she felt after reading Chester's letters in Harbin now seemed to vanish. Her exhaustion reignited her growing nerves about this rushed marriage. Thinking back to her first marriage—an elopement in her late teens to an Indiana lawyer that went against the wishes of her family because he wasn't Jewish—Bernardine couldn't remember feeling this unsure of herself even though she now knew she had also made a mistake back then. Before she knew it, there was no more time to wallow. Her train had reached Dairen.

"And then the train pulled in and I found myself shoving everybody aside in order to be the first one off."[12] Bernardine worried she wouldn't recognize Chester. They had only met that one time, more than half a year earlier. Perhaps he wouldn't recognize her? No, he would probably realize it was her from her turban and long earrings. No other foreign women on the train dressed the same, and Bernardine had not changed her fashion since she last saw Chester.

It was now or never. She stepped onto the platform, and there he was, as if he had known exactly where she would exit. They both

---

[11] By the time Bernardine arrived in Dairen, the city had undergone a number of different administrators, including Great Britain, China, and Russia. After the Russo-Japanese War in 1905, Russia ceded the southern part of Dairen to Japan, thus the Japanese train on which Bernardine traveled.

[12] Bernardine Szold Fritz, "The Trans-Siberian Railroad to Marriage in Dairen," unpublished manuscript, page 4.

stared at one another with no clue as to what came next, Chester with a tight-lipped smile and Bernardine speechless, perhaps for the first time in her life.

Chester quickly leaned in to kiss Bernardine on the lips, as if he worried she would change her mind. He then grabbed for her luggage like a nervous porter. On the platform, Bernardine heard a jumble of languages, which would have been various Chinese dialects, Japanese, Russian, English, and others from Europe. In one of his telegrams, Chester had billed Dairen as one of the most pristine seaside towns in Asia.[13] Now called Dalian, in the late 1920s, it was a city located in Manchuria, the massive region northeast of Beijing, between China and Soviet Siberia. Manchuria also bordered Mongolia to the west and the Korean peninsula to the east. The land hadn't always belonged to China, but when Bernardine and Chester married, it was run by a Chinese warlord named Chang Hsueh-liang, an opium addict also known as the Young Marshal, who would go on to unite the Nationalist and Communist sides to push back against Japanese aggression. He would also become a patron of Bernardine's Shanghai salon.

Bernardine found Chester thinner than when they'd met in Shanghai that winter. His three-piece wool suit seemed to hang off his body like a scarecrow's. As if Chester could read her mind, he volunteered that he'd been sick with malaria for a few weeks in the spring and was still regaining his strength. This was news to Bernardine, and it was worrisome, but in a way, she felt relieved they could rest up and she wouldn't be expected to jaunt around Dairen that day. She just wanted to take it easy after such an exhausting trip. After all, they had a wedding to attend to the following day.

Their ceremony at the US consulate was scheduled for ten-thirty in the morning, and to look at the pair, few would believe they were about to be married. The couple themselves were not entirely certain they were doing the right thing. Bernardine recalled, "We confessed to each other that each of us spent most of the night wondering whatever had

---

[13]   Ibid.

possessed us to decide to get married. Of something like that, fear and panic and doubts and doubts."

But Bernardine did not arrive in Dairen unprepared. Back in Paris, she had purchased a couture wedding dress created by the French designer Poiret. To celebrate his client's new home, Poiret designed Bernardine a red wedding dress, the color brides wear in China. Bernardine was already known in Paris for her clunky earrings and matching necklaces, along with the variety of turbans she wore over her long braids. She didn't have a conventional style and felt perfectly content wearing a red wedding gown.

Perhaps their trepidation was just pre-wedding nerves, for when Bernardine met up with Chester in the hotel's hallway that morning, both broke into wide grins. Chester took her hand, and they walked to the US consulate where a missionary would marry them in a short, nondenominational ceremony. Before leaving Shanghai, Chester had arranged the ceremony with the US consul, William Langdon, a career diplomat in the United States foreign service with a long tenure in East Asia.[14]

Even though a missionary was to marry them, the nondenominational service suited both Bernardine and Chester. Neither was religious. Her family was Jewish but celebrated Christmas in a secular way with a tree and large meal. What was more unusual was that her father had sent his four children to a Methodist Sunday school in Peoria, Illinois, when they were young, supposedly to keep them quiet. Bernardine and her siblings, Olga, Bud, and Aline, were all theatrically minded, so the Szold household was not a quiet one. Chester, on the other hand, was raised an only child by his aunt Kathrine and uncle Neil in North Dakota. In a letter to his aunt before his wedding, Chester told Kathrine that Bernardine wasn't Catholic, but he did not mention she was Jewish.

When Bernardine and Chester entered the US consulate on June 18, 1929, they found an introverted Christian missionary ready to officiate. In attendance were Consul Langdon, his wife, Laura, and

---

[14]   "William R. Langdon Dies at 71; Consul in the Far East until '51," *New York Times*, July 20, 1963, page 19.

their young daughters. Since their girls had never attended a wedding, Langdon and his wife allowed them to stay home from school that day to participate in the festivities.

It was the missionary's first time officiating a marriage ceremony, and it showed as he started to deliver his short homily. With Bernardine and Chester standing before him, the missionary's hands and knees began to shake uncontrollably, as if he were the nervous groom.[15] Bernardine tried not to stare but couldn't help notice his trembling. She found it endearing and was almost grateful for someone else's anxiety as it lessened her own nerves about leaving Paris, marrying Chester, and starting all over in Shanghai.

Chester had written short vows for them both, about six words each that omitted the promise of fidelity. Per tradition, Chester went first. Bernardine Szold then took Chester William Fritz to be her lawfully wedded husband. She would forever after be known as Bernardine Szold Fritz. Chester then presented Bernardine with a jade ring instead of a traditional diamond. The missionary pronounced Chester and Bernardine husband and wife. It would be her longest and final marriage. The same would not ring true for him.

Bernardine wasn't expecting any type of reception after their ceremony. It was her fourth wedding, after all. But Laura Langdon surprised them with a touch of Americana: strawberry shortcake and lemonade. The pièce de résistance was presented minutes later when Laura popped open a bottle of champagne. "We thought that the bride, coming from Paris, she might prefer champagne," Laura said, shyly.[16] The children looked on, aghast. They had never seen such luxury.

That evening, Bernardine and Chester entered the dining room at their hotel, "trying to look as if we'd been married ten years."[17] Arm in arm, the pair made an attractive couple. They weren't very tall—as she stood about five-two to his five-five—but together they possessed a com-

---

[15]   Ibid.

[16]   Bernardine Szold Fritz, "The Trans-Siberian Railroad to Marriage in Dairen," unpublished manuscript, page 5.

[17]   Ibid.

manding presence. Bernardine wore her light brown hair arranged in two braids wrapped around her head like a crown. As for Chester, he was clad in a three-piece suit. Like most men of that era, he dressed up at every opportunity, even on the polo field or at a paper hunt when he wore full equestrian gear—and his wedding night was no exception.

The Japanese maître d' intercepted the couple before they could get very far. He drew their attention and pointed to a spectacular cluster of lit candles in the middle of the restaurant. Perched upon a table was a giant frosted cake decorated with bows and topped with a pair of turtledoves. Bernardine had never seen such a large cake. It was to be the highlight of their evening.

For most brides in the 1920s, their wedding night would come with apprehension, excitement, and—in most cases—the unknown. But not for Bernardine. Sex wasn't new to her, and in fact, since her daughter Rosemary had turned fourteen earlier that year, it may have been something she would have discussed with Rosemary if the two had lived closer to one another. Bernardine hadn't seen Rosemary since before she and Barbara had set off on their travels a year and a half earlier. She and Chester had no plans for Rosemary to visit them in Shanghai.

As for Chester, he was also no stranger to intimate relationships. According to Bernardine, Chester had been one of the most sought-after expats in Shanghai. "A lot of women had tried to get him to marry them," she recalled.[18] As one would expect from newlyweds, Bernardine and Chester consummated their marriage. Yet as the couple were about to turn in for the night, Chester sheepishly faced Bernardine.

"Good night, dear. I'm heading off to sleep in the other room...."
What?

At first, Bernardine wasn't sure she had heard him correctly. Surely he would laugh, hitting his thigh with his hand, as if it were the biggest joke of the year. Maybe this was his idea of foreplay, although he hadn't behaved this way an hour earlier.

Yet Chester just stood there, as if he were about to take leave of a good friend after a long dinner. Did he really want to sleep in

---

[18] Lawrence Levin, Transcript from interview with Bernardine Szold Fritz, Tape 4, Side A, page 17.

another room? How could this be? After all the love letters he had cabled Bernardine, begging and pleading her to marry him and move to Shanghai, this was the last thing she expected.

"It's just that I'm not used to sleeping next to anyone," he finally said. "You know this is the first time I've been married and…"

Chester, in fact, had never slept next to another person overnight, even though he most certainly enjoyed the company of women. He just wasn't in the habit of sharing a bed with someone else for more than a couple hours.

"I'm also in training for the polo season and need my rest," he muttered.

The second reason seemed even more bizarre. As captain of the US polo team in Shanghai, Chester was claiming he couldn't hit a ball while riding a horse if he shared a bed with his wife.

A million thoughts raced through Bernardine's mind at once. Should she try to convince Chester to stay with her that night? She didn't want to be a nag, but it wasn't normal to sleep in separate bedrooms, especially on one's wedding night. On the other hand, it was true Chester had never been married before, so this was all new to him. But wasn't it time to start acting like a husband? Or should Bernardine just let it go for now and hope he would warm up once they settled in Shanghai?

When she looked into Chester's eyes, he no longer appeared a confident businessman, eager to make the next deal. Instead, with a slight pout of his lips, he appeared more like a timid child forced to hug an aging aunt. If Bernardine hadn't known better, she would have sworn Chester's eyes were tearing up. Just then, he turned away and headed out the door. Their discussion was over.

***

As in her other marriages, Bernardine faced strange and, quite frankly, selfish behavior from her new husband. This wasn't something she knew from her mother and father, Hermine and Jacob Szold, Hungarian Jews who immigrated to Peoria, Illinois, in 1890. Her parents enjoyed a loving relationship and modeled for their children a healthy partnership, so it took Bernardine by surprise when her first husband, lawyer Albert "Bert" Carver, instructed her to walk down their Gary, Indiana, street while he prowled behind her. Humiliated, she acquiesced until he eventually picked her up like a prostitute and took her home—the one they shared—so he could sleep with her. Bert also found other women and asked them to the movies while he ordered Bernardine to sit directly behind them in silence, as if she were a complete stranger and not his wife.

Bernardine was only eighteen when she eloped with Bert, but her younger cousin, David Lilienthal, saw her as a worldly woman even then. During part of his high school years, Lilienthal spent time with Bernardine's family after the Szolds had moved from Peoria to Gary, Indiana. Lilienthal was a young teenager and would sometimes join newlyweds Bernardine and Bert on outings to Chicago to hear Emma Goldman speak about birth control. He also admired Bernardine's acting at Chicago's Little Theatre and her work as a reporter at the *Chicago Evening Post*.[19] Bernardine, Lilienthal, and their siblings were all children of immigrants and excelled in their fields in ways their own children and grandchildren would not. Lilienthal would go on to become chairman of both the Tennessee Valley Authority and the Atomic Energy Commission.

A couple years after her divorce from Bert in 1917—and a grueling custody battle over Rosemary—Bernardine married the poet Hiram "Hi" Simons. She found Hi's idea of marriage even more extreme than Bert's. Soon after they settled into their converted garage on Huron Street in downtown Chicago, Hi asked Bernardine for an open marriage. Bernardine considered herself progressive, but an open marriage contrasted with her views of an equal partnership. It also went against her notions of romance and commitment.

Hi wouldn't let it drop and tried to explain that an open marriage would allow them each to reach their "nobility." To keep their marriage fair and equal, they would abide by certain rules and standards. For instance, if Bernardine wished to become intimate with someone else,

---

[19]   Bernardine had started acting in Chicago's Little Theatre during her marriage to Bert and while they lived in Gary, Indiana.

she would first discuss it with Hi and vice versa. They should never keep secrets from one another, Hi declared.

When Bernardine and Hi wed, the concept of marriage was undergoing great changes in the United States. With birth control, women could enter marriages without the main duty of reproducing. Some marriages in urban middle-class America became more egalitarian and served the needs of both partners. Couples had fewer children or none at all. Hi latched on to this concept but took it several notches further with his campaign to sleep with as many women as he wished. Bernardine and Hi knew socialist activists and journalists Louise Bryant and John Reed and certainly knew about their open marriage. Perhaps this was what inspired Hi.

Deep down, Bernardine knew what Hi was aiming for, so she continued to refuse him this wish. An open marriage was not the arrangement they had discussed when Hi proposed. Yet Hi wouldn't let it go. He kept insisting, and the more Bernardine disagreed, the more Hi would push it. Before long, Bernardine felt as if she needed to do whatever it took to make Hi stop nagging her. This issue had taken on a life of its own, and it was beginning to distress their marriage.

Maybe Hi was right. Maybe it could work. Bernardine did want to keep Hi happy. She loved him. No one she knew in Peoria or Gary had had an open marriage, but Chicago wasn't like those smaller cities. Bernardine felt caught between her Midwestern values and the easygoing lifestyle of her circle of friends in Chicago who spoke of "the free life of beauty."[20] The more she thought about it, the more she wondered if perhaps this was how relationships in the early 1920s had evolved.

Bernardine gave in and agreed to an open marriage.

She later recalled, "No matter what happened we'd see the other one through—it was to have been the proof of our nobility—we used words like that a lot in those days—the proof that we loved each other so much that we would understand and go through anything at all to help the other grow and enrich his life."[21]

---

[20] "Narrative of Bernardine Szold's Life," page 7.
[21] Ibid., page 8.

Not long into this new arrangement, Bernardine was out one afternoon and phoned Hi at home. Back then, people first dialed the operator who would connect the call. Since most people had party lines, which were non-private connections, the operator would often link the call into another conversation. When Bernardine was connected to Hi, he was already speaking to another woman. Before Bernardine could speak up, she realized Hi and this woman were engaged in a passionate discussion. They were so caught up in gushing over one another that neither realized someone else was on the line.

Bernardine felt like she'd just had the wind knocked out of her. This couldn't be happening, not with Hi. After all, he'd professed about informing one another about straying. Why hadn't he first told her about this other woman? That was the basic tenet of their terms.

Just then, Bernardine realized something else. The other woman's voice seemed very familiar.

It was her good friend.

How could Hi go behind her back like this, and how could her friend turn on her in the most awful way possible? Bernardine partly blamed herself for Hi sneaking around. "It made me feel I'd failed as a human being (Oh, my poor nobility!) as well as a wife—and so feeling it would have been adulterous otherwise, I left and went to New York."[22]

But it wasn't that simple, and Bernardine didn't, in fact, leave then. She stayed and tried to work on her marriage. When she attempted to talk to Hi about this affair, he turned on Bernardine and accused her of destroying his life, of ruining his chance for enhancing his nobility. She stayed with Hi long enough for him to grab a hammer from his workbench and throw it at her. At that point, she vowed to leave him, but again, she didn't divorce him right away. That happened in 1921, after two years of marriage. Bernardine was twenty-five years old.

As an independent woman who gave up the duties of motherhood for her journalism career and had the courage to leave an abusive first marriage, Bernardine continued to have a difficult time deciphering between love and manipulation. All along, Hi had tried to coerce her

---

[22]   Ibid., page 8.

into an open marriage, something she obviously felt wary of the many times he pestered her to agree. It's often difficult for women to say no when we've been conditioned since an early age to be nice and agreeable. Decades later, Bernardine still had a difficult time understanding that Hi may have promised one thing but was only after his own self-satisfaction and would blame her when he didn't get his way.

Even after her divorce from Hi, she wrote that he was "a very special person…and in time became one of the most important people in Chicago—in fact a gallery in the Art Institute was dedicated to him."[23]

Hi wrote a poem in September 1922, a year after their divorce, when he was at Union Pier, Michigan. Presumably he wrote it about her because she kept it for decades after they split up.

In "Maybe the Dead, too, Grieve,"[24] Hi wrote:

> If I should die before you come again—
> Who for love's sake alone, nor forgiveness',
> But your coming symbol I have attained
> Worthiness
> envisioned, unaspired to before you went—:
> if, I having died without the sacrament
> of your return, you afterward should stand
> upon a dune whose sand,
> in its eternal, nocturne, singing come and go,
> commingles ash—particular of me:
> then know
> the dead are not all blessed,
> do not all rest
> forever eased, ungrieving.

Bernardine had no reason to stay in Chicago after her divorce from Hi. In her first two marriages, she was swept off her feet. With her third

---

23   Ibid. I could find no proof of a gallery at the Art Institute in Hi's name, but the museum is large and it's possible there's a plaque somewhere in one of its many galleries.
24   Hiram Austin Simons, "Maybe the Dead, too, Grieve," unpublished poem, courtesy of Bernardine Szold Fritz's family, Union Pier, Michigan, September 17, 1922.

husband, Otto Liveright, she took longer to accept his proposal. When they met in New York after Bernardine moved there with Rosemary, Otto was in his early forties and for years had longed for a family. He appreciated Bernardine's love of literature and the arts. He asked Bernardine to marry him so he could take care of her and Rosemary. According to Otto, friendship counted more than love in the beginning; he felt that a solid friendship would lead to romantic love. Their sixteen-year age difference was not unusual, and because Bernardine wanted a father figure for Rosemary, she decided to give it a try.

Even though Otto wanted a family, Bernardine continued to send Rosemary to an Upstate New York boarding school where she'd been enrolled since mother and daughter had moved to Manhattan in 1921. Perhaps Bernardine kept Rosemary in boarding school after marrying Otto because she was used to that arrangement, or perhaps she thought it best for her daughter's education. Or maybe she felt too consumed with her newspaper job, bouncing around all five boroughs and beyond to report for the *New York Daily News*.

Otto joked with Bernardine about her absence from New York and their apartment when she needed to travel out of town for work. It could be that Otto implied something more serious behind his seemingly humorous words, yet without his side of the story, it's difficult to know for sure. In early 1922, he wrote her a pleading letter to return to New York. "Dee sweetheart dearest every day in every way I get lonesomer and lonesomer. It's 6:30 and I've finished dinner already. If you don't come home tomorrow I'm going to court and say that you are my wife and show the marriage certificate to the judge and ask him to get you back for me. It's all right during the day when I work, but here at home it's as dead and colorless as a Christian Science house of ill fame."[25]

Perhaps Otto was the first man Bernardine met who treated her decently and could give her a stable marriage. Maybe deep down, Bernardine felt she didn't deserve that, especially after her experiences with Bert and Hi, and she just couldn't handle a functional marriage.

[25] Letter from Otto Liveright to Bernardine, December 7, 1922, Beinecke Library, YCAL MSS 544 Box 3 f. Liveright, Otto, page 3.

By autumn 1924, Otto confessed to his friend, the writer Sherwood Anderson, that his marriage was all but over. "This will be a shock for you. Bernardine and I have separated irrevocably. We have been twisting and turning for a year trying to adjust ourselves to marriage and each other. No one has expected it but it was there just the same. We both have been miserable for several months. We are much better apart and I think we can be friends."[26] Bernardine moved to Paris with Rosemary the week her divorce from Otto was finalized the following May.

***

Now with Chester's odd bedtime behavior, Bernardine tried to make the most of their honeymoon. Dairen turned out to be a perfect place to transition into her new life in China, and Chester the perfect guide. He felt comfortable traveling all over China, because he had moved to Hong Kong, and later Shanghai, right out of college a decade before and had traveled to most of China's provinces in his twenties. He even wrote a book detailing these travels in the 1910s which spanned half a year.

The newlyweds spent a day at Hoshigara Beach, six miles from Dairen, and talked about everything but themselves. Bernardine looked almost girlish in her one-piece, sleeveless bathing suit that hit the top of her thighs. Chester photographed Bernardine on the beach with her hair in two long braids that fell to her waist. In another photo, she was sunbathing on a beach chair with her hair wrapped in a turban, Chester's shadow in the foreground. He appeared in some honeymoon photos at the beach dressed in a striped one-piece bathing suit fastened by a belt. His legs and arms were lean, pure muscle from his rigorous schedule of equestrian activities.

Chester taught Bernardine to count in Japanese because Japan had a concession in Dairen and one could hear the language everywhere. He took her, another day, to Port Arthur, now Lushun, a half hour

---

[26]   Letter from Otto Liveright to Sherwood Anderson, Newberry Library, Box 23, Folder 1179-1180, November 20, 1924, page 2.

from their hotel. They walked around the forts and visited a Japanese tea house at night. When they toured Chinese temples and parks, Bernardine appeared trim in a sleeveless sundress with an empire waist and pleated skirt that fell just below her knees while Chester dressed in a light suit, as was fitting for the season. Bernardine, with her wide smile and glittering eyes, always appeared happy in her photos, but apart from when he was on a horse, Chester did not smile for the camera.

It took them almost a week to feel used to the idea that they were married. Each seemed jittery and on the verge of panic. One day during their weeklong honeymoon, Chester turned to Bernardine and said, "Oh, I'm so happy to be married to you."

Still, they cut their honeymoon short and decided that, instead of continuing on to Japan, they would return to Shanghai. In his memoir, Chester insinuated that this change in plans was Bernardine's idea. "I had planned to go to Japan for a honeymoon, but Bernardine prefers to get settled in Shanghai as promptly as possible in order that we may get down to our regular routine as soon as possible."[27]

Whether that was the real reason for their abbreviated vacation, Bernardine didn't indicate one way or another in her papers. They both wrote about cutting their two-week trip down to one week, thereby foregoing Japan and heading to Shanghai earlier than planned.

The honeymoon was over.

---

[27] Chester Fritz, *Ever Westward to the Far East: The Story of Chester Fritz*, (University of North Dakota: 1982), page 140.

CHAPTER THREE

LOST IN SHANGHAI,
1929 TO EARLY 1930s

W hen Bernardine and Barbara visited Shanghai in late 1928, the winter weather had been cool and damp. But on her return with Chester, Bernardine found Shanghai to be hot and sticky. The air smelled more putrid than in the winter, as the odors from the night soil collectors' carts permeated the streets. The sewage system was still primitive, and rain drained slowly, leaving other liquids—cooking oil, urine, and dirty dishwater—to pool along the curbs and sidewalks.

The city was divided into three sections. The International Settlement was uniquely governed by fourteen countries then and dominated by Great Britain; the French Concession was governed by France; and the Chinese City remained in the hands of the Chinese government. Chinese residents lived in both concessions in traditional Shanghai lane neighborhoods.

The foreign concessions were located on lucrative pieces of real estate and were punctuated by a mélange of architectural styles, including Tudor mansions, Art Deco villas, Spanish Revival apartment buildings, Neoclassical banks, and a hodgepodge of Chinese and Western designs. These areas hardly looked like China. Several countries established extraterritorial treaties with China, meaning that their citizens were subject only to their laws, not the laws of China.

Besides Chinese, British, and American residents, Shanghai boasted sizeable communities of White Russians who had fled the Bolshevik Revolution, as well as Russian Jews, Baghdadi Jews, Japanese, Germans, Parsees, and Sikhs. Many Sikhs served as policemen in the International Settlement, typical in many British colonies back then.

Bernardine wasn't put off by the sights and smells of Shanghai. To her, they were as integral to the city as were its glamorous charms. She longed to revisit Chinese temples and gardens, with ancient buildings reflected in shallow pools adorned with deep green lily pads and soft pink lotus flowers. Although the International Settlement and French Concession were defined by colonial architecture, the Chinese City was still populated by traditional Shanghai shikumen or homes along narrow lanes with small front courtyards. Bernardine wanted to see it all.

Besides the architecture, Shanghai was—and still is—a mixture of East and West. Back in 1929, one could just as easily find a Viennese pastry shop as one could find a Chinese teahouse. Coffee shops and dance halls were as plentiful as Shanghai tailor shops and barbers. Overseas Chinese from Australia had built department stores that stocked the latest fashions, both Eastern and Western. Newspaper offices—publishing in over a dozen languages—were found all over the city, as were cinemas showing the latest Hollywood flick and Chinese smash hit. There was enough to see in Shanghai to keep one occupied for years.

Early on in their marriage, Bernardine and Chester would take strolls in the evening. These twilight walks became Bernardine's favorite time of the day. London plane trees lined the narrow streets of the French Concession, forming a shady canopy so days and evenings felt both cool and shadowy while walking under the leafy overhang. On these walks, Bernardine sometimes thought she was back in Paris. But then something would suddenly bring her mind back to Shanghai, like a shirtless man, as thin as a beanstalk, tottering along the curb with a bamboo pole balanced across his shoulder, two baskets of produce, eggs, or other sundries hanging from both ends of the pole.

Sometimes Chester would creep suspiciously close to a Shanghai lane home, peering into windows, even trespassing into the small court-yard as if to gather top secret information like the different dishes on a dining table. Bernardine squirmed in fear that they would get caught invading a family's privacy, while at the same time delighting in these new adventures one could seemingly only experience in a place like Shanghai.[28]

Bernardine also ventured out on her own to discover more of Shanghai when Chester was at work, but she couldn't help feeling extra lonely when she saw other women out for lunch or tea. As the weeks and then months elapsed, Bernardine found herself alone not just during the day but also most evenings.

Chester was indeed busy at work. In January 1929, he and two part-ners founded the investment firm Swan, Culbertson and Fritz, which would go on to become the most lucrative financial outfit in East Asia, holding seats on the New York Cotton Exchange and the Chicago Board of Trade. It also traded in the stock exchanges of London, Manila, and Winnipeg. Chester was a precious metals expert, special-izing in silver, which came in handy because China was on the silver standard back then and used the Mexican silver dollar as its currency.

The firm's office was housed in the new Sassoon House, a brick, Art Deco skyscraper topped with a copper pyramid roof built on the Bund, or the riverfront promenade along the Whangpoo River. The location was so prestigious that advertisements for Swan, Culbertson and Fritz simply listed their address as Sassoon House, Shanghai.

Victor Sassoon, or Sir V as Bernardine often referred to him, built Sassoon House in 1929 and was a Baghdadi Jewish real estate tycoon who was born in Italy with British citizenship. He was part of a fam-ily that had made its fortune in India and China, which involved opi-um-pushing in the mid-1800s. Victor arrived in Shanghai in the 1920s and became known for his themed parties and his monocle.

Located in Sassoon House was the Cathay Hotel, and Victor lived in the penthouse apartment just under the base of the hotel's pyramid

---

[28] Bernardine Szold Fritz, "Why Britannia Rules the Wave," unpublished manuscript, page 3.

roof. Rechristened the Peace Hotel in the 1950s, it still keeps watch over the Bund, and its current entrance faces out to the beginning of Nanking Road, one of the most lavish shopping streets in the city—then and now.

Chester did work long hours, but he also found plenty of free time outside the office. Yet he chose to spend that time with his horses. After their awkward reunion in Dairen and frustrating wedding night, Bernardine had grown to appreciate Chester and his enthusiasm for Shanghai. She wished for more evenings strolling along the plane trees, but at the same time, she also wanted to respect Chester's work obligations and his passion for polo and the paper hunt.

Wanting to accommodate Chester's interests, Bernardine started visiting the stables and polo fields to learn to ride. She had previously been terrified of horses but figured she would need to overcome this fear if she were going to ever see her husband. Bernardine tried her best, yet she never passed the beginner's level and could never keep up with Chester. Instead, she marched beside him in parades when he won at polo or a paper chase cup, yet felt awkward as a trophy wife. It wasn't easy for expat wives in Shanghai to forge their own identities, but she felt certain there must be something in the city she could enjoy and claim for herself.

If she couldn't find that soon, she was afraid she'd start to tear her hair out.

***

Early on in their marriage, the couple lived in Chester's apartment at 9 Route Kaufmann in the French Concession, but they hoped to find a new home that would be their own and not a vestige of his bachelor years. After a few months, they rented a grand home owned by a couple named Webb who were leaving the city for a year and offered it while they were away. Bernardine was delighted by this proposition after having met Americans and British who shipped whole interiors from their home countries to Shanghai so they could feel "at home." Bernardine had overheard these expats describing Chinese furnishings as "simply awful."[29] But the Webb home was something else. Bernardine fondly remembered the first time they invited her over. "The Webbs' house was huge, and the furniture, rugs, objects d'art, and lovely brocades and tapestries were all Chinese, fine Chinese things, beautifully arranged. I already saw myself walking from the large hall into the long drawing room, mistress of all I surveyed."[30]

Those months in the Webb house would shape the way Bernardine would set up her own home after she and Chester moved into a new apartment complex in the heart of the French Concession called the Cloisters. Before construction of the Cloisters was completed in 1930, the days dragged and Bernardine wondered how she would ever acclimate. Shanghai itself could seem so lonely. The lanes of the French Concession and International Settlement felt shadowy and oppressive and the reflections of the neon signs that illuminated shop windows made her feel small and invisible. She enjoyed venturing into the Chinese City with Chester when he was available, yet death, disease, and desperation were all around and weighed heavily on her mind.

The expats she met through Chester only seem interested in drinking gin and tonics at the Columbia Country Club, playing cards, and gossiping about scandals of the day. Bernardine wasn't averse to chatter, but she wasn't familiar enough with the foreign enclaves to understand whom these women were referring. It bothered her that she wasn't her usual outgoing self as she'd been in Chicago, New York, and Paris where she'd always flocked to the liveliest conversations and would inevitably find herself in the center of it all.

Without a core group of friends in Shanghai, Bernardine turned to the friends she had left back in Paris, namely Barbara Harrison, writer Glenway Wescott, art curator Monroe Wheeler, and photographer George Platt Lynes.

After Bernardine divorced her first husband, Bert Carver, in 1917 at the age of twenty-one, she found a reporting job at the *Chicago Evening Post* to support Rosemary and herself. It was during these years that she also attended a writers' group at Tower Bookshop and met Glenway

---

[29]   Bernardine Szold Fritz, "The Baroness de Pidol," unpublished manuscript, page 1.
[30]   Ibid.

Wescott, an undergraduate at the University of Chicago. Within a few years of their friendship, Glenway would become an author in the same class as Hemingway and would unwittingly serve as Hemingway's inspiration for Robert Prentiss in *The Sun Also Rises*.[31] Before Glenway reached great fame and around the time he met Bernardine, he began what would become a lifelong relationship with an advertising executive named Monroe Wheeler, another Midwesterner who went on to curate the Museum of Modern Art in New York. Bernardine seemed to follow the couple after each of her three divorces in the 1910s and 1920s, from Chicago to New York to Paris. It was in Paris where they met Barbara Harrison.

Barbara was independently wealthy thanks to her mother's inheritance as an heiress to the Southern Pacific Railroad, but this had come at a cost. When Barbara was only a year old, her mother had been killed in an automobile accident at the young age of twenty-seven. It was 1905, and Barbara and her four-year-old sister remained in the care of their father, Francis Burton Harrison, a US congressman from New York at the time. Francis would go on to marry five more times, including an eighteen-year-old college student when he was forty-five. When they divorced a decade later, he married her sister. He's best known for writing the bill that criminalized narcotics. Before his bill, heroin was an ingredient in many cough syrups and cocaine was still used in Coca-Cola.

For obvious reasons, Barbara had a complicated relationship with her father, but she didn't need to rely on him thanks to the inheritance from her mother. Barbara owned homes in and outside Paris, as well as Villefranche on the French Riviera, and generously opened these homes to her close friends, including Bernardine. In Villefranche, Barbara, Bernardine, Glenway, and Monroe met Jean Cocteau and W. Somerset Maugham.

Like many people back then, Monroe was a consummate letter writer. He often wrote home to Evanston, Illinois, and in one letter to his father from a trip to the South of France, Monroe penned:

[31] Jerry Rosco, *Glenway Wescott Personally: A Biography*, (Madison, The University of Wisconsin Press: 2002), page 40.

"Bernardine gave us tea, Jean Cocteau a luncheon, etc. At this time of the year, at the height of the season, Paris is so ravishing, so beautiful, and so costly, that it is ruinously expensive for us to stay for more than a week. I now know that the best way to enjoy Paris is to go, as we did, for a few days, concentrate all one's social activities in a few days, and then come back to the lovely serenity of Aix or Villefranche. We brought Bernardine Szold back with us to Aix for a few days so that Glenway could read some of *The Grandmothers* to her."[32] *The Grandmothers* was published in 1927 and would win Glenway the prestigious Harper Novel Prize. Glenway had sailed to New York with Monroe earlier that year to meet with his editors at Harper and had already built up a reputation as a writer to watch with his 1924 novel, *The Apple of the Eye*. In New York, the pair booked a room at the Hotel Lafayette in Greenwich Village. It was there that a nineteen-year-old named George Platt Lynes and his beau, Wesson Bull, called on Glenway and Monroe, explaining that they were sent by Bernardine.[33] Monroe was out on an errand, so Glenway met the pair.

Bernardine had indeed met George in Paris at Gertrude Stein and Alice Toklas' salon in the fall of 1925 when Glenway and Monroe were out of town. When she learned George would be heading to New York in early 1927, and Glenway and Monroe would be there, too, she wrote to George and suggested he look up her dear friends.

George and Wesson were close to Lincoln Kirstein, the future cofounder of the New York City Ballet. Wesson's full name was Harcourt Wesson Bull, the grandson of the cofounder of gun manu-facturer Smith & Wesson. The day after the young couple met Glenway, George returned to the hotel without Wesson and found Monroe alone. It was love at first sight.

George thought Monroe resembled Egyptian prince Ikhnaton with his dark, deep-set eyes and full lips. Not yet twenty, George felt

---

[32] Anatole Pohorilenko and James Crump, *When We Were Three: The Travel Albums of George Platt Lynes, Monroe Wheeler, and Glenway Wescott, 1925–1935*, (Santa Fe, Arena Editions: 1998), page 43.

[33] Jerry Rosco, *Glenway Wescott Personally: A Biography*. Madison: The University of Wisconsin Press, 2002, page 38.

perfectly comfortable professing his love for Monroe and living confidently as a gay man, which was unusual in an era when homosexual conduct was reviled and criminalized. This differed from Monroe's more cautious perspective. Although Monroe had been in a romantic relationship with Glenway for the better part of a decade at that point, he worked hard to present a straight identity in his public life.

Monroe and Glenway returned to Europe soon after they met George. They reunited with Bernardine and Rosemary in Villefranche, where mother and daughter were staying with Barbara Harrison. A year later, in 1928, George sailed back to Europe and met up with Glenway and Monroe. Bernardine had already embarked on her travels throughout Europe and Asia with Barbara, the trip during which they met Chester Fritz in Shanghai.

When the women returned to Paris at the end of that year, Glenway, Monroe, and George were inseparable. Monroe wrote to his father about Bernardine around this time: "Christmas was spent with Bernardine Szold, returned on Monday from her trip around the world with Barbara Harrison. Barbara has given Bernardine her two houses here for the winter, servants and all—a beautiful house on Vaugirard, and a country place at Rambouillet, outside Paris."[34]

Although George was romantically involved mostly with Monroe, he and Glenway were also intimate at one point. The men would live and travel together as a threesome for the next decade. And with Monroe's encouragement, George would go on to become one of the most influential American photographers of the twentieth century and a predecessor of Robert Mapplethorpe. He worked for *Vogue* and *Town & Country* and served as Alfred Kinsey's dedicated photographer when the famed scientist researched homosexuality in the 1940s.

In Shanghai, Bernardine often wrote to Barbara, Glenway, Monroe, and George, relaying her concerns about making friends and finding a purpose there. All that time alone seemed very disorienting, and she

---

[34]   Anatole Pohorilenko and James Crump, *When We Were Three: The Travel Albums of George Platt Lynes, Monroe Wheeler, and Glenway Wescott, 1925–1935*, (Santa Fe, Arena Editions: 1998), page 64.

understood very little of Chester's business and what he did all day. "I don't know what any of it is all about but Chester says if we live carefully a bit for seven years, we can retire forever and play about, going anywhere we like, so we'll have a caravan, yes, and all of us go to lovely and silly places and be as happy and good for each other," she wrote to Barbara soon after she arrived in Shanghai.[35]

Monroe encouraged her to find a passion in Shanghai and to make a difference. "I am certain that it is only a matter of time before your own interest in one or another of the arts or in human nature will become intense enough so that you will determine to become profoundly authoritative about it, and when that time comes no day will be long enough in Shanghai or Chicago or Gary or Timbuktu."[36]

When it came down to it, Chester wasn't the attentive husband he had proclaimed to be when he proposed. And as Bernardine got to know Chester better, she started to learn his true nature, which brought out the worst of her insecurities and jealousies.

She wrote extensively about her concerns in a letter to Barbara: "I wonder if I would have dared marry Chester, had I known before what I know now. I mean about his simply fantastic career with women. I've only been getting it inch by inch—it comes out at unexpected moments, and I am beginning to have the technique now for starting him off. But with my terrific obsession about this one thing—and my highly developed fears—and utter lack in any human security as it is— sustained only by the proof of Glenway's many years of faithfulness, which after all is quite another thing—I wonder, I wonder. I suppose when one is love infected, one does anyway, fears or not—and probably if I had known all I know now, it might have had the added effect of making me all the more passionate about him—or about having him for my own—I dunno."[37]

---

[35] Letter from Bernardine to Barbara Harrison, September 28, 1929, Beinecke Library, YCAL MSS 134 Box 126 f. 1969, page 100.

[36] Letter from Monroe Wheeler to Bernardine, February 7, 1933, Beinecke Library, YCAL MSS 134 Box 105 f. 1597, page 68.

[37] Letter from Bernardine to Barbara Harrison, August 1, 1929, Beinecke Library, YCAL MSS 134 Box 126 f. 1968, page 96.

Yet when Chester socialized with other couples, he expected Bernardine by his side, armed with a smile. He lightened up when they went out in groups, as if he were the most charming man in Shanghai. Bernardine tried not to hold Chester's moods against him and was just grateful to go out.

***

During that first year in Shanghai, Bernardine started to miss Rosemary and think about her more than she had when she lived in Paris. Bernardine truly believed boarding school was the best place for her daughter to receive an education, just as she had when Rosemary boarded in suburban Chicago and Upstate New York. She just wasn't used to being so far from her daughter. When Bernardine was still in Paris and Rosemary in Switzerland, the two often saw each other on vacations and other school breaks. Bernardine thought back to sunny beach days when she brought Rosemary to Barbara Harrison's house in Villefranche, where they socialized with Jean Cocteau and Pablo Picasso. Now that Bernardine was half a world away from Rosemary and no longer had the distractions from a writing career, she yearned to see her daughter again.

When Bernardine first met Chester on her trip with Barbara Harrison, she saw no reason to divulge details of her private life. There didn't seem to be much point to delving into personal details with someone she figured she would never see again. Yet after returning to Paris and finding that Chester had bombarded her with wedding proposals, Bernardine needed Chester to know that Rosemary would figure into their lives, even if she never lived with them in Shanghai. Communication back in 1929 made that easy in a sense because Bernardine would not witness Chester's reaction when she broke the news in a telegram. Many women and men do not feel comfortable telling a love interest they have children from a previous relationship, lest they scare away their new partner. Bernardine was certainly aware of the possibility that Chester could break off their engagement when he learned of Rosemary.

She decided to send her marriage acceptance before she informed Chester she had a teenage daughter at a Swiss boarding school. That telegram would come later, well after he had received her acceptance. To Bernardine's relief, Chester acknowledged the news about Rosemary in another telegram, but it was difficult for Bernardine to gauge how he felt. Chester expressed neither disappointment nor eagerness to meet Rosemary at some point. Instead, his response about Rosemary was more of an aside in his message to Bernardine, pining for the day the two of them would reunite in China. Chester didn't seem to feel deceived, and as far as he was concerned, Rosemary was Bernardine's problem and he was completely removed from that.

It wasn't as if Chester hadn't known Bernardine had been married before. He did claim in his memoir, however, that Bernardine had not been forthcoming about all three of her ex-husbands. His biographer wrote, "Bernardine had been married three times prior to her marriage to Fritz, a fact he claims he did not learn until later."[38]

It's difficult to know if Chester told his biographer the truth. According to the biographer, Bernardine's third husband was named Herman Liveright, the son of publisher Horace Liveright. Bernardine's third husband was in fact Otto Liveright, Horace's older brother. The biographer also noted that Bernardine and Chester lived at 9 Rue [sic] Kaufmann during their entire time together in Shanghai. That's also not true, as Bernardine and Chester mostly lived together at the Cloisters, which was at 62 Route de Boissezon.[39] The 9 Route Kaufmann apartment was Chester's before their wedding and for a few months after.

In any case, the two never discussed how Rosemary would fit into their lives, both when they corresponded by telegram and after Bernardine moved to China. Chester just assumed Rosemary would stay at school in Switzerland and during breaks would visit Bernardine's parents in Florida, where they had moved to invest in real estate. Bernardine, on the other hand, felt certain Rosemary could win over

---

[38] Chester Fritz and Dan Rylance, *Ever Westward to the Far East: The Story of Chester Fritz* (University of North Dakota: 1982), page 140.

[39] Ibid., pages 141–142.

Chester. The only question was when the two would actually meet. At this point, Bernardine hadn't seen Rosemary in almost three years.

Bernardine poured out her conflicted feelings to Barbara in a letter from autumn 1929, just months after she'd moved to Shanghai. "I so often am with the most woeful contrition and guilt about her. But I never mention her, nor does Chester, and we are both waiting I suppose to see how things work out. It seems a pity not to have her in the big house—and yet the schools aren't much good, and it isn't good for children to stay out here."[40]

It didn't help that Bernardine's mother, Hermine, encouraged Bernardine to keep Rosemary at her school in Switzerland "for a few years" until she could find a way to bring her to Shanghai.[41] Hermine figured Rosemary would be perfectly content away from Bernardine as long as she had food, shelter, and friends her own age. But Hermine had no experience raising a child from afar. She and Jacob had provided all four of their children with a comfortable home, no matter their financial situation, and the Szold children certainly gained plenty of confidence to pursue the fields of their choice. As it turned out, all four went into the entertainment industry. Bud became an actor on stage and in film, a stage director, and a Hollywood acting coach; Aline acted and ran Little Theatres in St. Paul, Omaha, and Dallas; and Olga was an actress on Chicago radio shows.

Her mother's blessings aside, Bernardine worried about the future, and rightly so. Chester had written a kind letter to Rosemary soon after he and Bernardine married, but it would be the first and last he would ever send to her. Bernardine would soon come to sense that Chester didn't want to talk about Rosemary at all, and she expressed these concerns to Barbara. "But the years fly and Rosemary will grow away from me so. I'm so afraid if she sees none of us she may lose our influence,

---

[40] Letter from Bernardine to Barbara Harrison, September 28, 1929, Beinecke Library, YCAL MSS 134 Box 126 f. 1969, page 98.
[41] "Narrative of Bernardine Szold's Life," courtesy of David Szanton, page 30.

bad as it is I prefer it to any other, I don't mean as it is, I mean bad as some people might call it, I prefer it to any other."[42]

Bernardine's saving grace came in the form of Chester's business partners. The Swans and Culbertsons loved children and could not understand why Rosemary had not yet visited Shanghai, let alone moved there. Once Chester started to feel pressure from his partners, he agreed to bring fifteen-year-old Rosemary for a visit the summer of 1930. Bernardine and Chester had been married for a full year by then.

---

[42]   Letter from Bernardine to Barbara Harrison, September 28, 1929, Beinecke Library, YCAL MSS 134 Box 126 f. 1969, page 98.

PART II

MADAME SALON

"The cicadas are wild this summer, screaming like sirens, yesterday at Kiangwan we watched a typhoon cloud gather, fly over us and burst just beyond it was the most thrilling and aweful [*sic*] experience I've ever had. I haven't been as happy in years as I was watching it."[43]
—Bernardine Szold Fritz

[43] Letter from Bernardine to Barbara Harrison, undated, Beinecke Library, YCAL MSS 134 Box 126 f. 1971, page 24.

CHAPTER FOUR

ROSEMARY SAILS TO SHANGHAI, 1930

ctress Claudette Colbert was visiting Bernardine the week Rosemary's ship docked on the Whangpoo River. Colbert was a new Hollywood star in 1930 and would go on to win the Oscar for best actress five years later in *It Happened One Night*. Also visiting Bernardine at that time were the newlyweds Rosa Rolanda and Miguel Covarrubias, she an American dancer and he a Mexican illustrator. They were contemporaries and friends of the painters Frida Kahlo and Diego Rivera and had become close to Bernardine during her New York years.

Bernardine still struggled to meet new people in Shanghai, but many friends and acquaintances from the US passed through the city and she felt more than happy to entertain them and show them around. Now, she would have a whole summer with Rosemary and looked forward to making up for their time apart.

Since the age of ten, Rosemary had traveled back and forth between Switzerland and Paris when Bernardine was living in France and across the Atlantic to the United States to visit her grandparents Hermine and Jacob in Daytona Beach, Florida. But Bernardine knew the trip to Shanghai would take longer and that the city seemed to attract people from all walks of life, including some who were up to no good. She decided to inquire with the French consulate in Shanghai to find a chaperone for Rosemary. As luck would have it, the consulate learned that the head of a French bank, a Monsieur de Bries, would be traveling from Paris to Shanghai early that summer and arranged for him to look after Rosemary. "He has four children and is a most reputable and respectable man—even for a Frenchman!" Bernardine wrote to Barbara and Glenway.[44]

The issue of money would become a larger issue. Even before she married Chester, money had always been a sore spot for Bernardine. She presented herself as much more well off than the reality, which was usually close to destitute. Before she married Chester, she confessed to Glenway: "I like people thinking I've lots of money, I know you and I have known of course that I haven't but other people think I have and I relished that deception…I am sure I am the only married three times young woman extant, who hasn't enough money to pay her carfares."[45]

Bernardine was able to pay her carfare but was otherwise completely dependent on Chester in Shanghai. Money was another thing she and Chester did not speak of when they first met. Some months later, when Chester wrote to his aunt Kathrine about his new bride, he explained, "Bernardine is not in love with me for what I am. The question of finances has never been discussed, in fact she does not have any idea as to how I am fixed in that regard."[46]

Chester insisted on providing Bernardine with a weekly allowance and felt it his duty as a husband, but he balked at paying for Rosemary's tuition or living expenses in Switzerland. The rationale behind not wanting to support Rosemary is common, even today, as many men are not eager to raise another man's children. Bernardine was hardly the only woman to deal with such a conundrum.

---

[44] Letter from Bernardine to Barbara Harrison and Glenway Wescott, undated, Beinecke Library, YCAL MSS 134 Box 126 f. 1968, page 59.

[45] Letter from Bernardine to Glenway Wescott, Beneicke Library, YCAL MSS 134 Box 103 f. 1572, page 13.

[46] Chester Fritz and Dan Rylance, *Ever Westward to the Far East: The Story of Chester Fritz* (University of North Dakota: 1982), page 140.

So to avoid asking Chester for extra money to pay for Rosemary's expenses in Shanghai, Bernardine quietly put aside part of her allowance month by month. Also in preparation for Rosemary's trip, Bernardine asked Barbara to arrange all the necessary travel documents and to help Rosemary pack appropriately for a hot and humid Shanghai summer. This wasn't the first time Bernardine had relied on friends to help Rosemary. Barbara had become almost a de facto parent even when Bernardine still lived in Paris. Since Bernardine was not in Paris to pay for Rosemary's ticket to Shanghai, Barbara also fronted the money for that. To Bernardine's relief, Chester insisted on paying Barbara back immediately.

Even with the logistics arranged for Rosemary's trip, Bernardine still lost sleep at night, wondering if her daughter and husband would ever get along. Without any close friends in Shanghai, she continued to spill her feelings in letters to Barbara and Glenway, especially when it came to her trepidation about that summer. "I am so happy about it; I do so want to get it over with too, the meeting between Chester and Rosemary, and next year will be even harder than this; it will be good for her too to have us established as her home, in her mind when she returns to school—and it will be good for me, for I have been in terror about this summer, with Chester so terribly busy that I'd probably be quite quite quite desolate...."[47]

On the day of Rosemary's arrival, Claudette Colbert and her husband, the director Norman Foster, stayed back at their hotel while Rosa Rolanda accompanied Bernardine to the Bund and stood with her on the pier. "We both almost fell into the water waiting for the boat to dock," Bernardine recalled of that day.[48] The last time she had seen her daughter, Rosemary was as skinny as a gangling fawn and stood just short of five-foot-two Bernardine.

---

[47]   Letter from Bernardine to Barbara Harrison and Glenway Wescott, undated, Beinecke Library, YCAL MSS 134 Box 126 f. 1968, page 59.

[48]   Letter from Bernardine to Barbara Harrison, June 23, 1930, Beinecke Library, YCAL MSS 134 Box 126 f. 1968, page 56.

But when Bernardine spotted her disembarking the little boat that took her from her ship to the pier, she saw that fifteen-year-old Rosemary had transformed into the woman who would become a stand-in for Katharine Hepburn the following decade. Tall and lithe, Rosemary seemed to float to her mother on the pier. She now stood a head above Bernardine.

Back at the Cloisters, Bernardine and Rosa made sure Rosemary bathed. They also supervised her clothing selection. Bernardine knew that Chester would only take to Rosemary if he had a positive first impression of her. If that failed, Bernardine worried Chester would never allow Rosemary to return. So in preparation for this critical first introduction, Bernardine gathered up the Covarrubiases, Claudette Colbert, and Norman Foster and put her plan into action.

Claudette Colbert and Norman Foster had sailed to Shanghai with the Covarrubiases and arrived at Bernardine and Chester's place from their hotel that evening just as Chester returned home from work. Introductions were rushed because they had dinner reservations and tickets to a Chinese theater. When Rosemary stole away to freshen up before they left the apartment, Chester claimed he could never dance with Rosemary because she was too tall.[49]

Height disparities aside, the group looked striking as they left 62 Route de Boissezon. There was Rosemary, tall and willowy, next to Bernardine with her hair tied in Swiss braids. Rosa Rolanda with her pert smile and sparkling brown eyes walked hand in hand with her portly husband, Miguel Covarrubias. Rosa was a year older than Bernardine and nine years older than Miguel, but her dancer's gait gave her the appearance of the youngest adult in the group. Chester's salt-and-pepper hair and slight underbite gave him the look of a stern elder. Claudette Colbert's smile rivaled that of Rosa's—both women were born for the stage. Colbert's husband Norman Foster, on the other hand, appeared a bit sinister with a beguiling smirk that made him seem not quite trustworthy.

---

[49] Ibid.

Foster was a Hollywood actor and director, and these two roles would come to a crossroads when he directed the 1936 noir, *I Cover Chinatown*. It was his first directing job and his last acting role. The film cast no Chinese actors even though it was set in San Francisco's Chinatown. Foster would go on to direct three Charlie Chan movies after this trip to Shanghai, all starring Sidney Toler, the second Hollywood actor to play Chan in yellowface. Foster also directed the Mr. Moto movies, starring Hungarian Jewish Peter Lorre as a Japanese secret agent. Foster turned what he had seen in Shanghai into a commodity of exotic fantasy and worked on these movies after he and Claudette Colbert divorced in 1935, five years following their trip to Shanghai.

Dinner that evening was lively and animated. Most of the adults quizzed Rosemary about her journey across the Mediterranean Sea and Indian Ocean. It was a long trip for a fifteen-year-old. Throughout their meal, Bernardine noticed Chester watching Rosemary like a silent hawk as she tried shark fin soup and crispy duck for the first time. Rosemary seemed to enjoy these delicacies and the attention from Bernardine and her friends. Yet Chester directed his conversations to everyone but Rosemary.

Chester's silence toward Rosemary continued, whether at home or in public. At the end of the week, Bernardine gave a garden party for Rosemary and included Claudette, Norman, Rosa, and Miguel again. Yet when Rosemary attempted to start a conversation with Chester, he would not reply or make eye contact.

Chester's behavior did not escape Bernardine for a minute. "I know he is watching her every move, to see if she is going to monopolize me altogether, or if her being here will change me toward him, etc. She's very sweet about it, and knows just what to do, which is a blessing, because in a strange way, Chester is jealous. No it isn't just that— he's terribly sensitive, in the way fearfully lonely and rather frightened people are, about the first person they've ever found and declared their own."[50]

Bernardine probably convinced herself that Rosemary was not bothered by Chester's treatment, but it's doubtful a fifteen-year-old would have the skills or experience to psychoanalyze someone who ignored her very being. Bernardine herself tried to understand why Chester behaved this way. From what she had pieced together about his background, she concluded that Chester could not accept Rosemary as family because of his own troubled history.

When Chester was ten years old, he and his parents lived in Fargo, North Dakota. His father, Charles Fritz, worked a seasonal job as a thresher and one day operated a defective machine without knowing it was problematic. Charles fell into the machine and suffered a terrible accident. "The bottoms of his feet were chewed up and they saved one foot," Chester recalled. "When the news came, I was in school and my mother came to the school house in Fargo and took me on the train out to Casselton to see my father. And I remember going down the hallway, I saw in a jar my father's foot."[51]

During Charles' recovery, he built a makeshift vehicle by tying two bicycles together side by side. This contraption allowed him to get around, but what Chester remembered most was that his father never earned much after the accident. "He just drifted along like a wandering minstrel. He liked to go and tell people 'how.' You see there were no media at that time, and he would ride from one part of Fargo to another and 'sound off' like a medieval minstrel."[52] Instead of feeling grateful that his father found a way to become mobile again, Chester grew embarrassed and bore no compassion toward Charles and his disability. At the same time, Chester's mother, Anne, grew tired of supporting the family through a variety of clerical jobs.

Two years later, his mother took off in the dead of winter one day and never returned. She left no note and didn't say a word to

---

[50] Ibid.
[51] Chester Fritz and Dan Rylance, *Ever Westward to the Far East: The Story of Chester Fritz*, (University of North Dakota: 1982), page 4.
[52] Ibid.

twelve-year-old Chester or Charles before she disappeared. Anne's younger sister, Kathrine, brought Chester south to Lidgerwood, North Dakota, where she and her husband took him in. "We never heard from her again," Chester recollected. "Some people thought a catastrophe had befallen her. After some time, my aunt and others decided that she had died, perhaps in an accident."[53]

Yet he had no interest in trying to find out what happened to his mother. "No useful purpose can now be served by further research in this regard. As Shakespeare once said, 'What's done is done,' and we should not introduce a Sherlock Holmes review."[54] Bernardine may not have agreed with suppressing such traumatic memories, but she deeply empathized with the pain Chester had been carrying for decades. She figured he didn't even know he was behaving badly toward Rosemary.

To make up for Chester's emotional absence, Bernardine tried to keep Rosemary occupied each day during her stay that summer. She watched over Rosemary like a cautious mother, refusing to allow her to swim at the Cercle Sportif Français, or French Club, because she had heard the pool water caused itchy eyes. Instead, Bernardine brought Rosemary to swim at the Columbia Club. The two played tennis and badminton in their backyard during the early morning or late afternoon. They also went to the polo fields to watch Chester putter around on his ponies. The oppressive midday heat of Shanghai summers made it impossible for Rosemary to remain outside all day, or so Bernardine worried. It wasn't like visiting Hermine and Jacob Szold in Florida, where one could stay at the beach from morning until night.

Bernardine kept Rosemary within her reach because most of the expat teens in Shanghai had left for the summer, and she worried Rosemary could fall in with the wrong crowd of young adults and the many "bad men" and foreigners in Shanghai who drank too much.[55]

Rosemary enjoyed ballet and the theater, so Bernardine enrolled her in dance classes that summer. It wasn't difficult to find a studio as

---

53 Ibid., page 7.
54 Ibid.
55 Letter from Bernardine to Barbara Harrison, June 23, 1930, Beinecke Library, YCAL MSS 134 Box 126 f. 1968, page 57.

many Russian dancers had fled to Shanghai after the 1917 Bolshevik Revolution. Rosemary revealed to Bernardine and Rosa her plans to go into acting, but both women warned it was a difficult profession and did not want Rosemary to assume she would succeed right away. Discouraged, Rosemary murmured she may as well just marry as soon as possible. "I seem to be too tall for anything else!" she remarked.[56]

Still, if Rosemary had remained in Shanghai beyond the summer, she could have experienced an education much more unique than what her boarding school provided. For the same reasons Bernardine had been attracted to Shanghai, Rosemary could have benefited from a cosmopolitanism not easily found in other countries. But Bernardine never tried to keep Rosemary in Shanghai after that summer.

Instead, Bernardine pondered her daughter's future and what lay beyond her education in Switzerland. At some point, Rosemary switched boarding schools and enrolled at King-Smith Studio School in Washington, DC. This may have started after her summer in Shanghai as she sailed from China to San Francisco, but there's a chance she visited Hermine and Jacob in Florida before returning to Switzerland. Bernardine also considered Carnegie Tech in Pittsburgh for Rosemary as it was renowned for its acting program, but then had second thoughts because she knew no one in Pittsburgh. She also wondered if Rosemary could study under Max Reinhardt, a director who ran a Little Theatre in Berlin and would remain there until 1933 when Hitler came into power.[57] Rosemary would end up studying at Carnegie Tech for a short time some years later, and it turned out very fortuitous that she didn't end up in Berlin as the child of a Jewish mother.

By the end of the summer, Bernardine confessed in a letter to Barbara that she actually looked forward to the day Rosemary was to leave Shanghai. Tensions with Chester had become unbearable. It wasn't anything Rosemary said or did to Chester, but her very presence just made him uneasy. "I'm all worn out, and look forward to her departure as a kind of liberation, although together, we have had a divine summer, she and I, became so much better friends than we ever

---

[56]   Ibid.
[57]   Ibid.

were, and she has quite enchanted and pleased me; in numerable ways. Chester is such an infant that you simply can't do a thing with him, in a situation like this. If one says anything at all, he is hurt to the heart, and his eyes fill with tears and he looks like an abused baby—he doesn't understand anything about himself, and he jolly well doesn't want to, with the uncanny cleverness of his type."[58]

The summer of 1930 would be the only time Rosemary would visit her mother in Shanghai. Chester obviously did not campaign to bring her back, but Bernardine also convinced herself it would be easier to deal with Chester if he did not have to share her attention. Yet Bernardine could not entirely blame Chester for her separation from Rosemary. It had begun more than a dozen years earlier, just after she divorced Bert Carver, when Rosemary was only two years old. Bernardine may have boasted about becoming close friends with her daughter in Shanghai, but Rosemary did not need another friend. She needed a mother.

This separation from her parents would forever scar Rosemary and her descendants. While Rosemary did end up acting in London and New York as well as serving as Katharine Hepburn's double in Hollywood, no amount of professional success would make up for being abandoned by both parents.

---

[58] Letter from Bernardine to Barbara Harrison, undated 1930, Beinecke Library, YCAL MSS 134 Box 126 f. 1968, page 48.

CHAPTER FIVE

TRAVELING WITH LIN
YUTANG, 1931–1933

Bernardine sometimes joined Chester for dinner when he entertained business associates. He mostly included her to impress his clients or colleagues with her mesmerizing stories of interviewing Sarah Bernhardt when she was a journalist in Chicago during her first marriage or rooming with the designer Elsa Schiaparelli when she first arrived in Paris after the end of her third. But she found very little in common with Chester's business colleagues as their interests revolved around investments and making millions. Bernardine had to force herself to stay awake during these conversations and often wished Chester hadn't asked her to come along. Yet Chester did have a few friends in other professions that interested Bernardine. Professor Hu Shih was one.

While Bernardine was still a teenager in Gary, Indiana, Hu Shih was enrolled as an undergraduate at Cornell University. When Bernardine lived in Chicago as a young mother, Hu Shih studied education under John Dewey at Columbia University in New York. Long before Bernardine arrived in Shanghai, Hu Shih had made a name for himself as one of China's most recognized intellectuals. Some years before he was named Chinese ambassador to the US and nominated for a Nobel Prize in Literature, Hu Shih had moved from Peking to his hometown of Shanghai around the time Bernardine married Chester.

When Bernardine met Hu Shih, she especially enjoyed listening to his ideas of how best to modernize China. Since China had become a republic two decades earlier, warlords contended for land and Japan had recently taken Chinese territory and threatened to grab more. This turmoil impaired China's progress, but Hu Shih held out hope for his country and that hope rested in education. He also promoted a written vernacular style of Chinese rather than the classical way of writing the language that differed greatly from the spoken. Hu Shih believed that literacy would be easier to achieve if one wrote the same way one spoke.

Bernardine proudly called Hu Shih her first Chinese friend in Shanghai.

"It was conceded that he was the foremost scholar in China, a truly rare, kind, generous man," Bernardine recalled. "Face was one of the things Dr. Hu Shih always said was the worst menace of China, though we actually have the same thing in the West, though by another name, perhaps. You always had to 'save face.'"[59]

She understood how a custom like face—doing whatever it takes to not offend someone else—could keep a culture down. Going back to her childhood in Peoria, she had once overheard adult relatives speak of an uncle's secret first marriage and relayed this news to some cousins, only to be beaten and grounded by her mother and aunt. Her uncle had indeed been married before, but for some reason, the family wanted to pretend it hadn't happened.

Hu Shih found in Bernardine a loyal friend who shared his views on justice. Years later after he had served as the Chinese ambassador to the US from the late 1930s to early '40s and the president of Peking University, he and his wife escaped to Taiwan. They also kept a home in New York, and from there, he wrote to Bernardine: "You are just

---

[59] Bernardine Szold Fritz, "Shanghai," unpublished manuscript courtesy of her family, page 3.

the same Bernardine who gets 'disturbed' on behalf of your unjustly victimized friends! More power to you!"[60]

Through Hu Shih, Bernardine met the writers Lin Yutang and his wife, Liao Tsui-feng, whom everyone in their set called Hong. Like Hu Shih, Lin Yutang was also educated in the United States, at Harvard, as well as in France and Germany before returning to China in the early 1920s, around the time Bernardine moved to New York after her divorce from Hi.

When Yutang learned that Bernardine had written for the *Chicago Evening Post* and the *New York Daily News* in her twenties, he asked her to join his staff at the *China Critic*, a weekly magazine he founded to cover the arts, politics, and society. It was just one of hundreds of publications in China at that time, a period when literature flourished, especially in Shanghai where much of the educated class could read and speak English. For this reason, Yutang decided to publish the *China Critic* in English. In fact, Yutang and his wife, Hong, each wrote many more books in English than they did in Chinese.

Hu Shih was also on staff for the *China Critic*, so Bernardine has credited him with introducing her to the Lins. But she also wrote that her actress friend, Tong Ying, connected her with Yutang after learning that Bernardine had been a journalist in the US and France. No matter the actual connection, Bernardine became the only foreign staff member at the *China Critic* in the early 1930s.

At the magazine, she wrote under the pen name Cassandra. She wasn't concerned about hiding her identity or protecting Chester's business interests but chose to write under a pen name because it seemed to be the custom of the time. In New York, she had sometimes written under the name Julia Harpman. From Paris, she used the names Argus and Genet.

Bernardine participated in editorial meetings at the *China Critic* every Friday night to plan out the next week's content. Dinner was

---

[60] Letter from Hu Shih to Bernardine, October 20, 1949, Beinecke Library, YCAL MSS 544 Box 4 f. Shih Hu, page 4.

often served at these meetings, and she felt no hurry to return home to Chester. More often than not, Chester would still be out when the editorial meetings finished. He continued to work late at his office in Sassoon House. Bernardine usually found herself at home with many servants—servants Chester had insisted on hiring—rather than sitting across the dinner table from her husband.

When Bernardine was still in her early twenties, she had taught at the Workers' Institute located in the Chicago stockyards. After this experience, she had never felt comfortable with hiring servants. Yet Chester explained that both foreigners and locals hired workers to take care of every household chore, even things like shopping and mailing letters. The wealth disparity in China was so much worse than in the United States at that time. Years later, Bernardine recalled, "We got very spoiled in a certain way, and also it was dreadful that none of us realized what a cruel life it was for the poor people. I think every decent person rejoiced when the system changed."[61] That change was Communism, which became the system of government in China starting in 1949.

When Bernardine married Chester, he insisted she stay home and not worry about working. He did encourage her writing career and her work at the *China Critic*, probably because Bernardine had told Chester that she was a novelist when they first met. It's true that she had been working on a novel, titled *The Dove*, but it was never completed or published and seems to be lost today. In any case, Chester must have fancied himself a patron of the arts by supporting his writer wife.

For the first time since she had moved to Shanghai, Bernardine no longer worried about finances. Her paid job at the *China Critic* allowed her to pay for Rosemary's tuition and living expenses without having to set aside most of her weekly allowance. Yutang and the other editors at the *China Critic* assigned Bernardine to write columns about women and foreigners in Shanghai. She enjoyed working with an editorial team and

---

61   Lawrence Levin, Transcription of interviews with Bernardine Szold Fritz, September 25, 1976, courtesy of Bernardine Szold Fritz's family, Tape 4, Side A.

appreciated the diligence of the *Critic*'s Chinese copyeditors, especially when it came to her writing. "I punctuate more or less the way I talk," she admitted.[62]

It wasn't until Bernardine met Hu Shih and Lin Yutang that she began to feel there was more to Shanghai than the small-mindedness of the expat communities. Yutang was especially warm and welcoming, unfailingly jovial with an expansive smile. One of the first things Bernardine noticed about Yutang was his cigar. He was rarely seen without one, often waving it in the air as he spoke, paced the room, or rocked back and forth on his heels. Yutang was known for his round glasses and wore a traditional Chinese changshan, or long robe, usually of a brown hue that matched his cigar.

Thanks to Yutang and Hong, Bernardine's social calendar soon became just as full as Chester's. The Lins often invited Bernardine to join them at dinners with friends. Hong spoke fluent English and wrote books about Chinese gastronomy. The two women became confidants and would correspond for decades after they all left Shanghai.

Bernardine delighted in spending time after work with the Lins and their friends, jotting down their conversations as soon as she returned home. She compiled vignettes about Shanghai and hoped to turn them into a book. Still in communication with her third husband, Otto Liveright, the only ex-husband she kept in touch with while she lived in Shanghai, she hoped he could use his literary agent powers to turn these Shanghai stories into a nonfiction narrative, separate from *The Dove*.

She also submitted essays to Harold Ross and Jane Grant, friends from her New York years and founders of the *New Yorker*. She had written a couple of letters from Paris that the *New Yorker* published in 1925—the year it was founded—but there didn't seem to be as much interest about the goings-on in 1930s Shanghai. Bernardine didn't receive another acceptance from the *New Yorker* until 1969, when she wrote about seeing Isadora Duncan shortly before the dancer's untimely death in 1927 when her scarf caught in her car tire and strangled her.[63]

---

[62] Ibid.

[63] Letter from Bernardine to Glenway Wescott, March 30, 1936, Beinecke Library, YCAL MSS 134 Box 103 f. 1574, page 31.

In her unpublished Shanghai vignettes, the person Bernardine wrote about the most was Yutang. She typed multiple drafts of articles dedicated to Yutang and mentioned in letters to friends and family that she hoped to publish an essay about him to further introduce him to people in the United States. It doesn't appear that any of these articles was ever published, but they all show how Yutang influenced Bernardine's views of Shanghai and China.

At one particular evening gathering, Yutang exhaled with relief after several in their group had left after dinner. The gathering had whittled down to five, including Bernardine. She figured Chester was still toiling away at the office.

"Now," exclaimed Yutang, "we can be ourselves." He lay down on a sofa, propping his head on a few cushions and his feet on the opposite armrest. Grinning ear to ear, Yutang never appeared without a smile. "Now, let us argue comfortably."[64] Yet Yutang would not remain on the couch for long. As he made his point, he would suddenly spring up, pace the room like a sleuth in deep thought, and return to the sofa while others took their turns in the discussion. Bernardine loved this about Yutang. He was so easygoing that it was difficult to argue with him.

Her thoughts drifted back to Gertrude Stein's Paris salon, where guests debated the most esoteric as well as the most pressing issues of the day. Sometimes, when Bernardine and novelist Zelda Fitzgerald tried to join in on a discussion, Gertrude Stein put up her hand and called on another participant, usually a man. Bernardine joked that Stein didn't like Zelda and her because they wore lipstick, but in any case, the discussions in Paris were never as carefree as they were with Yutang in Shanghai.

Through Yutang, Bernardine met many of Shanghai's most intriguing personalities. She soon started to invite them to her apartment at 62 Route de Boissezon, in part to show she wasn't one of those people who attended gatherings at other people's homes but never reciprocated. More than that, she found great joy in connecting people and

---

[64] Bernardine Szold, "Lin Yu Tang. Shanghai 1935," unpublished manuscript courtesy of her family, page 3.

had Chester's approval to start a salon. Their two front rooms with ample seating and standing areas served as the perfect space for such gatherings.

Yet it wasn't by happenstance that Bernardine hosted a salon. Although salons originated in France around the time of the French Revolution, Jewish women started their own salons in Berlin shortly thereafter. As it would turn out, Jewish women from France, Germany, and what was then Austria-Hungary disproportionately ran salons from the 1790s until just before World War II. These forums allowed Jews and other marginalized people to gather in an egalitarian setting— at a private home—and center their afternoons or evenings around conversation.

Some of the dignitaries Yutang introduced to Bernardine included members of the Soong family, headed by political financier Charlie Soong. Soong's three daughters were all educated in the United States and married some of the most prominent men in China. Bernardine became closest to the oldest daughter, Soong Ai-ling, or Madame H. H. Kung, wife of China's finance minister, among the other positions he held in the Nationalist government. Middle daughter Ching-ling had been married to Sun Yat-sen, the father of modern China, before he passed away, and the youngest, Mei-ling, was married to Nationalist leader Chiang Kai-shek. Bernardine knew all of them and also developed friendships with Charlie's sons, including T. V. Soong, who, like his brother-in-law, served as China's finance minister.

Before taking her job at the *Critic*, Bernardine had met with Soong Ai-ling, or Madame Kung, about taking an office job at Madame's new hospital. Bernardine felt she could use her free time for a worthwhile cause rather than loafing around her apartment all day while Chester was away at work. "The majority of women in town play poker every day, steadily from three to nine thirty, then dash home just under the curfew. Sometimes I wish I played 'something,' but it seems so sinful somehow to be trying to be flippant, when they ought to be making up their minds whether they mean to be loyal to China or not."[65] Yet when

65 Letter from Bernardine to Barbara Harrison, undated, Beinecke Library, YCAL MSS 134 Box 126 f. 1969, page 75.

Yutang offered her a job, the draw to writing again pulled her away from work at the hospital and toward the *China Critic*.

Unrelated to Charlie Soong and his family was another friend of Yutang's with the same surname. T. F. Soong was a banker by day with a passion for Western theater. One evening, Yutang invited Bernardine to a talk at T. F.'s home. They planned to meet there at a designated hour.

Just as a servant opened the front door, Bernardine quickly realized she had committed the gravest social faux pas in Shanghai: she had arrived on time. At this point, she still wasn't accustomed to Chinese social norms and found herself seated alone next to T. F.'s wife, who politely and quietly offered Bernardine tea. Mrs. Soong couldn't speak much English, and Bernardine did not know more than a few words of any Chinese dialect at that point. But the two were accustomed to this kind of language impasse and understood that one must adjust in order to mix with those who did not speak the same language.

The two women made do, and after an hour or two, the other guests trickled in, Yutang amongst them. Bernardine noticed the other guests were all men but wasn't bothered. She enjoyed T. F.'s talk about Western drama, a subject close to her heart ever since she and her siblings had spent their childhood putting together dramatic productions at home in Peoria and later when she acted at Chicago's Little Theatre during her first marriage.

In the living room, Bernardine was in the middle of a conversation with Yutang when he sprung up and headed toward a Chinese scroll hanging on the opposite wall. Bernardine found the scroll pretty, with giant brushstrokes of intricate and bold calligraphy. As Yutang examined the calligraphy, he praised the beauty of the Chinese characters and burst out in laughter. Bernardine couldn't read Chinese and asked him for a translation. If it was that funny, she wanted to know what it meant. But Yutang simply waved his hand in front of his face, as if shooing a fly, and called for the other guests to view the scroll. Soon they, too, began to laugh.

Bernardine wished she could read Chinese, but even if she had studied written Chinese for a few years, the classical characters on the scroll, brushed in sweeping strokes, may still have looked indecipherable. Educated Chinese like Yutang's friends had been taught this literary Chinese but its difficulty was part of the reason that Hu Shih was promoting a more vernacular style of writing.

In bilingual settings, Bernardine tried to remain patient and understand that her place as a foreigner meant she was the one who had to adapt. But here at T. F. Soong's, her curiosity got the best of her. Again Bernardine asked Yutang for a translation.

"Oh heavens! I am a parson's son," he said. "I can't tell you."[66]

"Really," Bernardine said, now laughing along with him. It was an excuse he often gave to get out of awkward situations. Bernardine never tired of Yutang's tales about his Christian upbringing and thought back to her own childhood experience of attending a Methodist Sunday school where her father enrolled her siblings and her. Jacob Szold thought his children would learn to sit still at the Methodist church, even though their family was Jewish. Bernardine enjoyed joking around with Yutang and replied, "I shall never speak to you again if you don't tell me. Such nonsense. You are acting quite as puritanical as a New Englander and after all, I know Chinese are not puritanical."[67]

Yutang put his hands up, claiming he wasn't shy about the meaning; it was simply a short poem to memorialize a nun who had given her life to the monks in her province. Bernardine sensed Yutang wasn't telling her the real message or perhaps there was something racy about the way the nun gave up her life. In any case, Bernardine often found herself in similar situations in which she couldn't understand conversations and would ask bilingual friends like Yutang to interpret the important parts.

At another evening gathering with Yutang at a mutual friend's home, Bernardine was not surprised when a young couple visiting Shanghai expressed an interest in trying opium. It seemed cliché, but she had seen this before with visitors from abroad. The pair wanted to smoke opium simply because they were in China.

[66] Bernardine Szold Fritz, "Lin Yu Tang. Shanghai 1935," unpublished manuscript courtesy of her family, page 4.
[67] Ibid.

In her papers, Bernardine claimed she never felt the desire to try opium. As if to prove it, she declared she couldn't even smoke a cigarette. But that's not true. While there is no proof that she ever tried opium, she was a heavy smoker for decades. Bernardine never wrote about her smoking habit—so it's not mentioned in her vignettes or letters—but she smoked so often that she developed emphysema later in life. Bernardine picked it up when she lived in New York after a man at a party told her she'd look even more elegant if she were holding a cigarette. Years later, she would often lament the vanity that had inspired her to begin smoking.

Opium was another matter, and Bernardine could see the devastating toll it took on people in Shanghai. Whether in the sinewy rickshaw pullers, their bodies whittled down to skin and bones, or in the dapper patrons of the most popular dance clubs, the dangers of addiction loomed before her eyes.

That evening, Bernardine watched as the Chinese host rested on an opium couch, facing the young foreign woman who was about to try opium for the first time. This woman faced him on another couch, posing in the same reclining position. Seated between them, the hostess rolled two small balls of opium and heated them over a small flame enclosed by a glass covering with an opening at the top. "These two lying facing each other somehow looked like brother and sister and several of us were struck by the likeness," Bernardine recalled. "They both have long narrow faces, lean and finely modeled."[68]

Bernardine looked on as the host demonstrated how to slowly inhale the smoke, speaking patiently to the foreign woman so she could better understand his instructions. The foreign woman attempted to inhale from the pipe. Bernardine peered over at Yutang, the both of them rolling their eyes and trying their best to suppress laughter. "She, in her excitement, puffed violently in and out like a toy steam engine," Bernardine recounted. "There is something fascinating about watching people smoke opium."[69]

---

[68]   Ibid., pages 5–6.
[69]   Ibid., page 6.

Just as the two were about to smoke again, Yutang meandered to the wall and flipped off the lights. Bernardine found the atmosphere even more alluring, as the light from the flame illuminated the host and the foreign woman, their skin glowing like phantoms. After taking another hit from their pipes, they both looked down at the floor. Bernardine thought of angels in reverie. "The young Chinese, whose beautifully drawn eyes spread like a pair of wings below his brow, would look down and then out at us, the whites of his eyes flashing and the pupils rolling back and forth like onyx marbles," she remembered.[70]

When the lights went back on after the smokers finished their pipes, the group turned to Yutang. Bernardine had never seen him smoke opium, nor had anyone else in their circle. Someone in the group suddenly cried, "Go on, Yutang, let us see if you have any skill."[71]

Yutang threw his arms out at right angles, laughing and backing away as if cornered by bandits. "I'm a parson's son," he said. "I simply couldn't."[72]

"Go on, this once," the group chided him. "You ought to try it once. Everybody else does."

"No," he replied, this time his smile turning downward. "I love to watch it. I find it a fascinating spectacle to watch, but I watch with the same feeling of horror that people say you get watching a snake. I'm sure it has to do with my early Christian training. Although the Christianity has gone, the moral training remains, and I know that I would be physically unable to put an opium pipe to my lips."

"But you couldn't get a habit from trying it once," the host claimed.

"Yes, but no one would have the habit if he hadn't tried it once. Go ahead, don't mind me," Yutang said, laughing once again. "My black cigar habit is just as bad as your opium habit, I'm sure. But the Bible didn't prejudice me against cigars!"

After Friday evening editorial meetings, Bernardine sometimes joined Yutang and friends at one of the many Shanghai dance halls. Their

[70] Ibid.
[71] Ibid.
[72] Ibid., page 7.

group would order cups of hot green tea, while some drank tall mugs of beer, peering over to the Western band at the far end of the room. Lining the three other sides of the room were Chinese and Russian taxi dancers dressed in elegant Chinese silk gowns or the latest in Western fashions.

As soon as the band leader struck up a new song, a stampede of men would sprint across the dance floor to pick their choice of dance partner. The men were required to buy a ticket and present it to their partner. They could buy three tickets for one Mexican silver dollar. If a man wanted to dance with the same woman for more than a few dances, the protocol called for him to buy several books of tickets so she would be compensated accordingly.

Bernardine did not write about dancing at the nightclubs herself and seemed to have only been an observer. It appeared that she and her friends frequented these venues to watch Shanghai society out at night. This included educated and wealthy Chinese; expats from Europe, Japan, and America; and Russian émigrés among others. But what impressed Bernardine the most about these evenings out was that Yutang would return home well past midnight, only to write for several hours before going to sleep.

At another dinner Bernardine attended with Yutang, Hong, American cartoonist J. P. McEvoy, and others, the group tucked into one of many Chinese delicacies Yutang had ordered in advance. He had painstakingly planned the menu—Bernardine counted two dozen dishes, including Honan ham, pine flower eggs, bamboo shoots, and pickled cauliflower. And those were just the appetizers. The waiters also served shark fin soup, a sparkling red suckling pig "with skin as crisp as celery," and seven desserts. The dinner had been the talk of Bernardine's circle for days beforehand, the friends all eager with anticipation.[73]

The dishes were so delicious and exceptional that hardly a sound was heard apart from the smacking of lips here and there. Yutang soon spotted on McEvoy's finger a metallic ring with wires and springs

---

[73]   Ibid., page 10.

poking out on all sides like wild hair. He recognized it as a trick ring popular in the markets of Peking and couldn't bear just to look at it on McEvoy's hand. Yutang asked to give it a try. Bernardine and the others soon switched their attention from the food to Yutang, twisting, turning, pushing, and pulling the silver chains in all directions in order to solve the puzzle.

"Go on eating, go on eating," Yutang said. "I'll have no appetite until I solve this. Oh, they were wonderful, these Peking fellows. You know, once I saw a chap on Foochow Road, he had a big basket full of every possible kind of trick ring like this, wonderful ones! What ingenuity! What do you think? I was such a fool, I only looked and passed on. Then afterward I thought what a fool I was, and I went back, but I have never seen him again. Oh, they were wonderful."[74]

Hong pulled the ring from her husband's hand and returned it to McEvoy. But Yutang could not concentrate on the grand feast before him, despite all of the time he had spent organizing it. He decided the other diners should come up with a game they could play at the table. Bernardine remained silent, as did the rest of their group. She wasn't sure what Yutang had in mind and, like the others, just wanted to get back to the delicacies on their plates.

"All right," Yutang said, "then here is one."[75] Everyone was to choose a compound word, like brushwood, and another word using the second part of the first word, like woodland. Then, each person gave a hint, like "brushland," and the others were to shout out the word that came in between—"wood."

Yutang grew excited as the other diners thought up their words.

"Stormy cap," someone shouted.

Without skipping a beat, Yutang called back, "night," for the center word. After several rounds, Yutang rolled back in his seat and admitted it was an old Chinese game. "I didn't make it up at all."

Of all her friends in Shanghai, Bernardine found in Yutang a kindred spirit who enjoyed discussing history, culture, and literature, but not all the time. "He has no sense of conventions. While he is happy

---

[74]   Ibid.
[75]   Ibid.

with people, he stays and chats and laughs and bubbles over all the time. The moment he is bored, he leaves. If he is invited to a party, Chinese fashion, he asks who will be the other guests."[76]

Bernardine only wished she had the same gumption to leave if she was bored by a group. For too long during her first two years in Shanghai, she had remained at gatherings that exhausted her. She marveled at the way Yutang spoke out if he didn't care for the other guests. "Oh please excuse me, I can't waste an evening with that old pest. I'd better stay home and work. I have to finish an article. I'll come another time."[77]

"He is rarely diplomatic," Bernardine remarked further, appreciating his honesty and bluntness. "He says instantly if he likes a person or an object. He says instantly if he does not, and why, always with waves and flourishes of his hands and arms, his indescribably gay smile and nodding head."[78]

She also marveled at the way Yutang found subject matter for his writing. For instance, he would observe an old man strolling along a street, a sparse white beard hanging from his chin like a waterfall. Carrying a little wooden birdcage with a small green bird hopping from the perch to the floor of the cage and back up to the perch, the old man crossed a chaotic Shanghai intersection as if traversing a tranquil field. This simple sight would inspire Yutang to race home and write a long essay about old Chinese men taking their birds for walks in the fresh air so the birds would be more inclined to sing. "Nothing is too trivial or humdrum to provide him with exciting material for speculation or comment," Bernardine noted.[79]

In 1935, Lin Yutang became famous in the US when his book, *My Country and My People*, became a bestseller. Bernardine took great pride in Yutang and his book because he had discussed much of the content with her while he was writing it. She delighted in seeing her name

---

[76]   Ibid., page 11.
[77]   Ibid.
[78]   Ibid.
[79]   Ibid., page 12.

SUSAN BLUMBERG-KASON

listed in the dedication at the beginning of the book. Yutang also dedicated it to Pearl Buck, author of *The Good Earth*, and the Baroness von Ungern-Sternberg, the Russian-born wife of an Austrian executive with the German conglomerate Siemens. Pearl Buck had introduced Yutang to her publisher, John Day Company, which went on to publish many of his books.[80] As for the baroness, she was another in their social circle.

Chiang Kai-shek's Nationalist government was not pleased with Yutang and the content of *My Country and My People*. The early 1930s was a unique time in Shanghai when citizens were free to criticize the Chinese government and Chinese customs. But Chiang Kai-shek had started cracking down on leftist writers as tensions with the Communists were coming to a boiling point and the Nationalists sought to portray a certain wholesome and flawless image in their New Life Movement, a social program inspired by Confucianism and his wife Soong Mei-ling's Christian upbringing. In the Movement, Chinese citizens were encouraged to respect their elders and live a clean lifestyle, which included bathing regularly, not succumbing to opium, and embracing a more disciplined work ethic. Yutang wrote of the benefits of modernization in China but also warned that blaming the West for China's woes was counterproductive and detrimental to actual change. The government didn't want to hear about this and felt shame and anger that a place like Shanghai was still partly run by foreign powers. France ran concessions all over China; Japan, Italy, and Russia did too, not to mention the Portuguese colony of Macau and the British colony of Hong Kong. The Nationalists took no action against Yutang at that time, other than putting him on a blacklist or two.

Other Chinese critics were not so lenient. Although Yutang had been educated at the prestigious St. John's University in Shanghai, these critics didn't think he wasn't the best person to write a book introducing China to the West because he had spent too many years outside China when he studied in the US, France, and Germany. Bernardine,

---

[80] Unpublished papers from Bernardine Szold Fritz, reproduced from a 'mosquito' paper in Shanghai, undated, Beinecke Library, YCAL MSS 544 Box 3 f. Lin, Yu Tang, page 16.

protective as ever, wrote extensively about literary critics and their disdain of Yutang. She thought they seemed nothing but envious of Yutang. This situation brought her back to her early days in Paris when Ernest Hemingway read aloud to her *The Torrents of Spring*, a new book he had written to satirize their mutual friend from Chicago, the writer Sherwood Anderson. Just as she had taken Sherwood's side, she stood firm in her defense of Yutang.

Bernardine could not see how Yutang's years abroad made him any less of a China expert. How could Pearl Buck, who would win the Nobel Prize in Literature in 1938, be viewed as an authority on China but Yutang was not? Most of China's leading intellectuals, including Yutang, Hu Shih, and others, had studied in the United States or England. These critics missed the central point: it was important for people in the US to learn about China. After all, China was America's largest ally in Asia, and it was a center of culture and the arts. If people in the West had no opportunity to travel or make Chinese friends, they could only learn about China by reading about it. Bernardine thought Yutang really was the best person to teach readers about his homeland. "Yutang sees his own people as he sees other human beings or other races, and he tells what he sees as fascinating, wonderful, awe inspiring material. He thinks a corrupt official no matter on what soil a menace to the good of the world."[81]

Chinese critics in Shanghai also worried Yutang would let the success of *My Country and My People* go to his head, but again Bernardine came to her friend's defense. Instead of spending the proceeds from his book on the type of material goods favored by many in Shanghai—fancy new American automobiles, pricy Swiss watches, and luxurious Russian furs—Yutang's only new acquisitions included a secondhand Ford and a traditional mandarin hat, or skullcap. Bernardine found it amusing that Yutang's wife, Hong, didn't care for the new hat and his daughters thought it looked funny. In any case, this was hardly the conspicuous consumption found among those with money in Shanghai.

---

[81] Bernardine Szold Fritz, "Lin Yu Tang. Shanghai 1935," unpublished manuscript courtesy of her family, page 12.

Bernardine looked on with joy at the way Yutang and Hong raised their three daughters. Yutang enjoyed flying kites in open fields and creating toys from the remnants of melted candle wax. The family also made outings to the cinema to watch the Marx Brothers. "Or you may see them strolling along the streets, Yutang carrying the baby, the other two little girls all eyes and ears, for he points out to them delightful street scenes, and makes such entertaining stories about each tiny thing that they are learning to love the most insignificant and commonplace aspects of Chinese life," Bernardine recalled.[82]

It's interesting that when she wrote about Yutang and his daughters, Bernardine didn't lament her missed years with Rosemary. She didn't even mention Rosemary. By the time Bernardine and the Lin family had become close, Rosemary was in her late teens and her childhood was all but over. Bernardine rarely saw her daughter, and instead of trying to fix their relationship, she only mentioned her in complaints to her parents, Hermine and Jacob; she was often angry Rosemary wouldn't return her letters. Bernardine couldn't see that she was the parent and it was up to her to mend the damage with Rosemary, not the other way around. It's not difficult to imagine Rosemary's anger, sadness, and feelings of rejection when she received Bernardine's letters describing the many intriguing people she'd met in Shanghai and the sights she had seen.

Bernardine was not the only parent of her era to send a daughter away to boarding school, as it was common then among wealthy and even middle-class families, though most children were sent to school hundreds of miles away, not thousands. Today it's difficult to understand why Bernardine thought that under these circumstances she and Rosemary might enjoy some semblance of a decent relationship. Perhaps Bernardine didn't think about it and was caught up in a never-ending attempt to gain Chester's attention and approval. After all, Chester had made it clear that he didn't want Rosemary with them in China. Or perhaps her separation from Rosemary was so painful that she couldn't allow herself to think about all she'd done and continued

---

[82] Ibid., page 9.

to do wrong as a mother. Or perhaps Bernardine was simply not a good parent, despite her best intentions. It does seem as though she always expected Rosemary to understand—with a maturity beyond her years—their relationship from Bernardine's point of view.

Looking back at Bernardine's own childhood, it's hard to see where her apparent ease of detachment came from. Hermine and Jacob doted on all their children, albeit strictly and with certain expectations, but there was nothing unusual about their parenting. Though raised in a home full of love, surrounded by many cousins, aunts, and uncles, Bernardine still viewed herself as an outlier who got in trouble for telling the truth or simply being herself.

She often joined the Lin family on excursions outside Shanghai. Sometimes Chester came too, but he mostly stayed back. No matter how emotionally and physically distant Chester became, Bernardine could not help but try to make their marriage work. He could be so damn charming walking into a party with her, his hand on the small of her back, as if they were Hollywood stars. The foreign set in Shanghai found them an odd pair—he reserved and stern, she spirited and curious. But people who got to know the couple—when they appeared together—saw they suited one another in their sense of adventure.

One weekend, Yutang invited Bernardine to join his family in Hangchow, a four-and-a-half-hour drive from Shanghai. The fabled city with its mountainous landscape and West Lake had long been a favorite of the Lins, but this trip would be special because they could travel on a newly paved road between the two cities. Mustard seed was in bloom, and for miles around, they saw nothing but a sea of yellow flowers. As they drove, Yutang spoke at length of the towering trees, majestic boulders, and enchanting birds they would find in Hangchow. Bernardine recalled, "He goes into rhapsodies whenever he is in a lovely spot and invariably rages against the stupidity of living in Shanghai."[83]

When they reached the coast, the ocean loomed off to the east. The final hour along the sea wall inspired Yutang to quote classical Chinese

---

[83]   Ibid., page 13.

poets. He also spoke of sing-song girls memorialized in tombs around the area they were about to reach. These sing-song girls were especially important to Chinese culture, Yutang proclaimed, because they were also poets and had sacrificed themselves for the men they loved.

"We will find their tombs," Yutang declared, "most of them in obscure spots. Some of them took me ten years to find, and then I will kowtow. Of course, you can all kowtow if you like."[84] Bernardine and Hong chuckled and politely declined.

"Of course you two women will laugh at me," he mocked. "But I don't mind."[85]

When they reached the hotel in Hangchow, Bernardine could not take her eyes off the scenery. The lakes, the mountains, the misty clouds in the trees—it all reminded her of a Chinese landscape painting. Most travelers to Hangchow spent their days hiking to temples and ancient tombs and climbing to a famous pagoda. Bernardine most looked forward to sailing on West Lake and on the many small lakes that fed into it, drifting in a large boat with a canvas cover to protect from the sun's rays.

After leaving her luggage in her room, she headed out to the hotel's courtyard, where she found Yutang taking in the scenery and fresh air. "Hong is unpacking and changing the children into warmer clothes," he told her. "Really, I feel sorry for women. How here I am not a bit the helpful husband, out enjoying this beautiful panorama and Hong is inside with the children." Yutang suddenly broke out into a wide grin. "But she loves it. Woman is happiest when functioning in harmony with her destiny."[86]

"Destiny, pooh!" Bernardine replied. She knew Hong was not a subservient wife but an accomplished writer and just as fluent in English as Yutang. Yet when Bernardine thought more about what Yutang said, she couldn't stay cross at him for very long. She enjoyed his sense of humor and knew he said these things mostly to cause a

---

[84]   Ibid.
[85]   Ibid., page 14.
[86]   Ibid.

stir. She also realized he spoke the truth. Hong truly loved their three daughters and would do anything for them.

Bernardine and the Lins had arrived in Hangchow just in time for the annual pilgrimage to Jade Emperor's Hill, a mountain dedicated to the father of the Chien Lung emperor during the Qing dynasty. The hike entailed walking up hundreds of stone steps wrapped around the mountain. It was not for the faint of heart, but the Lin daughters eagerly awaited the climb. Yutang grabbed a handful of copper coins, and Bernardine wondered why he didn't hand them out to the many panhandlers seated along the path. "Every two or three yards all the way up we passed beggars of every possible description from beautiful ascetic-looking monks to garrulous, scraggly old women, to the blind, the halt and the lame. Many of them kept up a continuous begging song which often was raised to substantial howls."[87] As Bernardine and the Lins passed the beggars, Yutang explained that hikers gave out money on the trip down the hill.

Once they reached the top, Bernardine found a cave. "The Chinese have a passion for caves like the French, and will travel hours to pay respects to some apparently insignificant hole in a hill."[88] Yutang took his youngest daughter, Meimei, and the middle girl, Wu-shuang, and stepped into the mouth of the cave, trying to make sense of what lay beyond the darkness. Bernardine and Hong stayed back with the oldest daughter, opting to pass on this adventure. Perhaps they knew something Yutang did not, for not a minute had passed before he reemerged with the two younger daughters. The girls didn't care for the dark, and Yutang didn't appreciate the slimy ground under his shoes.

When it was time to start back down the mountain, Bernardine noticed Yutang dividing the copper coins amongst his daughters. Bouncing with glee, they each dropped coins into the hands of what Bernardine called the "mendicants."[89] When they reached the bottom of the mountain, the Lin daughters begged to climb it again. They

---

87   Ibid., page 15.
88   Ibid.
89   Ibid.

wanted to give out more coins. The three adults put a quick stop to that idea, but Bernardine chuckled in delight at the girls' enthusiasm.

The following day, the group set off on a drive along a new road carved between cliffs along the Ch'ien-t'ang River. This would be Yutang's first time on this road, and it was all he had spoken of on their way to Hangchow.

Bernardine met the Lins early to start out on their excursion. "There is a roadway built through the center of the lake, and willows bend on either side of it, their lower branches trailing like fingers in the water," she wrote.[90] The other side of the lake was just as spectacular, with a winding road that led to a breathtaking view of the river. Since the riverbanks were so low, the river appeared to Bernardine as the most peaceful body of water in the world. The luscious trees on each side of the river contrasted with the ripples on the water as huge junks floated by with enormous sails.

Hong and the children admired the water while Bernardine silently took in the beauty of the hills, trees, and birds. She wished she could show Chester. Of course he had already seen Hangchow, but these sites could have been new to him since this road hadn't existed on his last visit. Still, Bernardine felt grateful she could enjoy these sights with the Lins.

As the driver meandered around the cliffs, one of the daughters noticed Yutang looking down at his lap. She suddenly cried out in surprise. Yutang had his nose in a book! The group went into an uproar, Hong, their daughters, and Bernardine imploring him to look up and enjoy the scenery he had so enthusiastically promoted up until that morning.

"Yes, yes, in a minute," Yutang replied, not looking up.

"You can read tonight," Bernardine said. "Scenery, Yutang, scenery!"[91]

He peered up for only a moment, holding his finger in place where he left off on the page. "But you see, last night before I went to sleep I began this novel, one that I never read before. Oh, it is so beautiful!

---

90   Ibid., page 16.
91   Ibid.

What poetry! How idyllic! I read until my eyes fell shut of themselves. But now I can't wait to see what happens. I MUST know if he gets her."

"Oh, you wretch!" Hong cried, laughing along with Bernardine. "You're the one who talked about this trip. Here you are with the finest scenery in the world before you! You can read your old novel any time. Put that book down!"

"In a minute, in a minute," Yutang said. And he continued to read. Bernardine, Hong, and the girls found the scenery like nothing they could find near Shanghai, and every few seconds one of them would shout, "Look, look, isn't that wonderful? Yutang, Yutang, look how beautiful! Yutang, scenery, scenery!"[92]

"Beautiful," he would reply, not looking up from his book. The drive lasted for hours, and Yutang remained glued to his novel. He did take his eyes away for a few moments when they stopped for lunch. Yet once seated, he continued to read, book in one hand and a sandwich in the other.

By late afternoon, the group approached Hangchow again, and Yutang suddenly exhaled. "He got her! Now let's see the scenery." But at that point, the scenery looked the same as what they'd become accustomed to from the hotel and on their mountain hikes. Yutang never lived this story down.

The following day, Yutang led his family and Bernardine to the tomb of the concubine who died for love, the same one he spoke of on their drive to Hangchow. At the tomb site, Yutang waxed poetic about the selfless concubine while Bernardine and Hong rolled their eyes, wondering why he was making such a fuss over her.

"Isn't it remarkable," he said, "I am a model father and husband. I really might be said to live a prosaic life, if you analyze it. And yet I cannot conceal the fact at heart I am a romantic man. I have a Western mind in many ways, but a completely Chinese heart. Also, what a lucky fellow I am; I am and will always be a cynic in my mind, but never in my heart."[93]

---

[92] Ibid.
[93] Ibid., page 17.

Bernardine found these words moving and felt they summed up Yutang perfectly. "And that is where he quite hit the nail on the head, for cynic that he is, it all comes from being obliged to rationalize that 'humbug' as he calls it, the cruelty of the world, in order to acquit himself with his essentially and incurably romantic soul."[94] She felt the same way about herself. Despite the pain and suffering she had endured through her first three marriages, Bernardine was as much a romantic as Yutang.

Bernardine would forever be grateful to Yutang and Hong for their hospitality in China and for accepting her into their literary circles when she had all but given up on adjusting to Shanghai. To remember her dear friend, Bernardine kept with her throughout her many moves a scrap of paper with a poem Yutang had scribbled for her.

> Busy for public, busy for private;
> to steal some leisure amidst business, drink a bowl
> of tea.
> Slave for wealth, slave for fame;
> to enjoy oneself in slavery, bring me a pot of wine.[95]

---

[94] Ibid., page 18.
[95] Poem from Lin Yutang to Bernardine, undated, Beinecke Library, YCAL MSS 544 Box 3 f. Lin, Yu Tang, page 2.

CHAPTER SIX

HAROLD ACTON DESCENDS
UPON SHANGHAI, 1932

The first thing British writer Harold Acton noticed when Bernardine brought him to the estate of Li Ch'ing-mai was a burly Cossack guard, his skirted coat and fur hat noticeably out of place in sub-tropical Shanghai. The second thing Harold noticed was another Cossack guard. Bernardine, used to the pageantry at Li Ch'ing-mai's, paid scant attention to the guards and walked right up to the owner, whom Shanghailanders called Lord Li. He was the son of Li Hung-chang, perhaps the most prominent Chinese statesman of the late Qing dynasty. The elder Li helped save China from further damage during both the Taiping and Boxer Rebellions. He attended the coronation of Nicholas II in Russia and urged the United States government to think twice about the 1882 Chinese Exclusion Act that banned emigration from China for six decades, to no avail.

Now at Li Ch'ing-mai's garden party, Bernardine presented her warmest smile and thanked him for the invitation. Lord Li, acting as maître d' of his own party, stood in his entryway dressed in a chang-shan and directed Bernardine and Harold to proceed around to the side of his mansion, toward the guests who had already arrived at his garden party.

Bernardine guided her friend, visiting from Peking, to the back of the grand estate. Harold was born in Italy to British parents and was a part of the Bright Young Things in 1920s London, a classmate of George Orwell, and a colleague of Evelyn Waugh. In 1932 when Bernardine learned Harold was to move to China, she invited him to stay with Chester and her for as long as he liked. They certainly had enough space in their apartment at 62 Route de Boissezon.

She and Harold became friends in the mid-to-late 1920s during her Paris years and brief sojourn at Cambridge. The two shared a demonstrative personality and always looked forward to catching up whenever they found themselves in the same city. With an interest in the Chinese classics, Harold had settled in Peking earlier in 1932. By the time he visited Bernardine in Shanghai in late 1932, he had already published seven books and would eventually write half a dozen more about China.

Now Bernardine was determined to introduce Harold to all the notables in Shanghai. Lord Li was especially generous in opening his sprawling English-style manor to acquaintances and visitors.

As the friends reached the garden, Harold stopped in amazement. No less than five hundred guests stood around, chatting and enjoying cocktails amidst a large marble fountain and an array of statues. Fuchsia and violet azaleas complemented the neatly manicured lawn, as if Lord Li were back in Austria, where he had served as the Chinese ambassador at the end of the Qing dynasty. And the lights! Thousands of fairy lights illuminated a lotus pool, summerhouse, and pagoda. They also lined gravel paths and wrapped around the many trees. Harold spotted two separate buildings on the grounds behind the sprawling manor— one housed a museum and the other a library. "Lord Li was reputed to be one of the wealthiest landowners in Shanghai," Harold wrote in his 1948 book, *Memoirs of an Aesthete*, "and he looked it. He never went out but in an armored car with Cossack guards, and Cossack guards patrolled his extensive domain."[96]

---

[96]   Harold Acton, *Memoirs of an Aesthete*, page 288.

Bernardine nudged Harold toward the fountain and pointed out Countess Ciano, or Edda Mussolini, daughter of the Italian Generalissimo and wife of the Italian consul in Shanghai. Bernardine had previously been invited to a reception hosted by the Italian couple but couldn't make it because she had come down with a cold. She now felt obliged to acknowledge them at Lord Li's. A small group had formed around Edda and Count Galeazzo Ciano, but Bernardine broke through to introduce Harold to the countess.[97]

Harold found Edda to resemble her father, especially with her prominent jawline. "She was trying to behave like royalty, surrounded by attentive myrmidons," he recalled. Bernardine described Edda in less endearing terms: "Her skin is very white and she looks as if she might have one of the diseases that eat out your insides in time."[98] Edda may have resembled her father, but Bernardine seemed harsh in her assessment: Edda was actually quite attractive.

When it came to Count Ciano, Bernardine seemed much more forgiving. She wrote to Glenway that the Count was "the perfect gigolo type, dark and sleek and charming looking and full of what the Chinese now call *ee duh*, which means *it* in Chinese."[99]

From the way Bernardine chatted about the Cianos, Harold could tell she was not especially close to the pair. One explanation is that Edda had been incorrectly credited as the first foreigner to bring together foreigners and Chinese in Shanghai, eclipsing Bernardine's accomplishment and standing in this realm. It was also rumored that Edda had become romantically involved with the Young Marshal, Chang Hsueh-liang, warlord of Manchuria and later general of the Nationalist Army. In her memoir, *My Truth*, Edda described her first meeting with Chang Hsueh-liang in Peking but didn't reveal any further interaction with him that didn't involve her husband. "Toward the end of the meal he sent me a little note asking me to visit the Summer

[97] Letter from Bernardine to Glenway Wescott, June 20, 1932, Beinecke Library, YCAL MSS 134 Box 103 f. 1573, page 21.
[98] Acton, *Memoirs of an Aesthete*, page 289.
[99] Letter from Bernardine to Glenway Wescott, December 17, 1930, Beinecke Library, YCAL MSS 134 Box 103 f. 1573, page 11.

Palace with him on the following day. I accepted, and for several hours one of the most important men in China acted as my guide and kept Ministers and other important persons waiting while he walked with me. Naturally, that was very agreeable for my ego."[100]

By the time of this garden party, Bernardine had already started hosting a salon in her apartment, and Chang Hsueh-liang himself enjoyed attending, discussing art, literature, and music while staying in Shanghai during his recovery from opium addiction. Several years later, Chang would orchestrate the kidnapping of China's own Generalissimo, Chiang Kai-shek, to bring together the Nationalists and the Communists to join forces against Japanese aggression just before the start of World War II. Chiang Kai-shek never forgave Chang for the kidnapping, even though it helped save China from a threatening invader. To punish the Young Marshal, Chiang put him under house arrest, which continued even after the Nationalists absconded to Taiwan in 1949. Whether or not Chang Hsueh-liang wanted to move to Taiwan, he had no choice and was under house arrest there until 1975 when Chiang Kai-shek died at the age of eighty-seven. Twenty years after that, Chang Hsueh-liang would move to Honolulu, where he lived out his last five years to the age of one hundred.

Bernardine and Harold mingled with the Cianos at the garden party a good decade before Mussolini would order a firing squad to execute his son-in-law and Edda would smuggle her husband's war diaries out of Italy and into Switzerland, disguised as a peasant. No one could have predicted any of these events on the grounds of Lord Li's estate that evening. Bernardine exchanged pleasantries with Edda before a porter announced dinner. She then took Harold's arm and led him to the buffet queue while a brass band played Gilbert and Sullivan.

Harold had traveled down to Shanghai by train with the British diplomat and writer Simon Harcourt-Smith and his wife, Rosamund Miller. On their arrival, Harold was stunned by the difference in climate

---

[100]   Edda Mussolini Ciano, as told to Albert Zarca, translated by Eileen Finletter, *My Truth*, New York: William Morrow and Company, 1976, page 102.

compared to the drier, dustier Peking. "Humidity saturated the atmosphere," Harold recalled. "The walls were sweating, and everything one touched was sticky; the humming of electric fans stunned one into listlessness till evening beckoned to a furtive and hesitant breeze."[101]

The Harcourt-Smiths had been living in Peking for two years on a diplomatic posting, and Simon in particular looked forward to Shanghai's fabled nightlife scene. So did Harold. Peking was a sleepier city in comparison, but then again, most cities around the world couldn't boast anything close to Shanghai's jazz clubs, ballrooms, and cabarets, which rivaled those in Berlin and Paris. Bernardine recalled that Harold "of course made a great stir."[102]

Long after the sun set on the Whangpoo and neon lights illuminated Nanking Road, Harold and Simon bounced from nightclub to nightclub. They hit the *ha-ha jing*, or funhouse mirrors, peep shows, and fantan tables at the Great World entertainment complex, a corner building with a skinny tower reminiscent of a distorted Pisa, appearing as if it would topple over with the next big wind. According to Bernardine, the two men "descending at once, quite drove people off their feet, and there has been a tremendous amount of talk."[103]

Poor Rosamund was left back at the hotel to fend for herself. Bernardine got along and empathized with her but didn't feel it her place to intrude if Simon wished to experience Shanghai nightlife with the bon vivant Harold. If there were issues between Simon and Rosamund, that was their business, not hers. Bernardine endured her own lonely nights as Chester continued to spend most evenings at the office. Their friends and acquaintances never told Chester to rush back to his wife, so Bernardine let the Harcourt-Smiths be.

Bernardine had lived in Shanghai for three years by the time Harold arrived. He was visibly impressed by her knack for connecting people; he had noticed it in the past but not to this extent. "Yet Bernardine,

---

[101] Acton, *Memoirs of an Aesthete*, page 287.
[102] Letter from Bernardine to Glenway Wescott, undated, Beinecke Library YCAL MSS 134 Box 103 f. 1573, page 29.
[103] Ibid.

ever within reach of a telephone, cool as a cucumber—'people talk about blood,' she said, 'I have no blood'—was organizing elaborate buffet-suppers and teas."[104]

Harold was also impressed with Bernardine's cast of friends. "No crowd could have been more jumbled, and one had to thank Bernardine for shaking up the old bran-pie. There were Chinese painters in Western style—one had exhibited at the Royal Academy; representatives of Western firms who welcomed an escape from business; the first German Jews aware of the trend at home; journalists and professors."[105]

Bernardine and Chester's apartment felt so different from Harold's home in Peking. Harold had become accustomed to the relative sprawl and cherished the traditional architecture of the former northern capital, a city full of low-rise homes and government buildings. He had even moved into a courtyard home, living like a mandarin. Harold learned Chinese brushstroke calligraphy and dressed in a changshan robe at home. Yet he appreciated Shanghai, a destination of architects who would become world-famous. The Hong Kong firm Palmer & Turner and Hungarian László Hudec had a strong presence in Shanghai, but many of the new buildings or those soon to be under construction like the Chinese YMCA, National YWCA, and Yangtze Hotel, were designed by architects Poy Gum Lee, Robert Fan Wenzhao, Li Pan, and Zhao Shen. The blending of Chinese and Western architecture in Shanghai can be traced back to architect Liu Jipiao, who introduced Chinese Art Deco at the 1925 Paris Expo.

Harold also admired the way Bernardine decorated her two front rooms, the area where her salon took place. Regulars at Bernardine's referred to her home as the red-and-black apartment because of the colors of the furniture and décor. She kept vases of fresh flowers on dark wooden Chinese end tables in these rooms. The walls were lined with several upholstered sofas so people could sit comfortably or stand in groups in the middle of the rooms. Guests traipsed over striped area rugs, laid on the hardwood floor to absorb Shanghai's unrelenting dampness.

---

[104] Acton, *Memoirs of an Aesthete*, page 287.
[105] Ibid., page 288.

Bernardine and Chester's unit had two fireplaces, but in subtropical Shanghai, they could only be used for a couple months each year. So Bernardine hung rattan fans in one fireplace instead of keeping firewood in it. Above this fireplace, she placed a dozen wooden Chinese masks, each with a different expression. She chose her artwork carefully and decorated the living room walls with Chinese landscape paintings and calligraphy. When she moved to Hollywood at the end of the decade, she would replicate her salon there and decorate her house with many of the same furnishings and artwork until she had to sell most of these pieces to pay the bills.

***

One late afternoon, Bernardine and Harold took a seat in the lobby of the Cathay Hotel to wait for Chester to finish work for the day. Chester had never met Harold before this visit but seemed pleased to open his home to one of Bernardine's writer friends. He could be generous when he wanted and had come to enjoy Harold's company and good humor. In fact, Bernardine had never seen Chester laugh so much. He appeared so at ease around Harold that Bernardine wished they could always have houseguests Chester admired.

Bernardine and Harold arrived early to take in the ambience of the Cathay. It was Art Deco heaven. Looking around the gilded lobby with its striking vertical lines and curlicue metalwork, they could have been anywhere in the world that could afford this latest craze in architecture and design. Guests from around the globe crisscrossed the marble lobby floor under the golden stained-glass atrium as the two friends fell into a deep discussion. Bernardine was in the middle of a story when a couple walked by and took the adjacent seats. She and Harold didn't look up until the man cleared his throat.

It was the Harcourt-Smiths, Harold's travel companions.

Without warning, Rosamund turned to Bernardine and Harold and began gossiping about the latest lesbian love triangles in the US and England. Simon looked on with interest, as if this were the first he had heard of it. Bernardine and Harold looked on in silence, wondering what brought on this topic. Most of Bernardine's male friends were gay, Harold amongst them, and some of her female friends and acquaintances were lesbian, including Gertrude Stein, Alice Toklas, and the writer Janet Flanner, all in Paris. There was an openness in 1920s Paris that Bernardine appreciated and thrived in when she lived there, but she knew Shanghai did not embrace this culture of acceptance. It was simply not a topic for a discussion in public.

Before long, Rosamund mentioned Barbara Harrison. Bernardine's ears pricked up. According to Rosamund, Barbara had seduced author Radclyffe Hall, a prominent British lesbian writer of the time. Bernardine knew this was not true but didn't know what to say. Should she speak up or keep quiet? Maybe Simon would interrupt or Rosamund would move on to another topic. But when Rosamund continued, Bernardine saw no other choice but to set the record straight and said under her breath, "That is the most preposterous fairy story I ever heard, and I happen to be able to speak with authority."[106]

The lobby was crowded, but sound didn't carry very far thanks to the ceilings that seemed to reach halfway to the sky. There was no reason for Rosamund not to have heard Bernardine, yet she carried on with her story.

According to Rosamund, Barbara had traveled to Asia four years earlier with two friends: a woman her age and an older, male foreign correspondent. "She went on a trip with Walter Harris of Morocco, and a friend, and of course she neglected Walter Harris for the friend."[107]

Bernardine could barely contain her anger. Harold was also close to Barbara and desperately tried to stifle his laughter. It took all his restraint to keep a calm face.

"You are killing me with mirth," Bernardine thought to herself, yet continued to keep quiet.[108] If Bernardine did tell the Harcourt-Smiths about her connection to the story, she didn't relay it in her writings.

When Bernardine and Barbara traveled extensively throughout Europe and Asia, they were joined by Walter Harris of the *London Times*.

---

[106] Letter from Bernardine to Barbara Harrison, undated, Beinecke Library YCAL MSS 134 Box 103 f. 1573, page 26.
[107] Ibid.
[108] Ibid.

The trip came about rather abruptly, and Bernardine recalled the urgency behind Barbara's need to get away when the two women were living in Paris. "Barbara was sitting on a terrace of a café with a young man when the police noticed a gun in the man's pocket and arrested them both."[109] Barbara's father wanted to get her out of town to quiet the scandal.

Barbara and Walter planned a trip abroad. Yet despite the openness of the decade, she could not travel alone with a man, even—or especially—one four decades her senior like Walter. At the time they were to depart France, Walter was sixty-one years old, and Barbara was only twenty-three. So she asked her good friend Bernardine to accompany her as a chaperon. Bernardine, eight years older than Barbara, jumped at this opportunity, knowing she would never have enough money to fund such a trip on her own. Whatever Bernardine earned from magazine and newspaper writing in Paris went to support herself and Rosemary, and that was barely enough to get by. Barbara's offer was a dream come true.

By the time the trio reached Singapore, Barbara had grown frustrated with Walter. He had professed his love for her before they set sail from Marseilles. Yet almost as soon as the ship departed, he all but ignored Barbara and refused to talk about their relationship. This was when the trip became even more exciting for Bernardine. Barbara penned a Dear John letter to Walter that Bernardine copied word for word to remember, calling it a "masterpiece of restraint."[110] In it, Barbara wrote, "I am going away. We could not have gone on as we were—our relations were impossible. If I have hurt you in any way with my foolishness, disloyalty, and arrogance, please try to forgive me. Perhaps we shall meet again someday and be friends. B."[111] The two women ditched Walter in Singapore and hightailed it to Saigon on a Norwegian cargo boat. Walter Harris would die five years later at his home in Tangier.

---

[109] Recounted to me by Bernardine's cousin, Nancy, including the Bernardine's exact words in telling the story, as recorded in Bernardine's writings.

[110] Unpublished manuscript, *Narrative of Bernardine Szold's Life*, commissioned by David Szanton, page 28, courtesy of David Szanton.

[111] Ibid.

After the mayhem in the Cathay lobby, Bernardine typed a letter to Barbara back in France to relay all that Rosamund had babbled on about, including the wild rumors about the two of them. She also offered Barbara her thoughts about the Harcourt-Smiths. "These two young people it seems are tearing each other to bits, emotionally," she wrote. "I don't know why, but I suspect she doesn't want to be married, and also that she must both attract and repel him. This is sheer speculation on my part, but they make one feel they'll kill each other presently in some rather awful way. I see so little of people of this kind anymore that it rather excites me."[112]

Turning her attention to just Simon, Bernardine continued, "Harcourt Smith who is a son of half a dozen lords and all of that, has one short arm and one long where it should be, and his face goes a bit to one side, the stories are that he was born that way, that he fell off a horse, that he got a disease, that he was inoculated with the wrong serum, etc.—anyway he IS that way, he also talks that way, a little to one side in a very high voice...."[113]

Bernardine may have had her opinions, but as a salon host, she was used to conversing with people of different backgrounds, at least when it came to those in prominent positions. Her salons continued to attract Chinese and foreign diplomats of different political persuasions, like the consul general of the Soviet Union and the head of Jardines, a Hong Kong business conglomerate that made millions in China during the Opium Wars. Bernardine strongly believed in the freedom to discuss one's opinions at will.

Still, she wasn't against divulging her thoughts about the Harcourt-Smiths in her letters to Barbara. She longed for Barbara to visit her in China and hoped to give the impression that Shanghai was every bit as exciting and story-worthy as Paris. "In Shanghai you see, people DON'T talk that way and now groups gather for the sole purpose of

---

[112] Letter from Bernardine to Barbara Harrison, undated, Beinecke Library YCAL MSS 134 Box 103 f. 1573, page 26.
[113] Letter to Glenway Wescott, undated, Beinecke Library YCAL MSS 134 Box 103 f. 1573, page 29.

repeating the things he said. Had he not been so British, I might have liked him."[114]

It wasn't that Bernardine didn't like the British or didn't have British friends, as exemplified by her particularly close camaraderie with Harold. She must have also appreciated Simon Harcourt-Smith's family background as his father Cecil was a former diplomat and director of the Victoria and Albert Museum in London. Rather, this was part of her humor, although deep down there may have been some truth behind her statement. In 1927, she enrolled at Cambridge as an "out student," or what we would now call a continuing education student.[115]

Before moving to Cambridge, Bernardine had become disillusioned that her work in Paris had not materialized in the way she had hoped. She had written for the Tribune News Service when she arrived in France, covering stories in France and the UK, and wrote a couple articles for the *New Yorker* and *Arts & Decoration*. But she just couldn't seem to focus on her writing as she had imagined. It was the first time she had truly been free of obligations since her late teens. With no husband to worry about and Rosemary off at another boarding school, Bernardine enjoyed a wide-open schedule, yet just couldn't write.

"I found I couldn't work in Paris, I couldn't write great books, or even facetious articles, and I was more unhappy than I'd ever been in all my life, all told. For months I was in almost a coma of despair and lethargy, and knew I ought to go back to New York, since I wasn't justifying my coming abroad by doing good writing, which had been my purpose."[116] Bernardine often went without food to save money in Paris, and after a couple of years there, she set off for Cambridge to study English literature, hoping it would help her writing career.

But during her time at Cambridge, she encountered a snobbishness she hadn't faced before as an adult. It wasn't so much a class issue as a steady stream of subtle antisemitism, which gave her less than savory

---

[114] Ibid., page 30.

[115] Sheila McHugh Simmons, "Bernardine Szold-Fritz" book proposal and "Chronology of Bernardine Szold's Life, undated in the 1980s, courtesy of Bernardine Szold Fritz's family, page 14.

[116] Letter from Bernardine to Barbara Harrison, undated, Beinecke Library, YCAL MSS 134 Box 126 f. 1969, page 40.

memories of that time. This was another reason she had so readily agreed to leave Cambridge and sail away with Barbara for more than a year. That trip would also lead to her meeting Chester in Shanghai.

***

Bernardine and Harold did not just dally away their evenings at dinner parties and garden get-togethers. They walked through all of Shanghai, even places foreigners refused to visit. Hunger and malnourishment were normal in these parts of the city, and it wasn't unusual to find dead people of every age on the streets when the sun came up, sometimes as young as newborns. Even though it was one of the densest and most populous metropolises in the world at four million and counting, the narrow, disease-infested lanes of the Chinese City contrasted with the manicured, affluent areas where Bernardine and Chester lived. Shanghai was certainly a city of pronounced disparities.

Most of the street traffic in the Chinese City consisted of human-pulled rickshaws and people walking on foot, right in the middle of the road. Cars, trucks, buses, and streetcars also competed for space, but they didn't make up nearly as much of the traffic as did people. "When the Japanese started coming, the people tended to disappear," Bernardine recalled from 1932. "They went to the sides of the streets, got out of the way as much as they could. But the Japanese would go around with big clubs and if a Chinese came along, man, woman, or child, they would just knock him over with a club."[117] The Japanese army occupied the Chinese sections of Shanghai in 1932, and even though China and Japan signed a treaty with the League of Nations that year, the brutality against Chinese residents continued for more than a dozen years.

Harold recorded his visits to Shanghai in *Memoirs of an Aesthete*, which included ideas about expats in China that read as if they could have come from Bernardine. Her influence was certainly apparent. "Thirty years—sometimes more—without troubling to learn the language, and these 'Old China Hands' pickled in alcohol considered

---

[117]   Lawrence Levin interview, Tape 5, Side 2, page 22.

82

themselves supreme authorities on the country and the people. They prided themselves on never mixing with the 'natives.' Was it due to the climate? They were inveterate grumblers. A traveler fresh from Europe who, instead of sozzling, went about sober with his eyes open, was plain 'green'; his views were worthless, and if he had learnt the lingo— well, the poor devil was past praying for. But some truths are evident to babes and sucklings."[118]

***

Bernardine had been begging Barbara to visit ever since she had moved to Shanghai. In one of these letters, Bernardine wrote, "Bobby darling DO come. Even if we are supposed to be the lesbians of the world, do come…the reputation sticks to me tighter and closer, and it will really amuse me now, to have us seen together and know the buzz buzz that goes on. Chester thinks it quite comic."[119]

By the end of 1932, Bernardine's wish finally came true. Barbara brought Monroe, while his two romantic partners, Glenway and George, chose to stick closer to their home bases in Paris and the South of France where all three lived together. Barbara and Monroe had recently gone into business together to create Harrison of Paris, a limited-edition press that prided itself on using the highest quality of paper from China, Japan, Madagascar, and Holland.[120] They published Glenway's work but also that of Katherine Anne Porter, Thomas Mann, Lord Byron, Shakespeare, and a translation of Dostoevsky. By coincidence, Victor Sassoon had booked passage on the same ship to Shanghai and ordered some of their books while on board.

Harold was in town when Barbara and Monroe arrived. They had all kept company in Paris, so Bernardine took extra joy in planning activities for her friends while they all visited her at the same time. Harold wrote about this reunion in his memoir. "Since the arrival of

---

[118]   Acton, *Memoirs of an Aesthete*, page 291.

[119]   Letter from Bernardine to Barbara Harrison, undated, Beinecke Library, YCAL MSS 134 Box 126 f. 1969, page 83.

[120]   Hugh Ford, *Published in Paris: American and British Writers, Printers, and Publishers in Paris, 1920–1939*, New York: Macmillan, 1975, page 323.

Monroe Wheeler, who had done an English translation of *Les Enfants Terrible*, Cocteau was the ruling topic at Bernardine's."[121]

He continued, directly quoting Bernardine, "'Oh, if we could only persuade Jean to join us,' sighed Bernardine hungrily, her eyes glistening with memories of the *Boeuf sur le Toit*. 'And I keep imploring Glenway Wescott to come over, but he can't tear himself away from Villefranche. It's just too bad! But Miguel Covarrubias will be with us soon, and that's something to look forward to....'"[122]

Cocteau had been part of Bernardine's group of friends, and she first got to know him through Glenway, Monroe, and George when they traveled together to the South of France. Cocteau turned out to be a Nazi sympathizer during the war. Given Bernardine's experiences with antisemitism at Cambridge, she may have picked up on his prejudice but doesn't write about it in her vignettes or correspondences.

As for her wish for Glenway to visit, that was an ongoing topic in their letters. But Glenway didn't wish to travel halfway across the world. Morocco was about the farthest he sailed from France while he lived in Europe. It was also true that Miguel Covarrubias and Rosa Rolanda would visit again in the coming year.

Bernardine appeared in Harold's memoir, but she also inspired his 1941 novel, *Peonies and Ponies*, a satire of the expat community in Peking. In this novel, a woman named Elvira held an "at home" event in which Chinese and expats mixed for the first time in the Chinese capital. Harold even incorporated conversations from Bernardine in the dialogue. "Monsieur Lefort had banished the Eighteenth Lohan to install a cocktail bar in his temples, with modish appurtenances in surgical steel. He called it *Le Boeuf sur le Tot*. It only lacked Jean Cocteau."[123]

When it came time for Harold to return to Peking, Bernardine hated to see him leave. Soon Barbara and Monroe left Shanghai too and traveled up to Peking to stay with Harold in the early part of 1933. Just before departing for France, Barbara and Monroe joined Harold and the wife of one of Chester's business partners for a farewell gathering.

---

[121] Acton, *Memoirs of an Aesthete*, page 321.
[122] Ibid., pages 321-322.
[123] Harold Acton, *Peonies and Ponies*, page 21.

Monroe wrote of this evening to Bernardine: "Harold came in afterwards to say good-bye and complicated packing with too much conversation, and convulsed us by being more butterfly than ever—literal
tra-la-las, and positively coloratura inflections. I don't think we have ever
laughed so hard at some of his stories the other night when we were
done at Hanforth's with Lucille Swan—not that the stories themselves
were so funny, but his versions above all his sincere personal asides were
little short of glorious. I sometimes wonder whether—and to what
extent—he is conscious of our being more amused by his mannerisms
than by his material, but since they amount to wit he shouldn't care."[124]

Even Chester missed Harold's company after he returned to
Peking. As Bernardine reported back to Barbara, "Harold has been
sweet and charming and great fun. He admires Chester very much
and Chester finds him very amusing."[125] Yet Harold also proved so
eccentric at times that Bernardine wrote to Rosemary promising
outrageous stories but warned she couldn't include them in a letter.
"I'll tell you more of him another time. I don't want to shock the
grandparents!!!"[126]

In *Peonies and Ponies*, Harold wrote that the hostess Elvira sought
to establish "a salon for the New China to congregate in and friends
who were Chinese to the core." Because his novel came out in 1941,
Harold had the luxury of time to see how Bernardine would go on
to bring people together in Shanghai in ways even she could not have
envisioned in 1932.[127]

---

[124] Letter from Bernardine to Monroe Wheeler to Bernardine, February 7, 1933, Beinecke
Library, YCAL MSS 134 Box 105 f. 1597, page 66.

[125] Letter from Bernardine to Barbara Harrison, undated, YCAL MSS 134 Box 103 f.
1573, page 26.

[126] Letter from Bernardine to Rosemary Carver, undated, courtesy of Bernardine's family, page 2.

[127] Acton, *Peonies and Ponies*, page 23.

CHAPTER SEVEN

FRIENDSHIP WITH SINMAY ZAU
AND THE INTERNATIONAL
ARTS THEATRE, 1933

It started with a party to honor George Bernard Shaw. When the Irish playwright arrived in Shanghai in February 1933 on his own around-the-world journey, PEN China hosted a garden party for him. Shaw was seventy-seven and one of the greatest living playwrights of his time. He did not want to be in Shanghai or anywhere but home in the British Isles, but agreed to this trip because his wife, Charlotte, wished to travel extensively before she was no longer able. Bernardine had performed in Shaw's plays at Chicago's Little Theatre sixteen years earlier and looked forward to the party. She had recently been named secretary of PEN China and arrived with Lin Yutang and a group of other Chinese writers. It's also probably where she first met the poet and publisher, Sinmay Zau.

Unimpressed with Shanghai, Shaw was noticeably bored at the party. Bernardine and a number of the guests guided him around the garden, hoping to cheer him up. Whether she was able to relay that she had acted in the first productions of his plays in the United States remains unknown, but he probably could not have cared less.

It was an unusually pleasant day in Shanghai as the weather fully cooperated for the party. The normal haze—from the many vessels on the Whangpoo, the burned coal from the trains, and the trucks, cars, and other gas-guzzling vehicles plodding through the dense confines of the city—somehow seemed to have disappeared that day.

"You don't know how lucky you are to see the sun in Shanghai at this season, Mr. Shaw," a guest remarked.

Shaw replied, "You don't know how lucky the sun is to see Mr. Shaw in Shanghai at any season of the year, Lady B—."[128]

Sinmay Zau made a greater impression on Bernardine than did George Bernard Shaw. A good decade younger than Bernardine, Sinmay had studied in Paris around the time Bernardine lived there, but they had not crossed paths back then. Sinmay was known for his wispy mustache and goatee, and Bernardine likened his looks to Jesus.[129] Married to wealthy Sheng Peiyu, Sinmay was already father to a couple of young children when he met Bernardine.

After the party for George Bernard Shaw, Bernardine and Sinmay began a decades-long correspondence. Other writers have intimated a romantic connection between the two, at the very least in their letters. But the timing of Bernardine's first meeting with Sinmay in early 1933 doesn't match up with something she wrote to Barbara later that year, a full twelve months after Barbara and Monroe had visited Shanghai in 1932. "About the thing I told you of here in this study, when you were here, that of course has absolutely nothing to do with the flesh. It means nothing at all to me, but there I am guilty of appalling infidelity of the spirit I suppose, because I idolize and adore him, but as a god and not as a man at all; if he weren't a poet, a sublime artist, he'd mean nothing more in the world to me than, well, just any nice man I know anywhere at all. Chester would never understand that, nor perhaps believe it. I have almost forgotten what the feeling of 'being in

---

[128] June Provines, "Front Views and Profiles," *Chicago Daily Tribune*, November 9, 1934, page 21.

[129] Letter from Bernardine to Barbara Harrison, July 20, undated, Beinecke Library, YCAL MSS 134 Box 126 f. 1971, page 23.

love' in that wild sickening way—perhaps it's just as well I never have cause to recall."[130]

She was not writing about Sinmay because the two did not meet until after Barbara and Monroe had left China, so the poet she was referring to could not have been him. Yet she did write to Barbara about her feelings toward Sinmay in another letter in late 1933. "Sinmay who is so beautiful that I always want to caress him, you didn't see him did you? Oh he is so beautiful."[131] Although Barbara had not met Sinmay, she certainly heard about him from Bernardine in their letters.

Instead, the poet Bernardine was referring to may have been Lin Yutang. Bernardine kept a typed excerpt from a Shanghai "mosquito" paper, or gossip rag, that appeared to be an English translation from the Chinese. "Lin Yutang has a pretty bosom friend. Good Gracious, it is No 1 IMPORTED GOODS, Bernardine Fritz. Inspired by the foreign ocean woman, he wrote his masterpiece, 'My Country and My People.' Our literary circle is always colored by peach blossom colored news."[132] Bernardine did write pages and pages about Yutang, but very little about Sinmay. Even so, mosquito papers were not to be trusted, and Bernardine's relationship with Yutang seemed platonic.

Yutang appreciated Bernardine's outgoing personality and wrote in a letter to her, early on in their friendship when he still addressed her as Mrs. Fritz, "You are an emotional soul, almost like a child it seems at times, as excitable, I must tell you that is the best part of yourself, the most likeable part."[133] Yet he kept her grounded and focused, something that certainly helped when she tried to bring people together. That was not the case with Sinmay.

Bernardine and Sinmay were both sprites. He compared himself to Verlaine, the French poet during the Decadent movement in Europe,

---

[130] Letter from Bernardine to Barbara Harrison, undated 1933, Beinecke Library, YCAL MSS 134 Box 126 f. 1969, page 27.

[131] Ibid., page 16.

[132] Undated typed newspaper excerpt, possibly a translation from the Chinese, "From the 'mosquito' paper, Shanghai', undated, Beinecke Library, YCAL MSS 544 Box 3, f. Lin, Yu Tang, page 16.

[133] Letter from Lin Yutang to Bernardine, February 28, undated, Beinecke Library, YCAL MSS 544 Box 3 f. Lin, Yu Tang, page 15.

and brought out the socialite in Bernardine. Sinmay relished in her connections to people like Gertrude Stein and Hemingway. During Sinmay's years in Paris, he had attended other salons, but he had yet to find one in Shanghai that brought together foreigners and Chinese until he met Bernardine. He soon became a regular at Bernardine's salon at 62 Route de Boissezon.

Not long after they met, Sinmay sent Bernardine fifteen copies of a pictorial—a popular type of publication in Shanghai at that time that included mostly photos and very little written text—published by his Modern Press. Bernardine in turn lent Sinmay a copy of Gertrude Stein's latest book, *The Autobiography of Alice B. Toklas*. A bestseller, the book caused a stir around the English-speaking world because, while Stein wrote the book, it appeared as if it were penned by her life partner, Alice Toklas. After Virginia Woolf's *Orlando*, this book was one of the first to reimagine the fictional biography. Hemingway found Stein's new book pitiful while Sinmay couldn't put it down. Yet Sinmay had some conflicting thoughts and expressed these in a letter to Bernardine that he included with the book when he returned it to her.

"I had an all-night reading of Gertrude Stein. Wonderful!" Sinmay wrote. "She used to please her people with her style, and she is now pleasing her style with her people. I don't like her 'commanding air,' which fits her (but doesn't fit me). Now, here is a lady who has no soul or has too many souls and misleads them all."[134] In another letter, he later wrote, "Bernardine, you are really adorable! Your letter means more to me than 100 autobiographies by Gertrude Stein. Do write your own someday. G.S. will be ashamed to death."[135]

As with Harold, Jean Cocteau appears in Sinmay's writings, namely in a letter to Bernardine when he lamented that Stein did not address the French writer enough in her book. Somewhere around the time Bernardine met Sinmay, she wrote to Glenway and referred to her new

---

[134] Letter from Sinmay Zau to Bernardine, undated, Beinecke Library, YCAL MSS 544 Box 5 f. Zau, Sinmay, page 17.
[135] Ibid., page 10.

friend as "the most beautiful human I've ever looked at."[136] To prove it, she sent Glenway a couple photos of Sinmay and asked him to pass one on to Cocteau.[137]

Bernardine had her own views about *The Autobiography of Alice B. Toklas*, finding it both amusing and irritating. "She has known only three geniuses and the first is G Stein *alors*. It makes me itch to write my experiences with her and I even think I may yet," she wrote to Barbara.[138]

Bernardine and Sinmay could spend hours talking about the state of Chinese publishing or the newest American authors. Through Sinmay, Bernardine started to meet more Chinese artists and actors. Less than two months after the George Bernard Shaw party, Sinmay attended Bernardine's salon and invited Butterfly Wu, China's most celebrated movie starlet.[139] Sinmay even came up with an endearing nickname for Bernardine: Madame Salon.

Early on in their friendship, Sinmay mailed Bernardine a letter, more of a drawing than a note. He had sketched a horse's head, writing underneath that it was his new signature. He wondered if Bernardine could read it. In Chinese romanization, his name "Zau" began at the horse's chin and "Sinmay" continued up to its ears and down its mane.[140]

As with Yutang and Hong, Bernardine joined Sinmay and his wife, Peiyu, for nights out. One evening, the Zaus invited Bernardine to dinner at the Sun Ya restaurant followed by a Peking opera at the Tien Chan Theatre.[141]

---

[136] Letter from Bernardine to Glenway Wescott, May 23, 1934, YCAL MSS 134 Box 103 f. 1572, page 21.

[137] In an undated letter from Sinmay Zau to Bernardine, he writes about Gertrude Stein's new book, *The Autobiograpy of Alice B. Toklas*: "Another impression I have of that book is that she has said too little about Cocteau." Beinecke Library, YCAL MSS 544 Box 5 f. Zau, Sinmay, page 17.

[138] Letter from Bernardine to Barbara Harrison, undated, Beinecke Library, YCAL MSS 134 Box 126 f. 1969, page 17.

[139] Sinmay Zau sent a letter to Bernardine, April 4, 1933, with a promise to invite to her salon the movie star, Butterfly Wu.

[140] Letter from Sinmay Zau to Bernardine, undated. Beinecke Library, YCAL MSS 544 Box 5 f. Zau, Sinmay, page 8.

[141] Ibid., pages 27–28.

Sometimes Sinmay suffered from writer's block and would write to Bernardine from out of town. His letters show how close they had become in the matter of a couple months. "You wonder why I signed my last letter as Sin? I could make it very simple. You know, I have already hidden myself here almost a month. I tried to craft something that could cause sensation to this world. Three weeks have gone; nothing blossoms. For there is no May in me any longer. This is why I sign with half of my name. It means that what I am now is not a complete representative of myself. O, I must stop now. Explanation always ends in nonsense! You said you could tell me something to make me smile. How do you know that I am not smiling (which is true)? Please tell me in your next letter, for I will not leave this cave until I have accomplished something."[142]

***

In an early letter to Bernardine soon after they met, Sinmay wrote about a meeting with Aaron Avshalomoff, a Russian Jewish composer who had studied medicine in Zürich before the Bolshevik Revolution. Worried about the instability at home, Avshalomoff's family insisted he not return home and rather move to the United States to practice medicine there. By the end of the 1910s, he became bored by the medical field and wanted to pursue classical music, both as a composer and a conductor. Avshalomoff knew about Russian enclaves in a number of Chinese cities, from Harbin in the northeast to Shanghai on the central east coast, as well as other cities in between. Some had been in China for decades to do business, while larger groups of White Russians and Russian Jews were more recent arrivals after fleeing the Bolsheviks. Avshalomoff felt it was worthwhile to give his music career a try in China. He couldn't have been more pleased when he started to collaborate with other Jewish musicians in Peking and Shanghai.

In the first half of 1933, Bernardine invited Avshalomoff to her salon and had already spoken to Sinmay of her desire to do something more for the Shanghai arts community. Her salons were seeing

---

[142] Ibid., page 22.

upwards of 150 people a night, and while she hated to turn people away, she just couldn't accommodate everyone in her apartment. When she invited Avshalomoff to her salon, she learned he had written a ballet, *The Soul of the Ch'in*, while living in Peking in 1925 and 1926. The ballet had been performed in Portland, Oregon, in the late 1920s but had yet to be produced in China.

Suddenly Bernardine had a new project she could take beyond her salon. She convinced Avshalomoff that together they could produce his ballet right there in Shanghai. She was not unfamiliar with the dance world and was friends with Ruth Page, the American ballerina, and her partner, Harald Kreutzberg, a pioneer in German modern dance.[143] Through George Platt Lynes, Bernardine was also connected to Lincoln Kirstein, who at that time was in the process of founding the School of American Ballet. And in Shanghai, Bernardine was close with Vanya Oakes, the pen name of American writer and librarian Virginia Armstrong Oakes, a friend of Glenway's, who was also involved in the dance community there.[144] Bernardine wrote that Vanya had helped Rosemary find dance classes in Shanghai during the summer of 1930, but it's unclear as to whether she ran her own ballet school or knew of ballet teachers in Shanghai.

Avshalomoff's experience in China—he had already lived there for almost fifteen years—and Bernardine's background at the Little Theatre in Chicago allowed the duo to bring a ballet to Shanghai that would appeal to all arts enthusiasts, both Chinese and foreign. Bernardine tapped into her connections in Shanghai's financial and political communities. Avshalomoff also knew Madame Chiang Kai-shek, or Soong Mei-ling, and Madame Sun Yat-sen, or Soong Ching-ling, both avid patrons of the arts.

---

[143]   Letter from Bernardine to Barbara Harrison, undated, YCAML MSS 134 Box 126 f. 1971, page 16. In this letter Bernardine mentions to Barbara that Ruth Page and her husband Harald Kreutzberg were to arrive in Shanghai later that year to stay with Chester and her on their way to performances in other parts of Asia.

[144]   Ibid., page 10. In this letter, Bernardine isn't sure if Vanya Oakes was closer with Ruth Weil or Lincoln Kirstein. Bernardine also mentions that Oakes was trying to open a dance and theater school in Shanghai. It's unclear as to whether she succeeded or not. Bernardine also wrote often about the Romanian dancer, Lizica Codreanu-Fontenoy, also in Shanghai during the time Bernardine lived there.

Bernardine did not write in her vignettes about the work she put into producing *The Soul of the Ch'in*, but she did keep a program from the performance on May 21, 1933, at 9:15 PM at the new Grand Theatre.[145] The list of organizers certainly included some of the most prominent figures in China, including—not surprisingly—Lin Yutang. Bernardine formed the general committee with three other expat women, including Jewish Slovakian Theresa Renner, who studied piano under Béla Bartók in Hungary and lived in Shanghai with her physician husband Alexander for almost thirty years before moving to Southern California.

The sponsor list contained mostly Chinese names with a sprinkling of foreigners: Georgette Chen, the painter and wife of diplomat Eugene Chen; Mei Lanfang, Peking opera star and a regular at Bernardine's salon; and T. F. Soong, the theater aficionado Bernardine met through Lin Yutang. Other sponsors included the founder of the Shanghai Conservatory of Music, the former head of the Bank of China, and the president of Peking University. Among the expats were the Baroness von Ungern-Sternberg, the wife of the US consul general, and the wife of a German shipping agent.

The Grand Theatre sat at the northern end of the Shanghai Race Course and was designed by Hungarian architect László Hudec. The Art Deco building was brand-new and had not yet officially opened as a cinema. It promised a state-of-the-art screen to provide simultaneous translation for the films that would start showing three weeks after the ballet.

Up until now, Bernardine had only organized cultural events at her salon. To put on an endeavor like this ballet, she felt that she and her group of friends should have a name. She called them the International Arts Theatre Group of Shanghai, but after this performance they would simply be known as the IAT.

---

[145] Special Chinese Programme, May 21, 1933, from the personal papers of Bernardine Szold Fritz, courtesy of her family, page 1.

The evening began with a "Ta Tung" Orchestra that played a selection of classic Chinese themes on Chinese instruments. According to the program, "The orchestra which appears to-night is well known for its faithful rendition of the ancient classical music, which though seemingly simple and monotonous, nevertheless reflected to the ancient Chinese people the subtlety of life and depth of thought. The music is selected from some of the old themes and played on thirty different instruments. It depicts generally the gaiety of life in the natural world, and how mankind lives peacefully and in harmony with nature."[146]

Musician Wei Chung Loh followed the orchestra's medleys with a solo on the pipa, an instrument that looks much like a lute. Wei was one of the most proficient pipa players in Shanghai and played a piece titled "Musical Description of a Battle."

Avshalomoff arranged the second part of the program, which included works performed by the Shanghai Municipal Orchestra conducted by Mario Paci. After a few pieces, the lights came on for a short intermission so the audience could stretch and the orchestra could set up for the final part: the ballet.

The Soul of the Ch'in was possibly the first ballet performed on a grand scale in China with a cast of Chinese dancers. The set designers, dramaturge, and stage manager were also Chinese. The only foreigners on the crew were the costume designer and the person managing the lights. While Anna Pavlova performed in Shanghai in 1922, inspiring scores of young Chinese to study ballet from the many Russian émigrés who had fled to the city after the Bolshevik Revolution, there didn't seem to be any large-scale ballet performances of Chinese stories in Shanghai or elsewhere in China before Bernardine and Avshalomoff produced *The Soul of the Ch'in* in 1933.

The ballet was set during a war. Trumpets announced the triumph of the victorious rebel general, Go Chai. The ousted emperor Yien Wang has retreated as his palace goes up in flames. By the shore of the Sai Nan Lake, General Go Chai hides in a boat to confront the emperor. The emperor has been joined by Kinsei, a devoted friend

---

[146] Ibid., page 5.

and renowned harpist. "See, there is a boat by the lake. Take it; cross the lake, reorganize your army and fight again," Kinsei pleads with the emperor.[147] The emperor instead attempts to commit suicide. Kinsei saves the emperor and guides him to a getaway boat.

Suddenly, Go Chai jumps from his boat to confront the emperor and kills him in a sword fight. Kinsei rushes to the emperor's side, but it is too late. General Go Chai declares that he is the new emperor and demands Kinsei play the harp for him. Still devoted to the fallen emperor Yien Wang, Kinsei begins to play his harp, enchanting Go Chai with the magic of the music. A dancing girl appears on the water, casting a spell on Go Chai and luring him into the lake until he drowns. Kinsei strums his harp, playing a song of despair. "The music waves like a pale line of ascending incense smoke, fading to infinity in the shadows of night." Kinsei tumbles over his harp and the emperor magically awakens. The emperor thanks the exhausted Kinsei, who tells the emperor he owes his gratitude to the harp. "Take it—it is my gift to my beloved master. I am ready to join my ancestors."[148] Kinsei dies and the emperor sheds tears as the curtains fall.

The audience jumped to a roaring applause.

Shanghai had never seen an evening like this with Chinese and foreign performers all working together. Bernardine knew she never could have produced a performance like this in Chicago, New York, or even Paris.

The International Arts Theatre would take a break for two years, but when it came back in 1935, it would revolutionize the arts in Shanghai for a brief period before much of the city would succumb to the Japanese invasion. As for Sinmay, Bernardine would indirectly change his life two years later, in ways neither he nor his wife, Peiyu, could ever have imagined.

---

[147] Ibid., page 10.
[148] Ibid., page 11.

CHAPTER EIGHT

MIGUEL AND ROSA RETURN
TO SHANGHAI, 1933

The *North China Herald* covered Miguel and Rosa Covarrubias' return to Shanghai in October 1933, and it all centered around Bernardine.

"It would have been difficult to name a nationality which was not represented at Mrs. Chester Fritz's cocktail party given last Tuesday in honor of Mr. and Mrs. Miguel Covarrubias. The large living room and dining room opening into one another, in her flat in The Cloisters, Route de Boissezon, were thronged. Mrs. Covarrubias, tall, beautiful and dark, was dressed in black, which set off to perfection her dark eyes. Among the guests were a large number of Chinese artists, several of whom had studied in Europe or America. And Mei Lanfang, consummate artist in his chosen vocation, was also present. Much interest was expressed in a collection of sketches of Chinese actresses and singing girls, done by Covarrubias, and pronounced by Chinese present to have caught with remarkable felicity the spirit of these women. A collection of curios, which Mr. and Mrs. Fritz have recently brought back from Peking, also drew forth a great deal of appreciative comment, particularly a fine example of the clay horses, such as have become the sought after pieces of Chinese art to-day."[149]

Headed to Bali for an extended stay, Miguel and Rosa spent a month at Bernardine and Chester's in 1933 and saw a Shanghai they could only have glimpsed on their first, quick trip in 1930. Besides the aforementioned cocktail party, Bernardine held a welcome lunch for the couple, inviting a dozen Chinese artists and writers including Sinmay, Yutang, and Hong. As conversation flowed and a group of illustrators probed Miguel with questions about his work for *Vanity Fair* and the *New Yorker*, Sinmay suddenly suggested they should all dash off to Soochow the following day. Soochow was a good three hours away by train.

Bernardine, picking up on Sinmay's excitement and just as impulsive, offered up Chester's houseboat, which happened to be docked in that very city and could comfortably sleep the whole group. Yutang and Hong declared they were in, as were illustrators Yeh Ch'ien-yu and two brothers by the name of Chang Kuang-yu and Chang Chen-yu.

"We traversed the canals in a red lacquer houseboat owned by the Fritzes, gliding under the bridges and observing the fascinating river traffic around us," Rosa remembered.[150] Although Chester did not join them, he was perfectly happy to lend his houseboat. Despite her difficulties with him, Bernardine found Chester most generous when he set his mind to it, especially when it would make him look good in front of their friends.

In Soochow, Sinmay and the Chinese writers and illustrators invited Miguel, Rosa, and Bernardine to the private homes of prominent painters, musicians, and other writers who welcomed them as guests. Miguel always kept a sketchbook on hand, and many of his drawings appeared in *The China I Knew*, a book Rosa published about their trip.

One illustration is a self-portrait along with Rosa and Bernardine seated in the dining car of a train.[151] Miguel is peering over his right

---

[149]   "Here and There," *The North-China Herald*, October 11, 1933, page 79.
[150]   Adriana Williams and Rosa Covarrubias, *The China I Knew*, (San Francisco, Protean Press: 2005), page 4.
[151]   Ibid., page 5.

shoulder as he brings chopsticks to his mouth. Rosa and Bernardine sit opposite, Rosa reaching for morsels of food with her chopsticks while Bernardine brings her rice bowl up to her mouth with one hand and her chopsticks with the other. With her signature turban and chunky earrings and necklace, Bernardine's wide eyes appear as hypnotic spirals.

One morning in Soochow, the group sailed under the many bridges that have branded the city as the Venice of China. Rosa wrote of their journey to the countryside, "Now and again the silence was broken by the woman in charge of the boat screaming loudly at her henpecked husband. Someone said, 'There goes Pearl Buck's oppressed womanhood.' We all had a good laugh. *The Good Earth* had just been published and the Chinese were a bit skeptical of the docile heroine of the now famous book."[152]

Sinmay insisted the group try all of the many delicacies in Soochow and ordered so many dishes one evening that Rosa diligently chronicled them all. This dinner began with tasting portions of starters, including candied walnuts, Chekiang ham, shirred eggs, roasted sparrows, raw crab in wine, bean curd, mushrooms in oil, cold boiled chicken, sliced gizzards, mushrooms stuffed with shrimp paste, sliced duck, and raw shrimp. Next came the hot dishes of white shrimp with new peas, ligaments of pig feet, "shrimp paste with fish centers on petals of ham and chicken," bamboo shoots with greens, and bird's nest soup.[153]

The group enjoyed four types of dumplings, their wrappers just as elaborate as the fillings. A pork dumpling was shaped like a leaf with red outlines over a white wrapper. Another resembled a phoenix egg, filled with rose leaves and decorated on the outside with the colors of the Mexican flag in honor of Rosa and Miguel. Yet another was modeled after a basket separated into four parts, each filled with mushrooms, shrimp, bamboo, and pickled vegetables. And the last was a puffed pastry with a sweet red bean filling formed into Buddha's hand.

That was just the beginning. The main dishes were then brought to the table: a whole duck cooked in soup, crab in red sauce, a whole chicken with scallions, a pork-based soup, sweet and sour baked fish,

---

152   Ibid., page 8.
153   Ibid., page 12.

Chinese cabbage, pigeon eggs, a soup with mushrooms that grow on bamboo, and rice. For dessert, they ate pomelo, melon seeds, and mint. "Finally we ended this extraordinary picnic with hot wine and tooth-picks!" Rosa wrote.[154] The others in their group returned to Shanghai after their memorable trip to Soochow, but Bernardine continued on to Peking with Rosa and Miguel. There, they visited with Harold Acton and enjoyed his tour of the city and his traditional Peking home.

When the trio returned to Shanghai, Bernardine took Rosa and Miguel to visit Lord Li's estate, the setting of the garden party where she and Harold chattered the previous year about Edda Mussolini and her husband, Count Ciano. Rosa was equally impressed with Lord Li's stately manner and also wrote about the immense garden. But the interiors captivated her the most. "In the living quarters the family altar was adorned with a lovely painting of peaches executed by the old Empress Dowager (1838–1908). In the dining room, where we were served tea, there hung huge slabs of white marble with dark forms of natural landscapes in very modern designs that impressed us all. Tea was served on a massive teakwood table accompanied by beautiful cakes that looked and tasted like fruits."[155]

Miguel's influence on Chinese illustrators—and vice versa—cannot be understated. Readers in Shanghai would have been able to view Miguel's illustrations in the *New Yorker* and *Vanity Fair*, as some bookstores, like Kelly and Walsh, catered to an international clientele.

Thanks to Bernardine, Miguel met journal editors in Shanghai, including Sinmay and Yutang. Their publications and others in the city started to publish Miguel's illustrations. Chinese artists also started to incorporate Miguel's style into their work. Some of these illustrators included Yeh Ch'ien-yu and the brothers, Chang Kuang-yu and Chang Chen-yu, the men on the Soochow houseboat.[156] They were the

---

[154] Ibid., page 14.
[155] Ibid., page 17.
[156] Paul Bevan, *A Modern Miscellany: Shanghai Cartoon Artists, Shao Xunmei's Circle and the Travels of Jack Chen, 1926–1938*, (Leiden, Brill: 2018), page 111.

premier illustrators and cartoonists in Shanghai, and their work began to reflect Miguel's style of bold, linear caricature.

Their illustrations contain more white space than ink. Chang Kuang-yu, for instance, drew a trio of women in 1934 that looks almost indistinguishable from Miguel's work. In Chang's *Folk Love Songs*, published in the Chinese magazine *Modern Sketch*, the three women each have bangs that fall in straight lines under their head coverings. But it's their caricaturized clothing that screams Covarrubias. Chang drew these three women each with loose trousers under tunics that fall to their knees. The creases of fabric at their elbows and the knotted buttons of the tunic are simple, yet just about the same amount of detail that Miguel used in his illustration, *Two Women Chatting*, published in Rosa's book.[157]

After his trip to Shanghai in 1933, Miguel sometimes used Chinese characters to sign his work.[158] In his illustrations from China, he exaggerated the mandarin collars in Chinese clothes, drawing them to reach the chin, often fastened by three knotted buttons. He paid attention to other details, illustrating a single jade bracelet, the blunt cut of a woman's bangs, almost touching her eyes, and the fuzzy claws of the famous Shanghai hairy crab. In a sketch titled "Sinmay Zau, poet and friend," Miguel highlighted Sinmay's thick mane and aquiline nose.[159]

After his two trips to China, Miguel illustrated a number of books about the country, including Rosa's *The China I Knew*, Marc Chadourne's *China*, and Pearl Buck's translation of Shih Nai-an's *All Men are Brothers* which is also known to some English readers as *Water Margin*. Through his drawings, Miguel brought China to audiences in the United States in ways that reach beyond words.

Rosa and Miguel's 1933 sojourn corresponded with the height of Bernardine's salon. On their previous visit, Bernardine had been full of

157   Adriana Williams and Rosa Covarrubias, *The China I Knew*, (San Francisco, Protean Press: 2005), page 13.

158   Paul Bevan, "The Impact of the Work of Miguel Covarrubias," *Anales del Instituto de Investigaciones Estéticas*, Universidad Nacional Autónoma de México, volumen XLII, suplemento al número 116, March 6, 2020, pages 42–43.

159   Adriana Williams and Rosa Covarrubias, *The China I Knew*, (San Francisco, Protean Press: 2005), page 3.

nerves over Rosemary's arrival and could concentrate on little else. But on this trip, Bernardine included the couple in her salon where they met her new friends, many of whom influenced Miguel in his art and vice versa.

By the time Rosa and Miguel had arrived in Shanghai on this second visit, Bernardine had already been coined Madame Salon by Sinmay, for good reason, and she had successfully produced the ballet with Aaron Avshalomoff at the Grand Theatre with her International Arts Theatre. Rosa and Miguel could see that Bernardine had made a name for herself in Shanghai and was also a passionate tour guide to other parts of China like Soochow and Peking. Bernardine had finally found a place for herself in Shanghai and looked forward to 1934, especially a trip to Bali to visit the Covarrubiases after they settled in there.

CHAPTER NINE

PANIC ON JAVA, 1934

B ernardine's original interest in Asia began in the drawing room of Blanche Matthias, a wealthy Chicago poet and close friend of Georgia O'Keeffe. In the late 1910s, Bernardine and Glenway met Blanche through Glenway's Chicago poetry circles. The two friends were delighted when Blanche invited them to her Chicago home to view her Indian silks. As Bernardine stepped into Blanche's drawing room, she felt as if she were entering a fairy tale. Swaths of silk draped over chairs and sofas, while others cascaded over the curtain rods.

"It looks like captured moonlight," Glenway remarked.[160]

Bernardine and Glenway sipped their tea while Blanche put her hands together as if in prayer. "But I haven't told you about Bali." She sashayed across the room to where she reached for two large, silver-bound books. "If you're done in by my Indian tissues, wait until you see the pictures of the island inhabited by angels."

Bernardine politely received one of the books, hoping to quickly fan through it so she could return her attention to the silks. Glenway appeared to do the same.

---

[160] Bernardine Szold Fritz, "It Seems Like Yesterday," unpublished manuscript courtesy of her family, page 1.

"Little did I suspect that that was a crucial point in my life," Bernardine recalled.[161]

For the next hour, the two friends carefully examined the pages, enraptured by the beauty and detail of the photos. "Occasionally one of us said, Oh My God. Sometimes the accent was on the first word, sometimes on the second, sometimes on the last...I have never been the same since," Bernardine recollected.

After that visit to Blanche's, Bernardine filed Bali in the back of her mind as the one place she would want to visit the most if given the chance, but she viewed it more as fantasy than possibility. "I've lost old illusions and collected new ones, for illusions are the manna of my life," Bernardine wrote.[162] Bali seemed so out of reach for her, even some years later after she had sailed across the Atlantic to live in Paris and had spent time at Cambridge. Dreams became reality when Barbara asked Bernardine to join her on that trip to Asia in 1927 and 1928.

With the opportunity to finally visit picturesque Bali in the Dutch East Indies, now known as Indonesia, Bernardine could not say no, even though it meant she would need to cut short her endeavors at Cambridge. "Barbara Harrison, you are a wretch. Bali is the only siren who could beguile me from London, where I've just settled down to a year of industry and accomplishment."[163]

Four days after Barbara proposed this trip, Bernardine, Barbara, and Walter Harris boarded their ship at Marseilles. It would take almost six months—traveling to Egypt, India, Sri Lanka, and Burma—to reach the Dutch protectorate of Bali but to Bernardine, the wait would be more than worthwhile.

"Bali lay before us, that April dawn, like a cool mysterious wreathe gently placed on the surface of untroubled sea. It was shrouded with an intense blue mist, as if a cover of Pompeian glass had been fitted over its contours, to protect them from mortal invasions. It was so unreal that for a moment I was afraid to clamor down the unsteady ladder to

---

161   Ibid., page 2.
162   Ibid.
163   Ibid.

the little row boat that stood waiting to haul us ashore."[164] These were Bernardine's first impressions of the island before she set foot on Bali.

When they reached shore, a local driver who called himself John met them in a Hudson automobile and whisked the trio away to the mountain village of Munduk. Bernardine fell into a trance and found the scenery even more majestic than she had imagined back in Blanche Matthias' drawing room. "The landscape curves and rolls and suddenly leaps into a mountain, the slopes of which are like a very formal terrace. These are the paddy fields, laid out in odd mottled peels, that shine like quicksilver in the sunlight, or where the tender rice shoots have pushed through, rise in regular accession of bright glistening greens."[165]

Soon they came across a procession along a sacred grove. A single file of women numbering in the hundreds stretched for half a mile. Each woman wore a sarong and carried a basket on her head, some holding their baskets with one hand and others balancing them hands-free. A line of men followed, each carrying cymbals or gongs suspended from bamboo poles. John stopped the car and guided Bernardine and her friends to where the procession was headed. "We clamored after them, and walked for a long way down a shaded jungle path. Hundreds of monkeys scampered about, and were being fed by priests. Without any warning, we suddenly found ourselves in a clearing, defined by colossal trees, whose bare silver trunks rose majestically upward, and finally, at an unbelievable height, were crowned by thick leaves, like lace parasols on impossibly tall handles."[166]

The travelers found thousands of pilgrims gathered in small groups, each surrounding a cluster of musicians playing instruments. Some of the women had walked more than twenty miles and were resting, while others headed through tapered carved gates to a shrine. "Grotesque demons now appeared—a weird creature, part tiger, part elephant, part dragon, with long peacock feathers and flimsy white streamers floating

---

[164] Ibid.
[165] Ibid., page 3.
[166] Ibid., page 4.

from his sides was carried over the heads of four men. His enormous bulging eyes were made out of mirrors, and he was truly terrifying."[167]

Blanche Matthias' photos had nothing on the many processions Bernardine observed during her stay in Bali, including simple early morning walks to the markets. Bernardine marveled at the stalls where vendors dressed pigs in green jackets of woven reed so they could easily be picked up and carried off when sold. "The creatures make so much noise," Bernardine recalled, "and their mistresses hold them just like infants, and pat them and say shh, hh, shh, hh, very tenderly. [sic]"[168]

***

Now six years later, Bernardine was about to head back to Bali. It was early 1934, and she and Chester would be visiting Rosa and Miguel before continuing on to other parts of Southeast Asia, the Middle East, Europe, and the United States. Chester had business in London and New York, and Bernardine made it her responsibility to ensure he enjoyed his time away from work and Shanghai. She felt extra nervous about keeping Chester happy because they planned to meet up with Rosemary in Europe. Bernardine had not forgotten the disappointing summer of 1930 when Chester completely ignored Rosemary during her stay with them in Shanghai. Now she wanted Chester to be in a good mood when they reached the West. Chester had seen Rosemary two other times—only for a few days—since 1930, when he and Bernardine traveled to Europe for his business. This forthcoming visit with Rosemary would be longer, at two to three weeks.

Soon after they arrived in Bali, Bernardine felt sluggish and took longer than usual to get out of bed each morning. She found herself struggling to muster the energy for everyday activities like walking in the fields with Chester or strolling to the market with Rosa. It was so atypical of her to possess less energy than Chester and her friends. Normally she was the one asking others to hurry along and catch up. This fatigue seemed to have come out of nowhere. At thirty-seven, she

---

[167] Ibid., page 5.
[168] Ibid.

was rather young to feel so incapacitated but figured she needed more time to rest after a couple days at sea since leaving Shanghai.

A day or two later, Bernardine noticed several spots of blood around her right nipple. She did not panic and immediately thought back to six years earlier when she was diagnosed with a swollen gland in the same breast. She was in the UK then, and her doctors believed it wasn't serious. Now in Bali, Bernardine figured it was more of the same. Perhaps the heat and humidity had brought on another swollen gland.

After she and Chester left Bali for Solo, now called Surakarta, in Central Java, Bernardine checked that breast again and felt a lump just under the nipple. This was new.

She touched it again and again just to be sure it wasn't her imagination. Each time she felt that area, she found the lump. It seemed the size of a quarter. Like most women who find a strange lump in their breast, Bernardine's mind shot directly to cancer. What else could explain it? And why was this happening now? She and Chester had just started their extended vacation.

Bernardine couldn't possibly disturb his peaceful time away from Shanghai with yet another health scare. Their first trip west together in 1930 seemed like yesterday, even though four years had passed. On that trip, when they reached Germany, Bernardine scheduled surgery for "adhesions," perhaps for uterine fibroids.[169] Although she was the one to go under the knife, it was Chester who fell apart. He claimed this simple surgery would be the end of Bernardine. He was so sure she wouldn't make it and that he would be left all alone in Germany and after he returned to Shanghai. She was now determined to keep Chester in the dark until she could learn more about this lump. Bernardine could not bear another of his doomsday breakdowns and worried she would destroy any chance of a peaceful vacation if she revealed her health issues before she knew for sure if this new discovery was indeed serious.

The need to keep the peace, sadly, was not unique to Bernardine. Historically, most women have been expected to make the caretaking of

---

[169] "Narrative of Bernardine Szold's Life," courtesy of David Szanton, page 32.

other people their top priority, putting their families first before taking care of themselves. Bernardine may have held progressive ideas when it came to politics and equality, but she was still subject to the same social and cultural constraints and expectations of her time, whether she realized it or not.

She racked her brain to think of someone she could ask for help. Rosa and Miguel were back in Bali, and Bernardine knew no one in Solo. A surge of nausea hit her like a tidal wave and she could barely stand. All she wanted was to get some sleep. But even then, she tossed and turned, thoughts of cancer and surgeries invading her dreams. The next morning, she and Chester boarded a train for Batavia, now known as Jakarta. Bernardine held on to the tops of each backrest, steadying herself as she made her way to their assigned seats. Once situated, she fell into a deep slumber. Her head tossed side to side, often colliding with Chester's shoulder, as the train rambled west.

"I've never seen you so 'all in' before," Chester remarked after they arrived in Batavia. "I can't believe you are *dozing* in the *day* time. Wonders will never cease."[170] Bernardine did not know how to answer Chester, so she remained silent. She needed to see a doctor immediately, but also sensed she would need surgery once they arrived in Europe. With a clear mind from sleeping on the train, Bernardine realized that Barbara could help her find excellent medical care somewhere in Europe. Bernardine could always depend on her dear friend Barbara, even though she was recovering from her own health issues.

Barbara had been diagnosed with tuberculosis sometime that year. There was no cure for TB, and the only treatment was rest. Barbara was confined to bed even though she felt well enough to shop for groceries and visit friends. Bernardine knew Barbara wasn't completely recovered when she wrote of her breast cancer scare, yet she had no one else to turn to during this crisis on her vacation.

As soon as Bernardine and Chester arrived at the Hotel Des Indes in Batavia, she typed a three-page letter to Barbara at her home in Paris. At the top of the first page, she wrote by hand, "Do not

---

[170] Letter from Bernardine to Barbara Harrison, undated 1934, Beinecke Library, YCAL MSS 134 Box 126 f. 1968, page 7.

read unless—or *until* you feel very fit—as it's full of *woes*, darling."[171] Desperate, Bernardine obsessed over her own mortality, trying to convince Barbara—and herself—that if she were to die from cancer or complications from the surgery, everyone she loved would be all right. Chester would remarry—Bernardine claimed she already knew who he would pick, but did not elaborate—and Rosemary would be fine on her own. Rosemary already got on so well without her, or so Bernardine told herself.

As luck would have it, Victor Sassoon was also visiting Batavia at the same time. Bernardine wrote to Sir V at his hotel and mentioned her dilemmas and how she needed to protect Chester. Victor knew Chester from before Bernardine moved to Shanghai in 1929 and agreed with her plan to keep it from him for now. Sir V tried to cheer her up and assured her it was probably benign. To give Bernardine ample time to consult with a doctor in Batavia, Victor asked Chester out for the afternoon. As she feared, the doctor advised her to see a specialist in Europe; he could not tell if her lump was malignant. If it were malignant, he warned Bernardine, she would need an immediate mastectomy to prevent further complications.

Bernardine could not pull off a surgery on her own, all while keeping it from Chester. Her need to hide it from him may seem extreme, but by this time, they'd been married five years and Bernardine thought she knew how best to deal with Chester's moods. She wrote to Barbara with a convoluted plan to divert Chester from the truth when they arrived in France. "MY idea is that you wire me before we land, asking if I would mind very much coming to see you alone, as you want very much to have me alone for a week or so—would I—I hate making you sound selfish, or willful which of course is the last thing you'd be, and I wonder how to do it, so that C won't think it odd that you want us to separate, on the beginning of our holiday—but as you are ill, I think he will find anything you say or do, most reasonable. And he can go on to London and do his business, and I'll come straight to Suisse, and get the first operation over."[172]

---

[171]   Ibid.
[172]   Ibid.

She mentioned a woman's hospital in Lausanne she had visited on a trip to see Rosemary before she married Chester. But in the same paragraph, Bernardine wondered if she should instead go to Vienna, which would require more planning to keep it from Chester. "I suppose I could go there, leaving letters with you to send to Chester and having you open my mail from C and reply if there are wires—it seems farfetched and dramatic, this scheme—but wilder ones have worked."[173]

Chester could easily learn the truth if Bernardine's plans didn't work perfectly, so she mentioned all possibilities to Barbara. She also wondered if "the boys could help with C, keep him in Paris, or take him on a trip that I could pretend I didn't want to take," referring to Glenway, Monroe, and George.[174] Barbara cabled Bernardine at a Batavian Thomas Cook travel agency office as soon as she received her letter and vowed she would do whatever it took to keep her secret and help her find the very best surgeons.

But before Bernardine received Barbara's telegram, she conferred again with Victor. This time, he urged her to tell Chester but cautioned her to underplay her condition. Without mentioning the word "cancer," Bernardine should tell Chester she needed to have a small cyst removed in Europe. Chester, of course, could deduce for himself the possibility of cancer, but as long as Bernardine did not discuss it, Sir V felt she could steer the conversation in a way that minimized the seriousness of her ailment.

If all went according to their plans, Bernardine could see a surgeon to have the lump analyzed and probably removed. And if she needed a mastectomy, it could happen during that same hospital stay so Chester wouldn't learn of the severity until after the surgeries were completed.

Sir V suggested Bernardine wait to tell Chester about the "cyst" until after they arrived in France. Bernardine remembered that before leaving Shanghai, Chester had mentioned he may want to consult a surgeon in Europe about widening his nasal passage. Now Bernardine realized they could both see doctors in Vienna at the same time. But after her unpleasant experience with Chester in 1930 following her

---

[173]   Ibid., page 8.
[174]   Ibid., page 9.

surgery in Germany, she still worried he would create a scene about her health scare, no matter the outcome.

Although Sir V had asked her to wait to tell Chester, Bernardine felt jittery in Batavia and worried Chester would wonder why she seemed out of sorts. So she decided to tell him then and there, before they left the Dutch East Indies. She would still downplay the seriousness of her condition.

For people who fear confrontation, it's very difficult to share news that may provoke a reaction they don't know how to handle or they want to avoid. So Bernardine turned to the medium of communication she found most comfortable for serious topics: letter writing. Just as she had divulged the existence of Rosemary by telegram five years earlier, Bernardine wrote a quick note to Chester about her "cyst." If Chester reacted in his doomsday manner, Bernardine could avoid his reaction because she wouldn't be near him when he read the letter. She left it in his hotel room before she stepped out to go shopping one morning.

When Bernardine returned an hour or two later, Chester enveloped her in his arms, consoling her with his gentle voice. This was not the reaction she expected, and it made her feel comforted for the first time in a long while. Chester sounded concerned, but not panicked, and assured her that the two of them would travel to Vienna to consult a doctor. Bernardine could tell he hadn't jumped to conclusions about cancer. He also wasn't blaming her for upsetting him with her health issues this time, and she felt grateful for that. It was this side of Chester that Bernardine craved and loved.

Yet she still blamed herself for causing this crack in their vacation plans. "I can't even bear to think how I hate it all, this happening with him, on our holiday, it is too wicked. I often wonder if any other man would be so sweet about things, and wouldn't reproach me, as if I did it on purpose, and think what a bother and expense I am—and wonder why he didn't marry someone else."[175] Bernardine certainly wasn't the first woman to think of her husband before her own well-being,

[175] Ibid., page 13.

and yet after finding the strength to leave her first three marriages, she somehow did not have the confidence to stand up to Chester. Perhaps there was so much more to lose this time.

Bernardine also worried that if she needed a mastectomy, losing a breast would cause a great rift in their relationship. She could picture it now: Chester would attempt to act normal with a wife missing a breast, but his little-boy face—his expression when he didn't get his way or felt threatened by Rosemary—would be sure to reveal his revulsion. "I understand so well, people in such a state are so dreadful," she mused to Barbara.

Bernardine needed a diversion from her worries and started her search for a doctor in Vienna. She wrote to a Dr. Reiss she knew back in Shanghai, asking him for a surgeon referral and making arrange-ments for any return correspondence to be sent to her at the Thomas Cook travel agency in Singapore, all while Chester was still in the dark about her true condition.

When Bernardine arrived in Singapore with Chester and Victor after leaving Batavia together, the city greatly contrasted with when she and Barbara had ditched Walter Harris there six years earlier. Bernardine met up with some mutual friends and reminisced in a letter to Barbara about the old days. "You can't think how I laugh, at places we've been together. X marks so many spots—they still talk of us—and how we've changed, especially you."[176]

Even surrounded by friends, Bernardine could not relax in Singapore. Could they sense she was different from before? Could they notice her lump? And if they knew about her lump, would they treat her any differently? She did feel somewhat relieved before leaving Singapore when her doctor acquaintance in Shanghai replied to her let-ter and suggested a Dr. Schmidt in Vienna.

Bernardine and Chester next sailed to Egypt, where he convinced her to fly in an airplane for the first time so they could quickly find her the proper medical attention. They took off from Suez and landed in

---

[176]   Ibid.

Cairo. It was a short flight, but a rough one nonetheless. "The plane was so tiny," Bernardine wrote to Barbara, "and we jiggled like a cork, all I could think of was please god don't let me get sick."[177] Chester had flown before but admitted after the hour flight that he never would have suggested it had he known the turbulence would be that awful.

Bernardine continued to lose sleep, wondering what the surgeon would find when she and Chester eventually reached Vienna.

---

[177]   Ibid., page 11.

CHAPTER TEN

EUROPEAN RECOVERY, 1934

T he day after her lumpectomy, Bernardine wrote to Barbara from the Sanatorium Auerspergstrasse, a hospital in Vienna that resembled a boutique hotel from the outside. The surgery to remove her lump went well, but she still had not received the pathology results. Instead of worrying about the results, she again turned her thoughts to her husband. "Chester hasn't the vaguest idea of what it's all about."[178]

Sometime during her recuperation at the sanatorium, the surgeon entered her room and announced the pathology results had come back. Speaking as if he were lecturing medical students, he informed Bernardine the lump did not contain abnormal cells, but there was still a worry. "We have taken so long because we wanted to be very sure," the surgeon said. "There is practically nothing there—and yet, the pathologist and I both to ourselves agree that were it anyone in our own families, we would operate again. The danger is that if something does develop it would be so fast that you would scarcely have time to do anything. You are going on a long journey, you are going far away,

---

[178] Ibid., page 20.

it is up to you." He sat on Bernardine's bed and took her hand in his. "Shall I send for your husband?"[179]

Startled by this question and stunned by the recommendation for a mastectomy, even though the physician in Batavia had also thought it would be necessary, Bernardine blurted out, "No, no, no. I must decide for myself. Anyway, whatever happens, don't let him know." She pictured Chester, unapproachable like a child and unable to face this news like an adult. She also worried if she did nothing now and later found another lump in Shanghai, it would be a thousand times worse. She wished she had a friend nearby, someone to consult or help her figure out what to do.

The surgeon advised Bernardine to take a night to think about it, but as soon as she heard that, she knew what she had to do. "I'd kill myself in the night," she told him. "I wouldn't live through the night. I'll decide, I'll decide now. Do it, but do it at once."

"It is very wise," he replied. "Truly my child if you'd seen what I have seen of these things, you'd take no chance."

Bernardine burst out crying. "It will ruin my life with my husband."

"But you are talking nonsense," the surgeon said. "This happens every day. I have never seen a man yet who didn't love his wife more for her affliction."

"He is not to be told," Bernardine warned, suddenly more anxious than sad. "I'll tell him you aren't sure and must make another incision."

That evening, the nurses gave Bernardine injections of morphine to quell the pain from the first surgery. As she waited for it to take, she realized there was nothing more she could do but remain calm and accept her predicament. "I look ahead and shudder—my teeth rattle— so I look behind, and say I must be grateful. I am astonished that I feel so brave and that I can be brave alone, but I know too I could not be brave if Chester knew. I feel somehow so intact, isn't it funny, and so resigned. So tired. Soon I'll wake again and it will all be over. All will be over."[180]

---

[179] Bernardine's unpublished diary, May 3, 1934, Beinecke Library, YCAL MSS 134 Box 103 f. 1575, page 37.
[180] Ibid., page 38.

Barbara wired Bernardine at the hospital to send her love and well wishes. Bernardine replied to Barbara in another letter, "I suppose I should rejoice that it's not worse. The only thing left is to try to behave well—not that I find that consoling."[181] But it wasn't just Chester she sought to protect; she begged Barbara not to tell any of their friends about her surgery. She worried about causing them sadness or perhaps she worried they would treat her differently after learning she had lost a breast. Decades after 1934, it's hard to say if this stigma has gone away even now.

Bernardine found some peace when her surgeon promised he would use only the finest stitches and that no one would be able to tell she had had a mastectomy when she was dressed. She didn't mention a prosthetic in her writings, but in 1934, that would have been common rather than the reconstructive surgery of today. Still, Bernardine could not ignore that she was without a breast. "I shall be a monster," she wrote to Barbara, "but still a live one."

After the surgery was completed, one of the doctors at the hospital insisted on telling Chester as soon as possible. If Bernardine waited any longer, the doctor claimed, her anxiety would only worsen. She agreed and allowed this doctor to take Chester outside for a walk along the path on the grounds. Ten minutes later, Chester rushed back to Bernardine's room, tears streaming from his eyes. He fell into her bed, sobbing. "Oh how could they," he cried. "How could they. My poor Bernardine."[182]

Bernardine couldn't bear to cause Chester so much sorrow. She stroked his hair, saying gently, "There, there." It was as if he were the one afflicted by a major surgery, not her.

The day after she was discharged from the hospital, Bernardine dressed to go bra shopping. She tried to arrange her clothes the same as always but cried when she saw her reflection in the mirror. She thought she looked like a bag lady living on the streets. Recalling the

[181] Bernardine letter to Barbara Harrison, undated 1934, Beinecke Library, YCAL MSS 134 Box 126 f. 1968, page 24.
[182] Bernardine's unpublished diary, May 11, 1934, Beinecke Library, YCAL MSS 134 Box 103 f. 1575, page 40.

way Chester constantly assessed women they passed in the street—no matter where they traveled—always criticizing something about their physical appearance, she knew he would judge her the same. And just as she'd imagined, when she knocked on Chester's hotel room door before going out, she could see in his wilted expression that he found her pathetic and felt embarrassed for her. Instead of telling her that she looked haggard, he suggested she put on a coat.[183]

Yet she still managed to find joy in Chester's good moods. One morning, he came into her room at the hotel and joked around with her until they broke into tears from laughter. "Oh Bernardine, you are so wonderful when you're feeling happy!"[184]

They traveled on to Paris and London after leaving Vienna. The day they left Paris, Bernardine wrote Chester another letter. She just couldn't confront him in person when she wanted to talk about serious issues. In this case, she needed to ask how he felt about her. The loss of her breast brought greater insecurity to her marriage, and she mentioned in her letter that she had divulged everything to Barbara. She noted to Chester that Barbara wished the couple could start "living a normal natural life."[185] Yet Bernardine added that if Chester could not bear her loss of a breast, he should tell her as soon as possible so they wouldn't need to prolong the inevitable: divorce. In her letter, she assured Chester that she would understand if he didn't want to stay married to her.

Upon reading the letter, Chester ran straight to Bernardine's room at their Paris hotel. "I can't bear it," he cried, convulsing uncontrollably. "I shall never get over it. You were so lovely. When you were happy, I used to look at you and think how wonderful you looked. Now I'll always think of that. I cannot forgive them for mutilating you." Chester begged Bernardine not to ask how he felt about her lost breast. He

---

[183] Bernardine letter to Barbara Harrison, undated 1934, Beinecke Library, YCAL MSS 134 Box 126 f. 1968, page 28.
[184] Letter from Bernardine to Barbara Harrison, undated, Beinecke Library, YCAL MSS 134 Box 126 f. 1969, page 94.
[185] Letter from Bernardine to Barbara Harrison, undated 1934, Beinecke Library, YCAL MSS 134 Box 126 f. 1968, page 28.

didn't know at that moment. But he did not want a divorce and made her promise to never speak of that again.

Bernardine felt relieved in a way that Chester wanted to stay with her, although in her mind, she had prepared for him to ask for a divorce. After marrying and divorcing three times, she had no plans for what she would do if he had wanted to split up. Yet now, she didn't have to think about this further because they could return to Shanghai at the end of the year and carry on as before. She had started to enjoy her time in China and still had big plans for her salon, perhaps helping with another performance along the lines of the Avshalomoff ballet. The stress over telling Chester about her mastectomy was over, but Bernardine still could not rest well. Rosemary was about to reenter their lives, and Bernardine had no idea how Chester would react this time.

***

According to their original plans, Rosemary was to meet Bernardine and Chester in Spain. But Chester's reaction to the mastectomy had caused Bernardine so much anxiety that she asked Rosemary to change her plans and sail to London as soon as her school term ended. Now nineteen, Rosemary was either finishing up at King-Smith in Washington, DC, or had already enrolled at the theater school at Carnegie Tech, where she also studied photography. She was more accustomed to spending time with her doting grandparents—despite their ailing health—and Bernardine's friends—like Barbara, Glenway, Monroe, and George—than with her own mother. Rosemary probably felt some apprehension about this trip.

Before mother and daughter could reunite in London, the stitches under Bernardine's arm somehow came out prematurely, perhaps from too much exercise. It hurt like "hellfire." Bernardine was terrified the entire incision would soon be exposed and that she had no way to protect it. In 1934, people didn't yet have the luxury of antibiotics to fight infection. On top of that fear, she continued to worry about Chester's and Rosemary's interaction. Just thinking about it gave her a headache. Instead, she tried to concentrate on her own reunion with Rosemary.

"How excited I am though to see her. Isn't it curious—it doesn't seem at all as if it's my CHILD though."

Almost as soon as the three met up in London, Rosemary regaled Bernardine and Chester with her adventures on the ship over. She had taken a dip in a hot tub for the first time while a male passenger insisted Rosemary completely disrobe before stepping into the water— as he stood by. Chester's face grew bright red in anger, yet he kept silent as Rosemary switched subjects and wondered if she had lost her keys since leaving the ship. Chester had no patience for such careless- ness and could no longer keep silent. "Haven't you a place to put such things like other people have?" he said more to himself than to her.[186]

Rosemary had no concept of money, and Bernardine worried about that, even as she reminded herself that her daughter was still only nineteen. When the three dined together that first evening, Rosemary ordered caviar and foie gras without looking at the prices. Bernardine felt pulled in two directions: Should she indulge the daughter she rarely saw, or should she stand up for Chester? She knew Chester could afford both delicacies and could comfortably treat every diner in the restaurant to the same, yet she was well aware he did not want to spend his money on Rosemary.

There was also the fact that Bernardine had just undergone trau- matic surgery. Perhaps a round of caviar and foie gras would have been a nice way to celebrate her recovery. Bernardine could sense that Chester wasn't thinking about her surgery or anything other than his annoyance and dislike of Rosemary. There was no reason for Chester to disapprove of Rosemary other than that he didn't care for children. Bernardine was aware of how quickly the friction between Chester and Rosemary could build up, and she felt she needed to do whatever she could to keep the peace. So she turned to Rosemary and said, "Darling, they're too rich for your skin."

[186] Ibid., page 32.

Chester always booked separate rooms for them while traveling. This went back to their wedding night five years earlier in Dairen when he insisted on sleeping apart because he was training for the polo season. Bernardine didn't write about their sleeping arrangements in Shanghai, but with so many rooms at their apartment at 62 Route de Boissezon, they may have kept separate bedrooms there, too.

In London, they could not find three single rooms and, instead, were given a large double with a connecting single. Chester insisted Bernardine share the larger room with Rosemary, but Bernardine claimed that she didn't want to tell Rosemary about her surgery yet, so Chester agreed that he and Bernardine would share a room. Bernardine wanted to get back to normal with Chester as soon as possible and felt sharing a room with him would force him to reconcile with her condition. Yet rooming with Chester still brought stress to Bernardine, as he hadn't yet seen her scar. She dressed day and night so she would always look "right" in case he walked in without warning. Bernardine had little to worry about in the end as Chester kept his distance, running from the emotions he couldn't bear to address.

Bernardine started to ponder the way Chester ignored her grief. And the more she thought about it, the more frustrated she grew. This wasn't just a squabble or a misunderstanding. It was her health and her life. Once again, she poured her heart out to Barbara: "I don't mean to be unfair, but at moments I think Chester could help me so much more. He makes me feel so constantly on the defensive, as if I had deliberately done HIM a great wrong. I suppose I want him to feel a little sorrier for me, and not quite so much for himself. No, that's not quite it, but I long to have him make me feel that my sorrow is his, in the same proportion and inevitably perhaps I'm too impatient. It's dreadfully hard."[187]

On their first full day together, Rosemary didn't wake until noon. She joined Bernardine and Chester at lunch and then announced after dinner that she wanted to turn in early that evening. As Rosemary departed for her hotel room, Chester's face suddenly turned pale with

---

[187] Ibid., page 29.

alarm. Bernardine worried she had done something to annoy Chester. Was her mastectomy still bothering him? Or had she said something to upset him during the day? Chester suddenly broke into tears, yet refused to tell her why. He dashed off to their room without saying a word. She knew he had his little-boy moments and figured he would just sleep it off. Still, it bothered her terribly not knowing what exactly was causing him so much grief.

Chester broke into tears again the next morning. Bernardine begged him to tell her what troubled him so much. "Oh, do tell me. We'll both feel better."

"Well," Chester said, "it's Rosemary. You know I can't get used to her being with us, and here she is all day on our laps. I can't see why you let her come so soon."

"But it's only been one day," Bernardine replied. "I'll find some friends for her, but I can't in one day. I'm sorry I let her come a little earlier."

Chester continued to cry like a child whose toy had been taken away for bad behavior. Bernardine couldn't bear to go through another summer like 1930 where she felt torn between husband and daughter. "Please don't make it hard for me, Chester. Everything is hard enough now, and I try not to bother you with my own sadness and concern, but do try to be nice to Rosemary. So many we know have stepchildren, and they don't seem to find it as difficult as you. Why do you think that is?"[188]

That only made him cry more.

It seemed the more Bernardine intervened to save Chester's feelings, the more her anger toward him escalated. She knew Chester only thought about himself and showed not an ounce of empathy toward her. Still, she wished she could muster the strength to demand that Chester help her for once and not just sit there and cry. She should be the one weeping on his shoulder. She was the one who felt lost. But she just couldn't confront him. Instead, she continued to do anything to avoid Chester's doomsday tantrums, which meant she spent hours

---

[188] Letter from Bernardine to Barbara Harrison, undated 1934, Beinecke Library, YCAL MSS 134 Box 126 f. 1968, page 32.

a day trying to hold herself together after her surgery and during her mediation between Rosemary and Chester.

Bernardine also worried about Rosemary's health. When they reunited in London, she had noticed that Rosemary coughed incessantly, supposedly from a cold she caught on the ship. Rosemary also appeared gaunt, pale, and always on edge. One can only wonder if she shut down because Chester refused to speak directly to her. She must have also felt dejected when Bernardine did not stand up for her at every opportunity. As poorly as Chester communicated, Bernardine was guilty of the same with Rosemary. With all the chances to repair her rapport with Rosemary, she failed to take hold of yet another opportunity to become closer to her daughter the summer of 1934.

Instead, Bernardine did everything in her power to appease Chester. Enlisting the help of a friend in England named Beth, Bernardine arranged for Rosemary to be sent off to Scotland for a week with this friend. In Bernardine's mind, a week without Rosemary would alleviate some tensions with Chester. His moods dominated their lives, and Bernardine wondered how the three of them would survive Spain together.

These worries boiled over in Bernardine's mind, and one afternoon, without thinking, she blurted to Chester, "You'd much rather Rosemary didn't come to Spain, wouldn't you?"[189]

"Yes!" Chester perked right up. Bernardine's exasperation was lost on him. He truly believed she was asking a legitimate question. His eyes continued to beam. This was not what Bernardine wanted, but she felt at her wits' end with him. She tried to explain that Rosemary did not even stay with them during the day since she usually went out with other people her age.

"I don't think I could bear it if I were being torn between the two of you at such close quarters for weeks," Bernardine replied, "and yet I had to leave Rosemary whom I've not seen for so long and shan't see again. I wondered if you could find someone to take the trip with and let me stay with Rosemary until you return."[190]

---

[189] Ibid., page 30.
[190] Ibid.

But Chester insisted Bernardine join him in Spain. He then began to sob. "I work so hard all the time and everything I have I've gotten through working. I suppose I'm selfish, but I want to enjoy my holiday, and I don't want to go off with someone else."

"Really dearest," Bernardine replied, "how AM I to divide myself? I know of course all I have to do is tell Rosemary and she shall understand and be a brick about it but it DOES seem so unfair, I adore her so. I love being with her. It will be so long again." As it would turn out, two years would pass before Bernardine would see Rosemary again.

It was starting to seem pretty evident to Bernardine that the three of them would not be able to travel to Spain peacefully. When Rosemary visited them in Shanghai in 1930, Chester could hide away in his office or run off to the stables. In Spain, he had nowhere to escape. And, frankly, he didn't think it was his job to make room for Rosemary when he was paying the bills. Bernardine still hoped after all this time that Chester would finally show he could be flexible, but this conversation put an end to those wishes. She knew the only way to prevent another mass struggle between her daughter and husband would be to send Rosemary away again.

Bernardine started to think of people who could watch over Rosemary while she and Chester left for Spain. As always, she turned to Barbara. Bernardine explained that Rosemary's smoking habit annoyed Chester and he couldn't stand to be around her for that reason. But Bernardine smoked too, so that excuse was just a way for her to feel better about not taking Rosemary with them to Spain. Bernardine was always thinking up many plans at once, and in the same letter to Barbara, she also mentioned Rebecca West, a renowned, British, feminist journalist and author. Rebecca was a friend from when Bernardine lived in New York where they socialized in the same circles with Charlie Chaplin and Harold Ross, cofounder of the *New Yorker*. Rebecca was back in London when Bernardine, Chester, and Rosemary visited. Bernardine mentioned to Barbara that Rebecca had been charmed by Rosemary.

She also wondered if Rosemary could stay in London for the summer to study ballet and theater with Maurice Browne, the founder of the

Little Theatre in Chicago and now a resident of London. As much as Bernardine had warned Rosemary against going into theater when she visited Shanghai in 1930, four years later Bernardine felt proud of Rosemary for taking to London. "She's in a state of perpetual excitement. She's never had this kind of life and is always in school or on beach summers."

Before Bernardine needed to make a decision about Spain, she had a week in London to herself while Rosemary was away in Scotland and Chester attended to business. She met the American movie star, Anna May Wong, through Madame Wellington Koo, the wife of China's preeminent diplomat. Madame Koo had treated Bernardine and Barbara to lunch in late 1928, just after they had returned to Paris from their trip around the world. Now in 1934, Madame Koo invited Bernardine to her apartment at Claridge's, a stately hotel going back to the 1850s. Bernardine found Madame Koo "old and jaded and bored, and was surrounded by the most reptilian people I've ever seen."[191] Madame Koo, who rarely went by her given name of Oei Hui-lan, was only seven years older than Bernardine, so hardly the biddy she described.

Bernardine had joined a group of Madame Koo's friends, many of them old and "mercurial." When Anna May Wong joined the group, Bernardine didn't know what to think of her. "Anna May stood out from them all. She seemed like a finely polished flint in the midst of a stack of moldy cornhusks. Her manner was almost rude, it was so direct and forthright. She didn't stay long."[192] Bernardine's relationship with Anna May would change two years later.

A decade younger than Bernardine, Anna May Wong was born and raised in Los Angeles. Her grandparents immigrated to the US from the southern Chinese county of Toisan, or Taishan, the hometown of the largest group of Chinese immigrants before the US passed the 1882 Chinese Exclusion Act. As a child, Anna May spent her free time observing Hollywood sets and peering on while silent films were in the middle of a shoot. She left high school to act and never looked back. By the time Bernardine met her, Anna May was a household name in

---

[191]   Ibid., page 31.
[192]   Bernardine Szold Fritz, "Fania Marinoff and Carl Van Vechten," unpublished manuscript courtesy of her family, page 6.

Hollywood who had moved to Berlin in the early 1920s after being shut out from leading roles and growing disillusioned by the typecast secondary roles she was offered—either Madame Butterflies or dragon ladies, both of which would invariably die at the end of the film.

In 1932, Anna May starred alongside German starlet Marlene Dietrich in *Shanghai Express*. She had learned German and French while working in Europe, but in *Shanghai Express*, she could speak her native English. And she lived at the end of the story. Although the film was set on a train from Peking to Shanghai, it wasn't filmed in China, and Anna May herself had not yet stepped foot in China at that point.

Also that week in London, Bernardine again felt a tugging sensation under her arm. Her surgery scar was still giving her trouble, but as far as she could tell, there was no sign of infection. While she had time to herself, she consulted with a physician. The doctor checked her wound and found it to be healing well after the earlier episode of popped stitches. But something else bothered him.

"There was no necessity for the drastic operation. Those Viennese doctors!" he said.[193] The British doctor thought it would have been sufficient for the surgeons in Vienna to remove Bernardine's benign lump, but there had been no need for a mastectomy. Bernardine burst into tears. Had she really gone through all that trouble for nothing? Now she was left with only one breast and a husband who refused to touch her.

When she and Chester moved on to Spain, Rosemary departed for France to visit Barbara. Rosemary may have appeared willing to spend time with Barbara, or perhaps that's what Bernardine wanted to believe. And as much as Bernardine found excuses for this separation—that Rosemary was desperate to see Barbara and that Barbara needed help packing for Salzburg, where she would attend the summer music and drama festival—it was another way she justified one more separation from her daughter. They had only spent a week together in London and, as usual, Bernardine picked Chester over Rosemary.

---

[193] Letter from Bernardine to Barbara Harrison, July 20, 1934, Beinecke Library, YCAL MSS 134 Box 103 f. 1575, page 34.

Yet after Chester begged Bernardine to never again talk about her mastectomy or the possibility of them splitting up, he continued to distance himself when it came to intimacy with her. The couple sailed to the United States, just the two of them, while Rosemary stayed in Europe, spending time dancing and acting in London and Italy. In New York, Bernardine stood for a photoshoot with Carl Van Vechten, an old friend. He socialized with many of the same people Bernardine knew like Gertrude Stein, Paul Robeson, and Isadora Duncan.

Bernardine was also close to Carl's wife, Fania Marinoff, an actress. Carl had affairs with men, and Bernardine could empathize with the pair as she had many gay male friends and was also a woman hurt by infidelity. She could see both sides to Fania and Carl's relationship.

Carl snapped multiple shots of Bernardine during this photoshoot. In one that comes up the most in online searches for Bernardine, she has crossed her arms over her chest, looking almost wounded. She seemed to be guarding her body against further destruction, although few who view this photo would know about her mastectomy.

Still troubled by the words of the London doctor who had seen her scar, Bernardine felt she needed yet another opinion and consulted with a surgeon in New York while Chester was off on business in Manhattan. This New York doctor told her the same thing as the one in London. "If some of these European surgeons were women, and had women surgeons operating on them and removing their testicles, there wouldn't be so many hasty operations. Not a good doctor in this country would have dreamed of making a drastic operation on you. You've plenty of time, they'd have put you under observation. There is not one word in this pathologist's report to warrant what was done to you. I don't think there was one chance in a thousand that anything would ever have developed beyond the small and very common tumor. That's damn little help to you, I'm damn sorry for you. You're a young woman, but luckily, you've got brains enough to find compensations."[194]

Bernardine relayed this story in a letter to Glenway, commenting that as she left his office, she patted her brains on the back.

---

[194]   Bernardine's unpublished diary, undated, Beinecke Library, YCAL MSS 134 Box 103 f. 1575, page 44.

Chester stayed back in New York, purportedly to attend to business, while Bernardine continued on to Daytona Beach to visit her parents. A year earlier, her sister Aline and brother-in-law Max both had to put their theater jobs on hold after they each contracted tuberculosis. To complicate matters, they had just had a baby, a daughter named Terry. Max insisted on recuperating on his own, apart from Aline and Terry. But it was difficult for Aline to stay alone with their daughter when she herself needed to rest. So Hermine and Jacob stepped in and cared for young Terry. They asked Bernardine if she could pay for Aline to recuperate at a sanitorium.

Bernardine always got along much better with Aline than with their older sister, Olga. In 1934, there was no treatment for TB, and it wouldn't matter where Aline recovered as long as she could get ample rest. Instead of paying for a sanitorium stay, Bernardine asked Aline to return with her to Shanghai and recuperate under her care. After living abroad for the last decade, Bernardine did not want to pass up a chance to spend time alone with her younger sister.

It took all of Bernardine's strength to ask Chester to help with Aline. The problem, as always, was money, and it pained Bernardine to ask for it. "I wept and wept until I thought my eyes would be loose in my head. I was so enraged, so bitter, so furious, so miserable, and so helpless. It is so difficult. My family after all means nothing to Chester. He's scarcely seen them, he has no 'family' or clan instincts, and I would rather die than ask for money anyway. What little I had I gave to him to do something with, and then forgot, for I know nothing about money and left it all to him. And then I cursed myself so for having relinquished it."[195]

Even though Bernardine came into her marriage with a little money, after she handed it over to Chester, she felt indebted to him for every expense. She had left her job with the *China Critic* more than a year earlier and continued to squirrel away part of her allowance from Chester to pay for Rosemary's tuition fees and other living expenses.

---

[195] Letter from Bernardine to Monroe Wheeler, December 28, 1933, Beinecke Library, YCAL MSS 134 Box 103 f. 1575, page 6.

Now, she needed to figure a way to convince Chester that Aline should return with them to Shanghai, which would inevitably involve money.

So as Bernardine did with other serious issues when she couldn't confront the person face-to-face, she wrote to Chester—still back in New York—and informed him that Aline needed to be guaranteed relaxation in order to recover and that could best happen in Shanghai with them. Chester agreed, perhaps because Rosemary would be oceans away from them at Carnegie Tech. All that mattered to Chester was that he was as far from Rosemary as possible. Aline probably didn't pose much of a threat to him.

By the end of 1934, Bernardine and Chester returned to Shanghai with Aline in tow. The couple had been away from China for the better part of the year, and on the ship back, Chester relaxed with a pile of books while Bernardine and Aline hatched plans for Shanghai.

In an unsent letter she wrote to Chester before continuing on to Florida to visit her family, Bernardine declared, "And if I go back to China, and if I am well, and go on living more or less for enough years to matter—I'm not going to try to change anymore but I'm going to return without resistance to whatever is left of me of what I was—and I swear that both you and I will be better for it. And that I'll find that way, the place for myself in China that I've been trying to find but wrongly by trying to reshape or change myself to fit into whatever spot I could find there, which seemed the least out of proportion and shape with my character and temperament."[196]

Bernardine never gave that letter to Chester but instead mapped out a role she wanted to play when she returned to Shanghai. She and Aline would reinstitute the International Arts Theatre with the help of Bernardine's friends and acquaintances. It was time for Bernardine to stop allowing her problems with Chester to get in the way of doing what she loved best.

So much for Aline's quiet recovery.

---

[196] Unsent letter from Bernardine to Chester Fritz, undated 1934, Beinecke Library, YCAL MSS 134 Box 126 f. 1967, page 5.

Bernardine, center front, at the IAT's Cabaret
Night on March 30, 1936 at the Cathay Hotel.
Photo courtesy of Bernardine's family.

Anna May Wong in China, 1936. Photo
courtesy of David Szanton.

Bernardine and Chester on their honeymoon in Manchuria, June 1929. Photo courtesy of Bernardine's family.

Bernardine in the last photo she took
with her granddaughter Wongmo in Los
Angeles. Photo courtesy of Wongmo.

Bernardine in the Chinese countryside.
Photo courtesy of Nancy Lilienthal.

Bernardine with her daughter Rosemary at the
Sam Sanzetti studio in Shanghai, 1930. This was
Rosemary's only trip to visit her mother in China.
Photo courtesy of Bernardine's family.

Portrait of Bernardine by Carl Van Vechten in
New York, 1934. Bernardine had just returned
to the United States following breast surgery
in Vienna. Photo in the public domain.

Bernardine, center looking down, at Shanghai's
fabled paper hunt, modeled after a fox hunt. Chester
won numerous paper hunt cups during his time
in Shanghai and Bernardine tried to show interest
in his horses soon after she arrived in Shanghai.
Photo courtesy of Bernardine's family.

Bernardine in Rambouillet, France, just outside
Paris in 1929. She would move to Shanghai to
marry Chester soon after this photo was taken.
Photo courtesy of Bernardine's family.

After leaving China, Bernardine recreated her
Shanghai living room at her Los Angeles home
on Heather Road. She would go on to sell many
of her Chinese artifacts and clothes to make ends
meet. Photo courtesy of Nancy Lilienthal.

133

Bernardine with her younger sister, Aline Sholes, who spent a year in Shanghai recuperating from tuberculosis and co-directing *Lady Precious Stream* at Bernardine's International Arts Theatre. Photo courtesy of Bernardine's family.

Bernardine with her mother Hermine, daughter Rosemary, and granddaughter Feather (later named Wongmo) in the late 1940s. Photo courtesy of Bernardine's family.

One of the many rooms at Bernardine and
Chester's apartment at 62 Route de Boissezon in
Shanghai's French Concession. Upwards of 150
guests would attend Bernardine's Shanghai salon.
Photo courtesy of Bernardine's family.

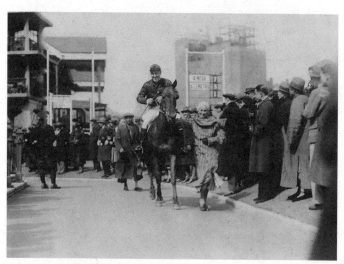

Chester was the captain of the US polo team in Shanghai
and took great pride in his horses. When Bernardine
moved to Shanghai, she went out of her way to spend
time at Chester's equestrian events even though she was
afraid of horses. Photo courtesy of Bernardine's family.

The International Arts Theater logo as seen
on a program for the IAT Ball, June 18, 1937.
Photo courtesy of Nancy Lilienthal.

Bernardine with Lee Ya-ching, China's first female
pilot. Photo courtesy of Nancy Lilienthal.

Bernardine, second, right, with Victor Sassoon, far right, and her sister Aline Sholes, third from right, with friends at an IAT reception for the pianist Arthur Rubinstein, May 5, 1935 in Shanghai. Photo courtesy of Nancy Lilienthal.

Bernardine and the IAT held an exhibit of Chinese landscape painting on March 6, 1936 to honor the visit of actors Charlie Chaplin, far left, and Paulette Goddard, third from left. Chaplin and Goddard eloped in Canton on this trip to China. Between Chaplin and Goddard is the silent film star, Butterfly Wu. Photo courtesy of Nancy Lilienthal.

A portrait of Rosemary by Carl Van Vechten in New York, 1936. Photo in the public domain.

Bernardine and Chester's living room at 62 Route de Boissezon in Shanghai's French Concession. Regulars of Bernardine's salon called her home the red and black apartment after the colors of the furniture and décor. Photo courtesy of Nancy Lilienthal.

PART III

BERNARDINE'S GREATEST ACT

"In general I believe in making a few deep immortal friendships. That's for the delight of the soul. But if people can come together in groups, through altruistic motives—I think there is no more fascinating experiment, and if I may say so, no more exacting social discipline."[197]
—Bernardine Szold Fritz

---

[197] Bernardine Szold Fritz, "I Am Not a Public Speaker," unpublished manuscript courtesy of her family, page 9.

CHAPTER ELEVEN

BERNARDINE AND FRIENDS, 1935

Tong Ying was one of Bernardine's first female friends in Shanghai. Fluent in English and several Chinese dialects, she painted, wrote poetry, and enjoyed both Chinese and Western literature. Bernardine was impressed with Tong Ying's embroidery skills, "the divinely elegant birds and flowers on bits of gauze, frail as moonbeams."[198] She also felt inspired by the way Tong Ying looked men directly in the eye and laughed without reserve. According to Bernardine, Tong Ying was the first woman in Shanghai to combine the classical arts with the modern outlook of New China. "She was known and loved from Peiping to Shanghai, so when I met her and listened to her adorable English, I decided to throw myself at her feet."[199]

In other words, Tong Ying was the type of friend Bernardine had desperately hoped to meet in Shanghai. They could discuss the arts and Chinese politics, but more than that, the two women could speak about everyday concerns like Bernardine's problems with Chester or Tong Ying's own marital issues. Although Bernardine credited Hu Shih with introducing her to Lin Yutang and the *China Critic*, she also attributed

---

[198] Ibid., page 4.
[199] Ibid.

Tong Ying with the same. Sometimes Bernardine would tell different versions of the same stories in her letters, vignettes, and in person. This is one of those cases.

"Oh, but there is a Chinese magazine, publishing in English, and they are just looking for a foreign contributor," Tong Ying said to Bernardine. "You will be their dream come true."[200] Bernardine claimed that Tong Ying introduced her to the staff at the *Critic* and was hired on the spot. "My adventure in China dated from that day."[201] And as Bernardine recalled in this version of events, she met Yutang at her first Friday night editorial meeting at the *Critic*.

Bernardine's group of Chinese women friends also included Lee Ya-ching, China's first female pilot. Before Bernardine arrived in Shanghai in 1929, Ya-ching had already starred in a number of Chinese silent films. A decade later, Bernardine would introduce Ya-ching to Hollywood, where she would be cast in the Dorothy Lamour film, *Disputed Passage*, as an aviatrix, or female pilot.[202] Lamour was a popular Hollywood actress who starred alongside Bing Crosby and Bob Hope. In *Disputed Passage*, Lamour dressed in yellowface to play the main female lead, Lan Ying. Ya-ching's role was small and mentioned at the end of the credits.

But her closest women friends in Shanghai were Daisy Kwok and Helene Chang. Like Tong Ying and Ya-ching, Daisy and Helene were fluent in English and from families that had lived abroad. Daisy was born in Australia to an overseas Chinese family that owned fruit and vegetable stores. At the age of ten, she moved with her family to Shanghai, where they helped run the Wing On department store with their Kwok cousins. Daisy's father was a supporter of Sun Yat-sen before the 1911 Revolution, and Sun was one of the reasons Daisy and her family relocated to China.[203]

---

[200] Ibid.
[201] Ibid.
[202] "New China Tiffin Club in U.S.A.," *The North-China Herald*, August 16, 1939, page 303.
[203] Daisy Kwok, Tess Johnston, and Graham Earnshaw, *Shanghai Daisy*. (Hong Kong, Earnshaw Books: 2019).

Helene's father was just as influential. Chang Ching-chiang had lived in Paris, where Helene was born, as well as New York, where his wife died suddenly after a tree branch struck her on a bench at Riverside Park. Helene was only eight years old when her mother was killed, and her father was left to raise five daughters. Helene was the youngest.[204]

Helene's Chinese name was Chang Tsing-ying. She also went by Helen. Bernardine called her by all three names. The two friends spoke at length about their dream of writing their autobiographies. By the time they met in the early 1930s, Helene's father had already retired as governor of Zhejiang Province and was trying to keep a low profile from Chiang Kai-shek, with whom he'd had a falling out.

Bernardine, Daisy, and Helene traveled together to Hangchow, where Helene's father kept a grand home sprawled across a mountain-top and reached by a staircase of two hundred steps. Daisy's husband, Y. H. Woo, and Chester joined them on at least one of their trips to Hangchow. Chester complained about the fog and attempted to stay dry under a yellow, oiled parasol. But Bernardine relished the sight before her, just as she had when Lin Yutang and his family brought her to Hangchow. "Drops of rain were dripping from the fine bamboo leaves like silver embroidery. As we got below the mist the view of the valley spread out in triangles of a hundred shades of green and yellow and as we jogged along I began to feel a deep and warm sense of poetic response of the Chinese to such scenes."[205]

Helene was also close to the pilot Ya-ching and became a licensed pilot herself before she met Bernardine. Through Bernardine's salon, Helene met Rosa, Miguel, Victor Sassoon, Harold Acton, and the actress Butterfly Wu. Helene's relatives in Shanghai did not approve of her friends or her fashion, as she often wore backless evening gowns and painted her fingernails black with green tips.

---

[204] Bernardine Szold Fritz, "Trouble in China," unpublished manuscript courtesy of her family, page 5.

[205] Bernardine Szold Fritz, "Tsingyi," unpublished manuscript courtesy of her family, page 2.

A year after Bernardine reinstated the International Arts Theatre in 1935, Helene and Daisy opened their dress boutique, Tsingi, a variation of Helene's Chinese name. At Tsingi, the two women hoped to bring contemporary design to classic Chinese fashion. Madame Wellington Koo had already made the cheongsam, or qipao, fashionable by wearing a form-fitting version of a traditional loose robe. Madame Koo also had her cheongsams tailored with a high mandarin collar. This style still remains in fashion today, almost a hundred years later. Helene designed the dresses at Tsingi and Daisy managed the operations, drawing from her family's entrepreneurial expertise.

Their boutique found the perfect home at the new Park Hotel, designed by László Hudec, the same Hungarian architect that brought the Grand Theatre, the venue of the *Soul of the Ch'in* ballet in 1933, to Shanghai. Across the street from the Grand Theatre, the Park Hotel was completed in 1934, a couple years before Helene and Daisy opened Tsingi. At the time, the hotel was the tallest building in all of Asia at twenty stories and towered over the Shanghai Race Course in the International Settlement.

Not long after they opened Tsingi, Helene and Daisy were involved in an attempted carjacking on a trip back from Hangchow. Daisy's husband, Y. H., was driving next to Daisy and Helene in the front seat, while an American couple sat in back. Down the road, three men appeared as if they needed to talk to the group, so Y. H. slowed down. Thinking they were police, Y. H. worried some kind of trouble loomed ahead. As the men neared, one of them suddenly jumped onto the car's running board, brandishing a pistol. They were not police but bandits out to rob the group. Y. H. stepped on the gas, throwing the one bandit from the running board, but not before another robber fired shots at the car, hitting the windshield and one of the car doors. Helene turned to Daisy and saw blood streaming down her face.

"My God, Daisy's been shot!" she screamed. But when Daisy looked at Helene, she saw blood on her friend's face and cried, "You're dripping blood!"[206] As it turned out, neither woman was shot. The

[206] Nelson Chang, Laurence Chang, and Song Luxia, *The Zhangs from Nanxun: A One Hundred and Fifty Year Chronicle of a Chinese Family*, (Denver, CF Press: 2010), page 304.

windshield had shattered when a bullet struck, spraying glass shards toward Daisy and Helene. The American couple in the back was left unharmed. Bernardine never wrote about this incident, so it's unlikely she and Chester were that American couple in the back seat.

The women were treated at a hospital, where two dozen pieces of glass were removed from Daisy's face. The group then headed to Jimmy's Kitchen, a popular Western restaurant near the Bund in Shanghai. Daisy phoned the English press, inviting them to Jimmy's Kitchen so she could relay the story and, while she was at it, put in a good word for their shop, Tsingi.[207]

When Bernardine returned to Shanghai in late 1934, she had all but abandoned the International Arts Theatre after the 1933 production of *The Soul of the Ch'in*. Now with Aline at her side, it seemed the perfect time to revive the IAT. But unlike in 1933, Bernardine found very little interest from the foreign communities in helping her rebuild the IAT. Daisy, Helene, and Tong Ying, on the other hand, were game and assisted with her plans.

They rented out space in an old warehouse on 50 East Nanking Road just off the Bund. It cost very little, because the building was in such tatters that Bernardine never knew if the thin wooden floor would be able to support all the people who made use of the studio. She modeled the IAT after the Little Theatre in Chicago and planned on presenting a broad range of performing arts, lectures, and visual arts. For their first event, Bernardine set her sights a little lower than the 1933 Avshalomoff music and ballet program. She had grander ideas in mind, but to get off the ground, she decided the IAT should relaunch with an event that would take little time to organize. For this, she recruited Dr. Max Mohr to give a lecture.

Mohr's story was unusual in 1935. A physician, psychoanalyst, and war veteran of the Weimar Republic, he was a friend of D. H. Lawrence and an author himself. Before Hitler came to power in 1933, Mohr

207 Daisy Kwok, Tess Johnston, and Graham Earnshaw, *Shanghai Daisy*, (Hong Kong, Earnshaw Books: 2019), page 45.

had penned over a dozen novels and plays. But as a Jew, Mohr was no longer allowed to practice after 1933 because of the new restrictive laws. He fled to Shanghai—one of the only places in the world to take foreigners without papers—and would be among the first group of Jewish refugees from Nazi-controlled Europe to flock to the city. By 1941, more than twenty-four thousand Jewish refugees would live in Shanghai.

Bernardine invited Mohr to discuss his friend, D. H. Lawrence, who had passed away five years earlier. In the *China Press*, the headline describing the event read, "Little Theater To Have First Lecture: Dr. Mohr To Be First To Speak To I.A.T. Group."[208] The title of the talk was "The Last Years of a Great Poet," but Mohr spoke mostly about Lawrence's scandalous novel, *Lady Chatterley's Lover*. Mohr met Lawrence in 1927, and the two connected over their love of literature and psychoanalysis. Bernardine was interested in Mohr because he owned a copy of the banned *Lady Chatterley's Lover*. She believed the English-speaking communities of Shanghai would be just as taken with Mohr's insider's look at Lawrence as she was. Admission to Mohr's talk was free, but seating was limited. As Bernardine predicted, the lecture drew a large crowd and the attendees talked about it for days afterward.

What did Bernardine think about Mohr fleeing Germany because he was Jewish like her? We will never know, but she certainly had profoundly mixed feelings about being Jewish. In Peoria, she felt like an outsider because the other students at school were all Christian and the only Jews she knew mainly consisted of her siblings and cousins. Her feelings of otherness seemed to dissipate when she lived in Chicago and New York, but in England, they bubbled to the surface again.

Sometime around 1933, Bernardine brought up the subject of antisemitism in a letter to Barbara that referred back to their fourteen-month trip. It is telling that she waited five years to tell Barbara about something she referred to as a "cruel episode," and that she still

---

[208] "Little Theater To Have First Lecture: Dr. Mohr To Be First To Speak To I.A.T. Group," *The China Press*, April 7, 1935, page 11.

didn't elaborate on the specific incidents.[209] In the mid-1930s as hostility toward Jews was heating up in Europe, Bernardine could no longer disconnect from her Jewish identity and felt the need to address this with Barbara in this letter. She brought up that, during their trip, Barbara and Walter Harris would mention in their conversations that certain people were Jewish. Bernardine wondered why it mattered so much.

"Other people don't say, when they meet one, How do you do, in case you can't tell on sight, I'm a Catholic or a Spaniard or whatever it is. And over and over. When people find out you're a Jew, they resent not having known. Sometimes it's because they remember they've said funny things or unkind things about Jews, and they feel abused that they were not let in for it before you.[210]

"The best one can do, if one tries to be funny about it, which isn't very easy, is to say it's a hell of a situation. You can't go about bearing banners, you don't go about wearing the yellow ticket as they used to have to do, you can't say, pardon me but if week after next you find out I'm a Jew please remember I was waiting for a proper opening in which to tell you myself. I don't know what to think anymore. I've gone through all the phases of hating it, of hating all Jews, of being proud of it and hating lots of Jews, of not minding one way or the other and having a few friends who are Jews, or deciding always to take the bull by the horns and in the most obvious way possible tell people right off, the 'now you know' kind of thing, or of never telling any except the people I like whose affairs I feel it is by virtue of my affection for them and my consequent desire to have no barriers, or what or what."[211]

Bernardine's ambivalence about her Judaism notwithstanding, she certainly surrounded herself with other Jews in Shanghai, like Aaron Avshalomoff, Dr. Mohr, and Victor Sassoon. That would soon increase with the arrival of an old friend from Chicago, the writer Emily Hahn.

---

[209] Letter from Bernardine to Barbara Harrison, undated, Beinecke Library, YCAL MSS 134 Box 126 f. 1969, page 37.
[210] Ibid.
[211] Ibid., page 38.

CHAPTER TWELVE

THE HAHN SISTERS, 1935

B ernardine stood at the Bund, the waterfront promenade lined with Neoclassical bank buildings and the Art Deco Cathay Hotel. It could have been any European city at a glance but for the rickshaws that competed with streetcars, automobiles, and lorries. To Bernardine, this scene was so familiar, so commonplace, now that she had lived in Shanghai for six years. The skyline and bustling activity along the Whangpoo River still dazzled her as they had when she was new to the city. Bernardine was accustomed to waiting for ocean liners bringing another friend, relative, or friend of a friend from Europe or the United States. She herself had also left with Chester from these piers, shipping out to Southeast Asia, Europe, or the US, almost on a yearly basis. But this day was extra special.

Emily Hahn and her sister, Helen Asbury, were scheduled to dock at any moment. Unlike some of the people Bernardine had met at the pier to show around Shanghai, the Hahn sisters were old friends from their Chicago days. Bernardine and Emily both started out in journalism around the same time, but by 1935, Emily's writing career had taken off, while Bernardine's had all but disappeared.

By the time she arrived in Shanghai, Emily had already published four books and was a staff writer at the *New Yorker*. Known by her friends and family as Mickey, after the popular comic strip character, Mickey Dooley, she and her sister Helen sailed to Shanghai for what was only supposed to be a stopover before Emily headed off to Africa.[212] She felt ambivalent about sailing back there after spending most of 1930 in the Belgian Congo, where a man was waiting for her. He was married, and that's why Emily delayed her return and entertained her sister's wish to see Asia. The women planned to stay in China for a couple months at most.

The Hahn sisters could have sailed into any port in Asia, but one of their motives for choosing Shanghai was Bernardine. She was a familiar face, and someone they could rely on to show them parts of this exciting city not found in guidebooks. Once the sisters stepped onto the jetty, Bernardine greeted them like long-lost family and shuttled them to a dinner party where they met Chinese and European dignitaries.

Aline seemed to have recovered from her TB by the time Emily and Helen arrived in Shanghai. The three women resembled one another, as they each wore their dark hair in wavy bobs and acted young and lively. Emily and Helen shared their every thought, no matter how risqué or inappropriate, especially when it came to men and sex. Emily was single, but Helen was very much married to a husband back home in the United States.

Bernardine was six to nine years older than them, with her greying hair braided into a crown, but the three women could barely keep up with her. Bernardine had regained her energy after her mastectomy and was excited to guide her sister and the Hahns around all of Shanghai, introducing them to larger-than-life personalities like Victor Sassoon and Sinmay Zau.

In her memoir, *China to Me*, Emily first mentioned Bernardine on page five: "There was one factor of Shanghai life which filled our days as

---

[212]   Ken Cuthbertson, *Nobody Said Not to Go: The Life, Loves, and Adventures of Emily Hahn*, (New York, Faber and Faber: 1998), page 15.

much as we wanted and a little more. Mrs. Fritz—Bernardine—had thought of and set into motion a sort of club known as the International Arts Theatre or, anticipating governmental habits, the IAT."[213]

It didn't take long for Bernardine to recruit Emily to give a talk about her career as a novelist at the IAT's second program in April 1935. In the *China Press*, the event with Emily and silent movie actress Pearl White, world-famous for the popular *Perils of Pauline* silent films, was billed as an "at home,"[214] which most likely took place in Bernardine's apartment at 62 Route de Boissezon. By 1935, Bernardine still held her salon but included it as part of the IAT's programming.

"Both the honored guests are visiting in Shanghai for some time," the *China Press* reported.[215] Pearl would return to Europe and die from liver failure three years after her IAT lecture. But Emily would go on to live in Shanghai and Hong Kong for almost a decade.

***

Sir Victor took to Emily almost as soon as he set eyes on her at Bernardine's. Emily stood out not just because she was young and beautiful, but also because she was sassy and outspoken in a way rarely seen among foreigners in Shanghai. Victor found her openness refreshing, if not a bit scandalous. In early May 1935, he invited Bernardine, Chester, Aline, and the Hahn sisters to sail on his boat around Shanghai. Bernardine soaked in the sun while Emily spoke to Aline, who was reading Emily's latest novel, *With Naked Foot*. In the book, Emily criticized the white men who tried to take advantage of the African female protagonist, although the "good" white male comes off as a white savior. The *New York Times* reviewed it in 1934 and concluded that "Miss Hahn makes Africans as well as Africa near and real to us. Her scenes of the natives when they are alone are rich and sly. Her novel is not

[213] Emily Hahn, *China to Me*, (Philadelphia, Blakiston: 1944), page 5.
[214] "I.A.T.G. To Sponsor Reception For Two: Miss White, Miss Hahn To Share Honors," *The China Press*, April 12, 1935, page 11.
[215] Ibid.

long, but it is continuously good reading."[216] Other reviewers noted the many sex scenes in the book.

Emily certainly found her share of male admirers in Shanghai. Sir Victor was known to take nude photos of women he fancied, although there were also rumors that he was gay. In his diary from April 25, 1935, he included photos of Emily and Helen but portraits in which they were both fully clothed.[217] Still, he lavished so much attention on Emily—buying her a car and fancy dinners—that she decided not to return to the Belgian Congo. Through Bernardine, she found a job with the *North China Daily News* after Helen left China in June that year.

Bernardine also introduced Emily to Sinmay at an IAT talk. They later saw one another again at a dinner Bernardine hosted, and soon the two became romantically involved.[218] Their relationship caused a scandal because Sinmay was married and it was "mixed race." There were very few cross-cultural romantic relationships in Shanghai at that time, and those that existed were usually between Chinese women and foreign men.

Other writers have criticized Bernardine for a deep jealousy of Emily, especially when it came to her relationship with Sinmay. These writers have referred to this rift as "The Great Bernardine War."[219] While it is true Emily often complained to other friends about Bernardine, it's also true Sir Victor enabled this rift. Sir Victor was supportive of Bernardine when she found the lump in her breast, and the two went on to write to one another until Sir V's death in the Bahamas in 1961. But Sir V was not always generous when it came to Bernardine.

In 1933, when she and Chester learned Sir V would be sailing on the same ship to Bali, Bernardine was determined to smooth the peace so their voyage wouldn't be plagued by awkward interactions. She went out of her way to mention they would be on the same boat. "We are undoubtedly the last people on earth he'd choose as intimates on a

[216] Emily Hahn's Novel of the Congo," *The New York Times*, September 16, 1934, page 49.
[217] Victor Sassoon, Southern Methodist University Archives, Personal Diary, May 4, 1935.
[218] Cuthbertson, page 140.
[219] Taras Grescoe, *Shanghai Grand: Forbidden Love and International Intrigue in a Doomed World.* New York: St. Martin's Press, 2016, page 182.

voyage to Bali—then also, being such a prima dona, he IS difficult, for we didn't want to annoy him (for being so feminine one always fears he'll turn against the firm for social reasons, and I'd hate to have that blamed on me)."[220]

Chester came to the conclusion that Sir Victor sailed this time without a companion, his usual practice, because he knew they would keep him company. If he wanted someone else to talk to on the voyage, he would need to hire a paid companion. Bernardine wrote to Barbara about it. "So I suppose he thought we'd be so honored that we'd pander to him in his anything, and be treated well or ignominiously whichever suited his convenience…well, as Glenway always said, you have to love people divinely to dare all of that."[221]

On the ship when the three were in a conversation, Sir Victor asked Chester if he thought Bernardine "was really a gold digger under the guise of childlike innocence sort of thing?"[222] Mortified, she ran off to calm herself, counting to "ten and twenty and five hundred" and willing herself not to break down in tears. Chester hated to see Sir V treat Bernardine this way, but she made him promise not to give Sir V the satisfaction that they were even aware of his harassment.

Still, Sir Victor helped Bernardine during her breast scare. And Bernardine admitted that Sir Victor always brought them back little trinkets from his travels and sold Chester a camera at cost, yet he still "goads and pokes and prods at me until I am really nearly hysterical."[223]

As Bernardine tried to put the IAT back together in 1935, she asked Sir Victor—along with many friends in Shanghai—for help with sponsoring events, such as a lecture, a one-act play, a film, or a tea. In a letter to her a couple months after Emily and Helen arrived in Shanghai, Sir Victor informed Bernardine that he could not help her with any of that.

---

[220]   Letter from Bernardine to Barbara Harrison, undated, Beinecke Library, YCAL MSS 134 Box 126 f. 1969, page 89.
[221]   Ibid., page 90.
[222]   Ibid., page 91.
[223]   Ibid., page 90.

It could be that he was turned off by the way she pushed her ideas for the IAT on most every influential person she came into contact with, or maybe he felt threatened by her ability to bring people together in the business world and party circuit and wanted that role all to himself. Or it could have been a combination of both. In any case, Bernardine could never predict if Sir Victor would be generous to her or if he would mock her.

"I think I have never grown to 'despise' any human being so much as I have to despise him, in these few weeks," Bernardine wrote. "I am apparently among one of those who arouses in him his most diabolical tendencies—I understand it when he picks on 'socially' intent women, who try to 'use' or 'do' him (to quote himself), and whom he so glibly delights to tick off. But from his point of view I am, after all, an utter fool, and it is so stupid for him to waste his talents on a fool."[224]

Bernardine knew it wasn't just in her head because Chester also sensed it and made a point to avoid Victor when they knew they would run into him. And when they couldn't avoid Sir V, Chester sometimes felt like fighting back. To Chester's credit, he could have just ignored this conflict because Sir Victor was his landlord at Sassoon House and if there were problems with Chester and Bernardine, Sir V could very well cancel the rental agreement of Swan, Culbertson and Fritz. Yet Chester supported Bernardine in this conflict.

One afternoon, the couple ran into Sir V at lunch and Bernardine cowered from him. After Sir V walked over to another group, Chester turned to Bernardine. "Insult him, go back at him," Chester said. "Would you like me to?"

"Oh my God, no," Bernardine replied. "How he'd love it if you quarreled with him for me."[225] Chester did not end up confronting Sir V, but Bernardine fretted over the tension with their friend and willed herself to act naturally around him and not let it show that he rattled her.

The so-called Great Bernardine War took off when Emily had been in Shanghai for a year. Bernardine worried about Emily's reputation

---

224   Ibid., page 89.
225   Ibid.

and thought back to her own problems of fitting in when she first arrived in 1929. At dinners and gatherings, Bernardine often overheard Emily bragging about her sex life and felt this kind of behavior crossed a boundary. At a dinner the two women attended, Emily walked in late and made a grand show with a revealing dress. Bernardine wrote to Monroe that the dress was "cut to her navel in front."[226] Shanghai was the most open-minded city in 1930s China, but it wasn't Berlin. "No one knew where to look all evening. I said laughingly the next day that she had better not take that dress to Hong Kong." Yet Emily decided to pack it just because Bernardine warned her against it.

Bernardine also admitted to Monroe that Emily had done a little too much opium in Shanghai. "She is taking an opium cure now, having smoked herself almost into a real habit. I'm sure her book about her affair with Sinmay will be interesting, spectacular, and I imagine once it is ready she'll leave, though if you suggest that she goes into fits."[227] Though Bernardine had cut a path as a very modern woman, Emily was far more bold, adventurous, and liberated, much to Bernardine's consternation and concern.

"I like to tell stories on myself sometimes," Bernardine confessed to Sir Victor, "but I am shy about telling them before people I don't know well or care for. I don't in general ever like speaking of whatever my sex life has been to any but a few intimates. You won't find anyone in Shanghai who knows my past sex life, and I'm quite happy that it's so."[228]

Believing she could trust Sir Victor as she had with her breast cancer scare, Bernardine shared her worries that Emily was setting herself up for a difficult time in Shanghai. Instead of keeping this concern to himself as would any loyal friend, he ran to Emily and reported that Bernardine was gossiping behind her back. Emily usually didn't let other people get to her, but in this instance, she felt betrayed by

[226] Letter from Bernardine to Monroe Wheeler, February 19, 1936, Beinecke Library, YCAL MSS 134 Box 103 f. 1574, page 2.
[227] Ibid.
[228] Letter from Bernardine to Victor Sassoon, undated, YCAL MSS 544 Box 4 f. Sassoon, page 31.

Bernardine. Although Bernardine was wrong to gossip about Emily, she had every right to feel angry at Sir Victor for divulging her confidences. The Shanghai rumor mill never rested, and Emily's disappointment in her friend eventually got back to Bernardine.

Again Bernardine went to Sir Victor about this misunderstanding. He tried to console her in a letter, but his words came off as condescending. "I think I appreciate your good qualities even although I realize that you, like everyone else, have your weaknesses. This being so, I am probably a little more lenient than others who are not so understanding. And as you know, Shanghai is not charitable. Without any hesitation I should say that your unflagging energy is probably one of your greatest points, but naturally like everyone else who is very energetic, you come across people who cannot maintain the same pace."[229]

Sir Victor then turned to women's relationships in general. "Personal relations between women are always such that it is dangerous for any mere man to interfere. All I will say is that it seems a little strange, after taking all the trouble you have done in warning one of your friends to be careful what she says in public, that you should somewhat lightheartedly repeat the very things which you deprecated being mentioned in the first place."[230]

Although Bernardine did not owe Sir Victor an explanation, she felt the need to stand up for herself. If Emily was really angry at her, she should have approached Bernardine directly. Also, Bernardine felt Emily was perfectly capable of damaging her own reputation and did not need Bernardine's help with that. "I love Mickey and I always shall. There is no one whose companionship I enjoy more and it is for that reason that I don't dare see her much for she disarms me utterly and I loathe having to feel cautious with people I'm happy with. Mickey isn't worried that I've ruined her reputation in Shanghai, Sir Victor. If you think back, my very first situation with Mickey was caused by you telling her what I'd supposed I was telling you in confidence; that I wished

---

[229] Letter from Victor Sassoon to Bernardine, April 30, 1936, Beinecke Library, YCAL MSS 544 Box 4 f. Sassoon, page 16.
[230] Ibid., pages 16-17.

you, who had influence with her would try to keep her from telling her sex life to the town."[231]

Sir Victor may have used Bernardine to punish Emily for her relationship with Sinmay; he was not happy Emily had drifted so close to Sinmay and away from himself. Sir Victor even told Emily, "What you need is to get married, if you had a husband of your own instead of having somebody else's, you'd get over trying to shock people all the time."[232] Emily and Sir V remained friendly, but the close rapport they had developed soon after meeting certainly dwindled after Emily became Sinmay's common-law wife.

One day, Aline reported back to Bernardine that Emily, Sinmay, and Sinmay's wife, Peiyu, were all headed for a week to Wu-hsi, a city a few hours from Shanghai. "Heavens how mad of Mickey," Bernardine wrote to Glenway, "but I've learned not to oppose her for it only makes her a thousand times worse. Little did I think when she began rolling her eyes at Sinmay that it would end at this."[233]

Emily also may not have had much time for Sir V simply because of all the work she poured herself into in Shanghai, thanks in part to connections from Bernardine. She started a couple of bilingual magazines with Sinmay and worked at his Modern Press. She also enjoyed a growing readership in the United States for her popular column in the *New Yorker* relaying the antics of a Mr. Pan Heh-ven, whom she modeled after Sinmay. "Pale and wraith-like, bearded with a few wisps of real Chinese hair, gowned in sober brown, his long, narrow eyes blank and faraway, he is calculated to make the most hardened tourist gape and gasp."[234] Though Emily used him as fodder for her writing, Sinmay was supportive of her successful writing career.

While this was just a snippet of her writings about Mr. Pan, in her column she claimed Mr. Pan felt dismayed by a Mrs. Manners, obviously

---

[231] Letter from Bernradine to Victor Sassoon, undated, Beinecke Library, YCAL MSS 544 Box 4 f. Sassoon, page 31.

[232] Letter from Bernardine to Glenway Wescott, September 5, 1935, Beinecke Library, YCAL MSS 134 Box 103 f. 1574, page 37.

[233] Letter from Bernardine to Glenway Wescott, undated, Beinecke Library, YCAL MSS 134 Box 103 f. 1574 page 10.

[234] Emily Hahn, *Mr. Pan*, (New York, Doubleday: 1942), page 5.

modeled after Bernardine. "Mrs. Manners, however, is not so easily set-tled. She never tarries in her ceaseless search for Art, and because she is so kind, and because Heh-ven is so kind, complications ensue."[235]

In the beginning of the book, *Mr. Pan*, compiled from Emily's columns, she wrote more about the Bernardine character: "Surprised for a moment by the crowd, Mrs. Manners grew openly delighted at her good fortune. This was *China*, these were *philosophers*. She settled down in the best chair, beaming, and proceeded to be One of Them. She was Broad-Minded; she was a Good Sport; she was Hands Across the Sea and marvelously international. The party turned impercepti-bly into a high-toned affair, and sadly, dispiritedly, everyone followed Mrs. Manners' lead and talked of Art. Manners told us how she loved Chinese theater, and what a shame she thinks it that the young Chinese maidens have taken to curling their hair, and of how they should all wear the old Peiping silks instead of newfangled patterns. She shook her finger severely at Heh-ven for using English shoes instead of Chinese slippers; it spoiled the effect, she said. Heh-ven said he was sorry."[236]

Though this is a perfect though sarcastic description of Bernardine in many ways, she did support Chinese women wearing Westernized cloths, which can be seen in the pride she took of her friends, Daisy Kwok and Helene Chang, owners of the popular dress boutique, Tsingi.

Soon, Emily became even more tied down to Asia after she met Madame H. H. Kung, or Soong Ai-ling, the wife of China's finance minister. There are conflicting reports as to whether Bernardine or their mutual friend, newspaper reporter John Gunther, introduced Emily to Madame Kung, but in any case, this connection resulted in a trust the Soong sisters would bestow upon Emily to pen their biogra-phy, something they would not allow just anyone to write. Emily would stay in China to work on this book until war broke out there in the late 1930s. She retreated to Hong Kong to continue working on it and stayed there until the early 1940s.

While in Hong Kong, Emily would become involved with another married man—the head of British intelligence in Hong Kong, Charles

---

[235] Ibid., page 6.
[236] Ibid.

Boxer. Once he convinced his wife to divorce him, Boxer and Emily were married. After the war and Boxer's release from a POW camp in Hong Kong, the couple would have two daughters and live across the Atlantic from one another, Boxer in the UK and Emily in New York. They would stay married for more than fifty years until Emily died in 1997 at the age of ninety-two. Charles Boxer passed away in England three years later at the age of ninety-six. Emily would continue to write for the *New Yorker* almost until the month she died. She would go on to write more than sixty books, including novels, memoirs, and biographies of Chiang Kai-shek, D. H. Lawrence, and Leonardo da Vinci among others.

Sinmay stayed in touch with Emily, writing to her in 1958 at the start of the Great Leap Forward, the political campaign that caused famine and around forty-five million people to die over the next three to four years.[237] He was imprisoned for writing this letter, a taboo connection with the West and suffered greatly during the three years he was locked away. Sinmay died seven years later in 1968, and Emily didn't learn of his passing until many years after that.[238]

The Great Bernardine War did not last long. Bernardine and Emily's letters, which continued for decades after they both left Shanghai, show a deeper friendship than has been portrayed in previous biographies. Bernardine even apologized years later to Emily for their disagreement in Shanghai, but mostly the two women reminisced about the good old days in China.

This friendship can also be seen in the work Emily took up at the IAT. She reported on some IAT performances in the Shanghai press and even starred in a production of *Lysistrata*. But before that, the IAT would put on its greatest show yet: Shih-I Hsiung's West End hit, *Lady Precious Stream*.

---

[237] Grescoe, page 352.

[238] Gloria Bien, *Baudelaire in China: A Study in Literary Reception*, (Newark, Delaware, The University of Delaware Press: 2013), page 125.

CHAPTER THIRTEEN

LADY PRECIOUS STREAM, 1932–1935

W hen Shih-I Hsiung sailed to London in 1932, he dreamt of becoming an authority on Shakespeare.[239] He was about to begin a BA in English literature at University College London and had already translated works from George Bernard Shaw and J. M. Barrie, the creator of *Peter Pan*, from English to Chinese. Hsiung notified Shaw of his presence in London shortly after the Irish playwright had returned from his own 1933 trip to Shanghai; Hsiung hoped to write plays, too.

But the message in London was clear. Hsiung would be better off crafting stories with Chinese settings rather than Anglican ones. Chinese culture had become fashionable in London and other places in the West, as seen by the rising stars of American actress Anna May Wong and Australian actress Rose Quong. But an interest in Chinese culture did not mean that English or American playwrights wrote realistic Chinese characters or that Chinese actors were cast in lead roles. More troubling, in the 1930s Chinese actors in Hollywood could not by law even kiss white actors on-screen. The 1934 Hays Code that

---

[239] Diana Yeh, *The Happy Hsiungs: Performing China and the Struggle for Modernity*, (Hong Kong, Hong Kong University Press: 2014), page 31.

prohibited interracial relationships in films was abolished in 1968, but the practice in Hollywood has not changed much over the decades.

Hsiung didn't give up hope of being produced on the West End and took the advice of friends in London to write a play based on a Chinese story. He decided to adapt the much beloved Peking opera *Wild Horse with Red Mane* to the English stage. This opera had been performed for centuries and included traditional songs, dance, and costumes. It was so lengthy that performances were usually spread out over a couple days, although some audiences didn't mind sitting through a seven-hour opera in one day. Bernardine's friend, the Peking opera star Mei Lanfang, performed *Wild Horse with Red Mane* as part of his repertoire.

Shih-I Hsiung knew English audiences had shorter attention spans and couldn't sit through multiple daylong performances, so he cut his adaptation down to two hours, removing all song and dance. Hsiung named his adaptation *Lady Precious Stream*, after the lead female character. He started writing *Lady Precious Stream* in the spring of 1933 and finished in six weeks. In June, he sent the play to his literary circles in London. Much to his dismay, George Bernard Shaw did not reply.[240]

Lady Precious Stream premiered in London on November 27, 1934 at the Little Theatre in the Adelphi and was described as "the first European production of a traditional Chinese play in four acts."[241] Despite the traditional Chinese story, instruments, and costumes, every single actor in *Lady Precious Stream* was white. So despite his best wishes of casting stars like Anna May Wong, Rose Quong, Mei Lanfang, or the Chinese film star Butterfly Wu, the only way Hsiung could stage it was to abide by the producers' wishes to hire an all-white cast.

It ran for a thousand nights on the West End.

Future British prime ministers Churchill, Chamberlain, Attlee, and Eden each attended during its three-year run. George Bernard Shaw came around and nominated *Lady Precious Stream* for the Malvern Festival, commemorating his eightieth birthday in 1936. London had never seen such a spectacle.

240 Ibid., page 33.
241 Ibid., page 47.

There is a chance Bernardine met Shih-I Hsiung during her stay in London while Chester attended to business and Rosemary was sent away to Scotland for a week. Whether or not this happened, she would have heard about his new hit play when she, Chester, and Aline settled back into Shanghai in late 1934. Bernardine enjoyed connections to the London theater scene, namely through her former boss, Maurice Browne, from their Chicago Little Theatre days. Maurice had moved to London, and Bernardine had visited with him on her trip earlier in 1934.

Bernardine couldn't stop thinking about *Lady Precious Stream* once she returned to Shanghai. Like *The Soul of the Ch'in*, she found in *Lady Precious Stream* the perfect opportunity for the IAT to stage a play to be enjoyed by Chinese and foreign audiences alike. She was determined to show expats in Shanghai the beauty of Chinese culture and contacted Hsiung in early 1935 to request permission to adapt his play.[242] Bernardine did not have to look far to find someone to help with the logistics of a large-scale production like *Lady Precious Stream*. Her sister Aline was an experienced director in the Little Theatre movement in the US. Although Aline was supposed to be recuperating from tuberculosis in Shanghai, that plan was short-lived. Aline must have felt better by then, or perhaps she just couldn't say no to Bernardine. It wasn't long before the sisters got to work.

The first thing they did was to hire S. Y. Wong as codirector. Although Wong worked at the Asiatic Petroleum Company during the day, he possessed a great interest in and knowledge of traditional Chinese drama. Between Wong's expertise in Chinese theater and Aline's theater experience back home, Bernardine felt *Lady Precious Stream* was in good hands. Aline's personality was also a selling point to the production. Calm and amenable, she complemented Bernardine's nonstop energy. Aline also happily deferred to Wong when it came to sticking to Hsiung's vision of *Lady Precious Stream*.

In the original opera, Wang Baochuan, or Lady Precious Stream, is an upper-class young woman who falls in love with Hsieh Pingkwei,

---

[242] Da Zheng, *Shih-I Hsiung: A Glorious Showman*, (Vancouver, Fairleigh Dickinson University Press: 2020), page 107.

a beggar. Of course, this pairing goes against social norms, and Lady Precious Stream is forbidden from marrying Hsieh. Nevertheless, she marries him against her family's wishes, and Hsieh is soon drafted into the army, leaving home for eighteen years. All that time, Lady Precious Stream longs for her husband and awaits his return. In the original Peking opera, Hsieh is captured by the enemy and survives, marrying another woman: Princess Dazhan. When Hsieh and Princess Dazhan return to Hsieh's hometown and Lady Precious Stream, the reunion is a merry one and all three live together happily ever after.

Hsiung knew that British audiences would not accept a polygamous happy ending, so in his adaptation, he has Hsieh return to Lady Precious Stream without marrying Princess Dazhan.[243] Besides eliminating song and dance, Hsiung also took out references to the supernatural and made Hsieh's character the family gardener, not a beggar.

These changes paid off, and Hsiung's play was staged in Amsterdam and Dublin after finding success in London. Other productions were planned for 1935 and 1936 in New York, Norway, Finland, Sweden, Denmark, Germany, Australia, Hungary, France, and Hong Kong, although not all of them came to fruition. Unlike the London production, Bernardine and her directors were determined to have an all-Chinese cast. Theirs would be the first production of *Lady Precious Stream* with no yellowface. The only non-Chinese involved in the IAT production were Aline and some of the stage crew.

Bernardine made sure the press knew about *Lady Precious Stream* and that it would garner much attention before opening night on June 25, 1935. Almost two years to the date after *The Soul of the Ch'in* premiered in Shanghai, Bernardine's IAT was in full rehearsal for *Lady Precious Stream*. At the IAT studio on 50 East Nanking Road, laughter could be heard as the cast and crew went through their lines and stage direction. The play was a comedy, and the directors needed to make sure the dialogue, movement, and facial expressions were delivered as such. Most members of the cast were amateurs.

---

[243] Yeh, page 41.

The *China Press* reported on the activity at 50 East Nanking Road. "The studio of the International Arts Theater is rapidly assuming the aspect of the offices of a combined 'big business' enterprise and social center. All day long persons intent on IAT activities are hurrying in and out, singly or in groups; typewriters are clicking, telephone bells jangle, and eager voices try to urgently make themselves heard."[244]

At the same time that *Lady Precious Stream* was in rehearsal, Sinmay held court in another part of the studio, presiding over a caricaturists' club. Yet another group in the studio taught Chinese stage makeup. Bernardine and the IAT board also met regularly with business leaders to discuss financing and sponsorship. Perhaps because he noticed others in the business community lending their support or maybe because Emily was involved, Sir Victor graciously offered to help with fundraising. Besides securing donations from individuals and companies, the IAT also started a membership program, which eventually grew to 250 Shanghai residents. Membership dues helped pay for the venue rentals and costume expenses.

***

For the lead role of Lady Precious Stream, Aline and S. Y. Wong cast Tong Ying, one of Bernardine's closest friends and one of the people she credited with introducing her to Lin Yutang. Henry H. Lin starred as Hsieh Pingkwei. Although he wasn't an actor by trade, he was tall and dashing and had earned an MBA at the University of Southern California. He went on to become the president of Shanghai University eleven years after his acting stint in *Lady Precious Stream*.

Daisy Kwok played the second leading female role of Lady Silver Stream. Elsie Lee Soong, no relation to the powerful Shanghai Soong family, starred as Princess Dazhan. An avid tennis player in Shanghai, Florie Ouei played a character simply referred to as Madam. Other cast members included Nates Wong, an editor and translator, and a Mrs. Peter Chang. While the name Peter Chang was very common in 1930s

---

[244] "I.A.T. Studio Hums With Activity Daily: New Projects Launched, Dreams Come True," *The China Press*, May 12, 1935, page 11.

Shanghai, the warlord and general Chang Hsueh-liang also went by the name of Peter Chang. Given his friendship with Bernardine, there is a chance that his wife was the "Mrs. Peter Chang" who acted in a small role in *Lady Precious Stream*.

Bernardine and the directors stayed true to Hsiung's script with one exception. Without the natural breaks of the original Chinese opera, Hsiung had developed the role of the Honourable Reader as a way to inform the audience of scene changes and to interpret some of the symbolism that a non-Chinese audience wouldn't necessarily understand. But S. Y. Wong and Aline felt that Shanghai theatergoers wouldn't need such explanations. Much of the audience would have a basic understanding of Chinese culture, with the exception of the most sheltered foreigners. So the role of the Honourable Reader was eliminated in the IAT's production.

In early June, the IAT announced that *Lady Precious Stream* would be performed on June 25 and 26, 1935 at the Carlton Theatre, near the Park Hotel where Daisy Kwok and Helene Chang would open their dress shop the following year.[245] The Carlton was also close to the Grand Theatre, site of *The Soul of the Ch'in*. It was a modest two-story building without a marquee but rather a second-floor sunroom adorned with metalwork much like that in Bernardine's home at 62 Route de Boissezon. The theater is no longer standing today.

Tickets for IAT members went for two dollars and the general public paid four dollars.[246] To protect the voices of the actors and to keep the audience from coughing during the performance, the IAT prohibited smoking even though it was normally allowed at the Carlton.

As the opening day approached, Chester became disgruntled by the amount of time Bernardine spent on rehearsals and production matters. He had been supportive of her endeavors with the IAT, but the difference between the 1933 production of *The Soul of the Ch'in* and the 1935 staging of *Lady Precious Stream* was pretty simple.

---

[245] "I.A.T.S. To Give Play At Carlton: 'Lady Precious Stream' To Be Produced On June 25 and 26," *The China Press*, June 8, 1935, page 11.
[246] Ibid.

It was Aline.

Chester blamed his sister-in-law for taking Bernardine's attention from him, although they all lived under the same roof at 62 Route de Boissezon and Chester continued to spend the bulk of his free time with his horses. Yet Aline's presence bothered Chester so much that his biographer wrote about this issue. "The theater brought Bernardine considerable notoriety. Her husband had no objection until Bernardine's sister, Aline Sholes, and her husband arrived for a visit from Omaha, Nebraska. The visitors, however, became permanent residents when Bernardine hired the couple as the executive directors of the theater group."[247]

Chester's biographer was correct in his assessment of Chester's dislike of Aline. Similar to his jealousy of Rosemary, Chester possessed little tolerance when it came to Bernardine's close family relationships. Aline was the sibling Bernardine felt most attached to and the one she got along with the best. But the biographer was incorrect when he wrote that Aline and her husband arrived from Omaha. Max Sholes had stayed back in the US, recuperating from his own bout with TB. Perhaps if Max had accompanied Aline to Shanghai, Chester may not have felt so threatened by her presence. But with Max in the US, Aline could devote all of her attention to her big sister. Bernardine could see how Chester envied her family and wrote about it to Glenway. "Though he cares for some of my friends very much, he cannot bear me to have family—any kind, in any relationship, and only manages to be amiable and interested at a great distance."[248]

Bernardine was far too occupied with *Lady Precious Stream* to let Chester's jealousy get to her this time. After all the anxiety he'd caused her with his disdain of Rosemary and during her breast cancer scare, Bernardine would not allow herself to become derailed by a needy husband again. She needed *Lady Precious Stream* and the IAT to succeed now that she had the opportunity to work on such a large production. This was her big chance to bring the expat and Chinese communities

---

[247] Fritz and Rylance, *Ever Westward to the Far East: The Story of Chester Fritz*, page 143.

[248] Letter from Bernardine to Glenway Wescott, July 22, 1936, Beinecke Library, YCAL MSS 134 Box 103 f. 1575, page 56.

together through the arts, and failure was not an option. Bernardine had never felt more at home in Shanghai as she reveled in the happiness she saw in others when they came together around a performance, lecture, or exhibition. Even as *Lady Precious Stream* was deep into rehearsals, Bernardine scheduled other events at the IAT to build momentum for the theater company.

The pianist Arthur Rubinstein passed through Shanghai in the late spring of 1935, so Bernardine arranged a tea reception for him at the IAT studio.[249] Someone found a piano to borrow, and the commotion around its delivery caused a disruption to rehearsals for *Lady Precious Stream*. The *China Press* poetically described the scene following the arrival of the piano. "All this time there is an undercurrent of activity; phone bells peal, messengers come and go, printers arrive with stationery for approval. And when, as occasionally happens, there is a momentary lull in this furious tempo, and the coolie is left alone to watch the premises, he straightens the disorder left by this tornado of energy; and, fired by the same spirit, as if it were loath to leave the premises, he sits at the typewriter and practices, painfully pecking at the keys, copying announcements and keeping up still the busy sounds that represent the spirit of the International Arts Theater."[250]

Around that same time, in early May 1935, Bernardine arranged a controversial debate around birth control in Shanghai, newly available over the past five years. At first, the Nationalist government supported birth control to provide relief to poor families, but as Chiang Kai-shek and Madame Chiang launched their New Life Movement in early 1934, influenced by Confucianism and Madame Chiang's Christian upbringing, the government suddenly gave less support to birth control than in recent years.

Before Bernardine started writing for the *China Critic*, the magazine published a front-page editorial in May 1930 supporting the Birth Control League. The League was organized with the explicit purpose

---

[249] "Many Hear Discussion At Studio: Pros and Cons Of Birth Control Viewed At I.A.T. Meeting," *The China Press*, May 7, 1935, page 11.
[250] "I.A.T. Studio Hums With Activity Daily: New Projects Launched, Dreams Come True," *The China Press*, May 12, 1935, page 11.

of helping to "improve the quality of children, to protect motherhood, and to enrich family life."[251] Further on in the editorial, Lin Yutang and his editors expressed the need for such measures. "Enlightened people have long felt the necessity for such an institution, and we have more than once, both in these columns and in special articles, called the attention of our readers to the fact that birth control, like other far reaching social endeavors, must first come under public control, if we are to reap full and legitimate benefit from it."

Bernadine moved to Shanghai just when birth control became legal in China. She dared to bring voice to this topic at the IAT, and instead of enlisting passionate believers and naysayers to support their own views, she chose a different tack. She asked Dr. J. R. B. Branch to give the opposition's argument even though he was a strong proponent of birth control and a physician who researched brain injuries of Chinese victims during Japan's 1932 bombings in Shanghai. To praise the benefits of birth control, Bernardine picked Dr. P. T. Chou of Honolulu, who supported birth control but personally believed China was not yet ready for it.[252]

The event drew a large crowd, some of whom were visibly upset by the topic, such as Father James Kearney and his colleagues from Gonzaga College, a local school established in the French Concession in 1931, not to be confused with Gonzaga University in Washington State, also founded by Jesuits. In attendance on the other side of the spectrum were Dr. F. C. Yen, the president of Shanghai's Birth Control League, and Mrs. Anna Chung Chou, the director of the birth control clinic.[253]

The *China Press* reported, "The International Arts Theater Studio, which ordinarily attracts the group of people whose interests tend toward the artistic, yesterday afternoon was the scene of a varied

---

[251] The Birth Control League," *The China Critic*, Volume 3, Number 21, May 22, 1930, page 1.

[252] "Many Hear Discussion At Studio: Pros and Cons Of Birth Control Viewed At I.A.T. Meeting," *The China Press*, May 7, 1935, page 11.

[253] Ibid.

assembly. Doctors and religious people were seen at the meeting and took part in the general discussion which followed the talks."[254]

Lest one think Bernardine held a grudge against Catholics, ten days before *Lady Precious Stream* opened, she helped with a charity ball to raise money for the Catholic mission at Nanyang in Henan Province, one of China's poorest regions then and now. The gala also raised funds for the Anti-Tuberculosis Society.[255]

Bernardine assigned the production of the ball to other prominent figures in Shanghai. This was a trademark of hers. She was skilled at delegating and finding the right person for the job. Bernardine named Maria Lojacono, the wife of the Italian ambassador, as the president of the ball committee. About a decade older than Bernardine, Countess Lojacono spoke French and Italian but no English. At her side as vice president of the committee was Madame Wu Te-chen, the wife of the mayor of Shanghai.

Bernardine listed herself as just one of the committee members, along with a mixed group of Chinese and foreign women, including the wife of T. V. Soong, the former finance minister of China; Princess Giulia Ottoboni, sister-in-law of Victor Sassoon; and Madame de Weydenthal, the wife of the Polish ambassador.

The ball ushered in a night of international pageantry with a Venetian carnival, a Louis XV waltz, a Cuban rumba, a Hungarian czardas, a Spanish dance, a children's dance, and an American barn dance arranged by Aline. Sinmay put together the Chinese entertainment of the evening. As the *China Press* reported, the ball raised money and awareness for these two charities, "both institutions being, needless to say, highly deserving of the funds that are always so necessary for the furtherance of their wonderful work."[256]

The IAT also held a number of lectures before the premiere of *Lady Precious Stream* as well as an exhibition of photographs from Edward

---

[254] Ibid.
[255] "I.A.T.S. To Sponsor Benefit: June 12 Charity Ball To Have Patronage Of Prominent Women," *The China Press*, May 18, 1935, page 11.
[256] Ibid.

Weston, one of the most notable early-twentieth-century American photographers. Weston sent fifty photos with a friend who was traveling there, which marked the first time photography was viewed as an art in Shanghai.[257] The IAT sent out postcards to members announcing the show. "The International Arts Theatre announces an exhibition of prints by Edward Weston, foremost American photographer, at their studio, Nanking and Szechuen Roads (top floor, Asia Realty Building) from May 29 to June 12. Open daily except Sunday from 11 to 5. The public is invited. No admission charge."[258]

The *China Press* reported, "To photograph a rock and to make the print a subject of interest, a graphic composition, reflecting skill and mastery in handling light is no easy task. But Edward Weston has accomplished this in almost every one of his photos. Hardly a print on display does not have an essential fineness, firmness, and distinctiveness of its own."[259] The exhibit was a unique opportunity for Chinese and foreigners in Shanghai to be treated to a show from such a renowned artist back in the United States. Bernardine may have crossed paths with Weston in the mid-1910s when she wrote alongside Carl Sandburg at the *Chicago Evening Post.* Weston photographed Sandburg around that time.

Bernardine helped arrange these lectures, exhibits, and the fundraising ball to showcase all that the IAT was capable of producing. The flurry of activity in the months and weeks leading up to *Lady Precious Stream* was part of the IAT's plan to advertise the big production opening on June 25, 1935.

---

257 Edward Weston, *The Daybooks of Edward Weston*, vol. 2, edited by Nancy Newhall, (Millerton, New York, Aperture Press: 1973), page 276.

258 Postcard announcement for Edward Weston exhibition in Shanghai, Collection of the Edward Weston Archive, Center for Creative Photography, University of Arizona, Scrapbook A.

259 "Photographs By Weston Now Seen At IAT: Fine Exhibit Of Camera Studies Being Displayed; Collection Not Complete," *The China Press*, May 30, 1935, page 3.

CHAPTER FOURTEEN

OPENING NIGHT AND
AFTERWARDS, 1935

The lobby was packed at the Carlton Theatre. All around, Bernardine greeted familiar faces as well as people she had never seen before. It seemed as if all of Shanghai's well-educated Chinese and foreigners had turned up that evening. Exhausted and running on adrenaline, Bernardine greeted Sir Victor who was dressed in a tuxedo.[260] The rest of the crowd wore a mix of Western and Chinese fashions and intermingled in ways that were rarely seen on such a large scale in Shanghai apart from the racecourse. Even Chester, at Bernardine's side, grinned widely at the turnout. His business associates shook his hand as they walked by, and Chester basked in the Chinese custom of gaining face. He felt so proud of Bernardine for her involvement in the program, even though it meant Aline had been living with them for more than half a year.

It was opening night of *Lady Precious Stream* and the IAT's largest production to date. Guests arrived early as the IAT did not offer reserved seating. Each seat in the audience was filled, and the following

---

[260] Allen Krause, Untitled, *The China Press*, June 30, 1935, page C1.

night was sold out too. The Carlton was normally used as a cinema and its patrons enjoyed the building's air-conditioning. By June 25, the Shanghai evenings would have been blanketed in heat and humidity, so this modern luxury came in handy to the hundreds of theatergoers in the audience. Bernardine wanted to schedule a third performance because many people were unable to buy tickets for the first two, but the theater wasn't available. So she scrambled to make arrangements for a third performance to be held on June 28 at the Lyceum Theatre, a corner, red, brick building in the French Concession.[261]

On opening night, IAT members served as ushers, standing in the lobby and passing out elaborate bilingual programs with the IAT logo front and center. Bound with red thread, the programs were printed in English if read left to right. If someone were to open the program to read from right to left, she would find those pages printed in Chinese. The program pages were not numbered, so neither Chinese readers nor English readers would feel their language came second.

Bernardine asked Lin Yutang to write the program's introduction with more information about Chinese opera for the English version as this audience was less familiar with the story and art form than the Chinese attendees. Yutang explained that traditional Chinese opera was often performed outdoors and thus competed with barking dogs and the shouts of merchants advertising their goods. Gongs and drums would draw the attention of an audience, so these instruments became a part of Chinese opera.

"With the change of theatre conditions and the influence of Western dramas, it is inevitable that the Chinese theatre of today should evolve a new technique. Modern audiences will no longer sit through a programme of six or seven hours, and this fact alone must produce a change in the tempo of acting."[262] Yutang appreciated Shih-I Hsiung's shortened version of this classic opera as well as the modern adaptation to appeal to conservative Western audiences when it came to polygamy. Although Hsiung wrote the story with British audiences

[261] Da Zheng, "Lady Precious Stream Returns Home," Journal of the Royal Asiatic Society China, Volume 76, Number 1, 2016, page 28.
[262] Ibid., page 26.

in mind, the Chinese government's puritanical New Life Movement most likely supported this change, too. The audience, Yutang advised, should be prepared for experimental theater because that was exactly what they would be seeing that evening.

Bernardine held her breath as the curtain began to rustle. She knew some members of the audience had seen the original in London, and she was eager to hear their thoughts about the IAT production. When the curtain opened, it would stay up until the end of the play. S. Y. Wong and Aline instructed the stage crew to simply make changes in the lighting to indicate a new act instead of lowering and raising the curtain. The stage set included a stark display of wooden Chinese chairs, with a banner of red characters attached to the back curtain.

The actors soon took to the stage, dressed in elaborate robes, hats, and headdresses. Elsie Lee Soong, starring as Princess Dazhan, wowed the audience with her enormous headdress flanked by two long pheasant feathers. But Tong Ying was the actress who stole the show. Poised and pert, she kept the audience captivated with her endearing smile and catchy dialogue. It was almost as if Shih-I Hsiung had written the role just for her.

The performance did not involve much action but rather included a series of scenes where the actors sat in the parlor on stage, discussing the mismatched pairing of Lady Precious Stream and the gardener, Hsieh Pingkwei.

Bernardine silently cheered as Daisy Kwok marveled the audience with her rendition of Lady Silver Stream. Daisy had not acted since high school, but she embraced the IAT's vision of engaging Shanghai residents in the arts. Daisy made the most of these opportunities and wrote about the IAT in her memoir, *Shanghai Daisy*. "We did all sorts of programs, and since I was always interested in dramatics, I did several plays with them. These were Chinese plays translated into English. I had an instructor to teach me all the techniques, etc., and it was fun. We even did puppet shows and made our own puppets."[263] Bernardine's

---

[263]   Kwok, Johnston, and Earnshaw, page 34.

work with the Little Theatre in Chicago inspired her to bring puppetry to the IAT.

When the curtain finally closed, the audience leapt to a standing ovation. The performance had exceeded Bernardine's grandest hopes for the IAT. She glowed, just thinking about all the many hours dozens of volunteers had put into every detail of the production. Their hard work paid off in ways she had only dreamt of five to six years earlier. As exhausted and overtaxed as Bernardine felt, it was all worth it. Perhaps in the future she would find someone to take over more of the daily operations of the IAT, but for now she would soak in the moment.

Lin Yutang reviewed the production for the *China Critic* a week later. He began by congratulating the IAT "on its presentation of *Lady Precious Stream*, which was the first performance by a Chinese cast of an old Chinese play in English rendering."[264] Yutang quickly compared Hsiung's translation with the original Chinese opera, *Wild Horse with Red Mane*, but explained in his review that instead of delving more into the work of Hsiung, he wished to address the "brilliant cast of Chinese amateur actors."

Yutang highlighted the significance of Chinese actors performing a Chinese play in English and how he found that so transformative. It simply hadn't been done before, and Yutang saw great hope for Shanghai theater because of this performance. "The Princess, for instance, as played by Elsie Soong, has got a Hollywood touch to her that may well be envied by Clara Bow. No conflict exists for her; she has just thrown the Chinese theatrical technique to the winds. If one would like to see what the modern Chinese woman could come to under a different breeding and social environment, the best way is just to look at the Princess. But it should be realized that her part requires such a freedom as a necessary contrast to the Chinese matron in the Celestial Empire at home."[265]

---

[264] Yutang Lin, "Lady Precious Stream," *The China Critic*, Vol. X, No. 1, July 4, 1935, page 17.

[265] Ibid.

His assessment of Tong Ying glimmered even more.[266] "We mustn't forget Lady Precious Stream herself, played by the beautiful and vivacious Tang Ing. She was a sweet, young thing and a spoilt daughter, as Lady Precious Stream should be, and her overflowing vivacity gave a basic sustenance of jollity so essential to the play. I was struck, however, more by her tragic parts, for it is easy with Tang Ing to be gay and giggling, and I had rather trembled for her tragic moments, in which she did rise to the occasion. If anything, she inclined just a little too often to relapse into her gay natural smile. And I should like to see her changed, in Act Three, into a mature woman after eighteen years of parting and absence. If the Chinese stage tradition requires that she remain a sweet, young thing after eighteen years of hardship and sadness, then to hell with Chinese tradition."[267] He went on to predict that Tong Ying would go on to a great acting career. Yutang also felt the IAT now had much to live up to after the success of these performances.

Bernardine was in contact with Shih-I Hsiung at some point during the IAT production, if not throughout. He did not travel to Shanghai to see it, perhaps because *Lady Precious Stream* was still in the midst of its successful run in London and also because Bernardine's theater company was still viewed as an amateur one. It probably didn't seem worth the trip across the ocean for a three-night run when the London production was attracting all the big names in British politics and literature.

After the IAT performances, Bernardine wrote to Hsiung about its grand success. She had discussed the differences between the Shanghai and London shows with friends who had attended both and relayed to Hsiung that "it was so infinitely more delightful in Shanghai BECAUSE

---

[266] There were many ways to romanize Chinese names then, and Yutang used a different spelling from the way Bernardine spelled Tong Ying's name in the many letters she wrote to friends and family.

[267] Yutang Lin, "Lady Precious Stream," *The China Critic*, Vol. X, No. 1, July 4, 1935, page 17.

of the atmosphere, grace, charm and *style*, all so CHINESE…that Westerners of course could not possibly imitate."[268]

It wasn't just that Bernardine thought S. Y. Wong and Aline did a superior job in their casting, but also that Shanghai was better situated for *Lady Precious Stream* because of the choice of actors and the knowledge of the costume designers. The London production had a difficult time sourcing costumes and learning the techniques of Peking opera makeup. None of these things was ever an issue in Shanghai. The IAT production was so successful that the Nationalist government invited the cast to perform in the capital city of Nanking. From there, the IAT hoped to bring the play to Peking, Tientsin, and Hangchow in 1936. But none of these plans would pan out, and the IAT's *Lady Precious Stream* ended up only running those three nights in Shanghai. Bernardine was exhausted after the Shanghai performances and didn't seem particularly disappointed these other Chinese productions fell through. But she did try to assist a little in the Broadway production.

Less than a month after the IAT production, Anna May Wong contacted Hsiung about taking his play to New York. She was the most well-known Asian American actress in Hollywood and offered help in producing it. But Hsiung instead turned to Jewish immigrant theater producers in New York: Morris Gest and Lee Shubert. Incidentally, Gest's wife, Reina, was the daughter of theater producer David Belasco. When Bernardine was a reporter living in New York, she was one of many guests at a dinner party at Belasco's home. He was charmed by Bernardine. She reminded him so much of his daughter Augusta, who had died in 1911 at the age of thirty-one. He was so taken with Bernardine after the dinner that he said he had a gift for her and walked her to a large trunk filled with beautiful shawls that had belonged to Augusta. He told her to select her favorite, and when she had trouble choosing between two of the many exquisite shawls, he gave her both. She cherished the shawls and shared this story for the rest of her life.[269]

[268] Da Zheng, "Lady Precious Stream Returns Home," Journal of the Royal Asiatic Society China, Volume 76, Number 1, 2016, page 28.

[269] Bernardine's cousin Nancy told me about this and how Bernardine treasured these scarves and spoke about them often.

The New York producers were determined to right some of the wrongs of the West End production. First, they would order costumes from China and not try to reproduce them on their own. They also asked Mei Lanfang to design the set. And for the main role of Lady Precious Stream, the Broadway producers offered it to Tong Ying. Shih-I Hsiung and his wife, Dymia—a novelist who also wrote in English—would travel to New York to be there in person. The couple set sail from the UK in the fall of 1935.[270]

Around the time the Broadway production was in the planning stages, Tong Ying found herself in the middle of a rough divorce. As much as she wished to reprise her role as Lady Precious Stream, she just couldn't leave Shanghai. Her troubles had started even before the IAT production was staged in June 1935. According to Bernardine, after five years of marriage to insurance executive Lee Tsufa, Tong Ying began an affair with a married man. "I met him and found him the work of the earth," Bernardine recalled. "Her husband, Tsufa, being very Chinese and a fatalist said, 'what can I do, it is destiny,' and let her go on. But it got worse and worse, and she went out dancing with her lover to all the public places cheek to cheek, etc. It has got in the mosquito papers a hundred times. They are blackmail sheets and scandal sheets which are printed in fly by night presses, with no editor known to god or man, hundreds of them exist. You pay a yearly tariff to be let out of them."[271]

Bernardine also wrote to Glenway that Tong Ying's new love interest was the husband of a Mrs. Yung. When Mrs. Yung found out about her husband's affair, she threatened suicide if Tong Ying divorced and married Mr. Yung. At the same time, Tsufa threatened to divorce Tong Ying if she starred in the IAT's production of *Lady Precious Stream*.[272] Bernardine and Lin Yutang tried to make sense of the different sides of this love triangle. It was none of their business, of course, but

---

[270] Da Zheng, "Performing Transposition: *Lady Precious Stream* on Broadway," *New England Theatre Journal*, Volume 26, 2015, page 88.

[271] Letter from Bernardine to Glenway Wescott, undated, YCAL MSS 134 Box 103 f. 1574, page 14.

[272] Ibid., page 15.

it threatened to disrupt the IAT's rehearsals. In the end, Tong Ying remained the lead in Shanghai, but her life was too chaotic for her to leave for New York.

After Hsiung went with the New York producers and Tong Ying couldn't leave Shanghai, Anna May Wong decided to campaign for the lead role herself. Again, it appeared that Hsiung turned her down. It's not clear why this happened, but he probably felt pressure from his producers, Gest and Shubert, to cast a white woman in the lead. And that's exactly what happened. Helen Chandler, known for her work in the 1931 film, *Dracula*, became Lady Precious Stream on Broadway—in yellowface.

But Shih-I Hsiung did insist on one Chinese actor for the Broadway production. The role of the Honourable Reader had been cut from the IAT performance but reappeared in the New York shows. Although the producers could choose from a number of qualified Asian actors, they chose Mai-Mai Sze, a friend of Bernardine's and the daughter of the Chinese ambassador to the US. This choice could be viewed as a political move to further diplomatic bonds between the US and China. Or it could be seen as a way to engage a Chinese artist who was very familiar with Broadway theater.

Mai-Mai's background was suitable for this role. Born in Tientsin, now called Tianjin, she spent her formative years in the UK when her father served as the Chinese ambassador to the UK. Later, she moved with her family to Washington, DC, when her father was posted to the Chinese embassy there. Mai-Mai graduated from Wellesley College in 1931, where she enjoyed a liberal arts education of literature, art, philosophy, Western history, and religion. A lifelong friend of Bernardine's, Mai-Mai took up painting after graduation and, at some point, began a decades-long relationship with the costume designer, Irene Sharaff. The women lived together until they each passed away a year apart in the early 1990s, both over the age of eighty. During her younger years, Mai-Mai posed for *Vogue* and was photographed by Bernardine's friends, Carl Van Vechten and George Platt Lynes. Her performance in the Broadway version of *Lady Precious Stream* was the highlight of the production as her style of narration alone had the audience in stitches, a tone reminiscent of the IAT's shows.

Lady Precious Stream ran for only 105 nights at the Booth Theatre in New York. Eleanor Roosevelt attended toward the end of the run and enjoyed it immensely, yet the Broadway production never caught on as it had on the West End or in Shanghai. The play enjoyed a short revival in the 1950s and '60s with productions in Ghana, Kenya, South Africa, Israel, and Wales, usually connected to nascent political movements or nation-building, perhaps due to the message that perseverance pays off.

Bernardine blamed the New York producers for not listening to her when it came to casting Chinese actors. In a letter to Glenway, she complained, "It looks as if the NY performance was a washout— why they did it like child's play instead of seriously I can't think, and the dodo Gest NOT to have taken a Chinese cast as I suggested.... It would have been superb."[273] She held out hope that Aline could direct *Lady Precious Stream* at another theater in the US, but that never materialized.

Anna May Wong felt the same about the New York production, although at that time, she and Bernardine were still just acquaintances after meeting the previous year in London. Wong's frustrations with Broadway stemmed from her experience in Hollywood. The film studios had no problem typecasting her in roles that portrayed Chinese in derogatory ways. She was seen as an outsider in the US entertainment industry, although she was an American and had never even been to China. So in early 1936, she decided it was time to finally visit her grandparents' birthland and to make her own movie there. It was time to show Hollywood she was the right person for authentic leading Asian roles. To prepare for her high-profile trip and documentary, she contacted that acquaintance of hers, Bernardine Szold Fritz.

---

[273] Ibid., page 29.

CHAPTER FIFTEEN

ANNA MAY TAKES CHINA
BY STORM, 1936

nna May Wong suffered her greatest professional setback the year Bernardine reached her career apex. In 1935, while *Lady Precious Stream* took Shanghai by storm, the film adaptation of Pearl Buck's bestseller, *The Good Earth*, went into production in Hollywood. Anna May had become one of the most celebrated movie stars in the US and Europe even though she mainly starred in stereotypical roles like Dr. Fu Manchu's daughter, Princess Ling Moy, in *Daughter of the Dragon* with Swedish-American actor Warner Oland in yellowface as Dr. Fu Manchu. Oland went on to make a career of working in yellowface, as the Eurasian villain Chang in *Shanghai Express* and as detective Charlie Chan in sixteen films.

When Hollywood refused to cast Anna May in the lead role of *The Good Earth*, she took it personally. Instead, the character O-Lan would go to the German Jewish actress, Luise Rainer, a refugee from Nazi Germany who never took to Hollywood even though she won two Oscars for Best Actress, including for the O-Lan role. The only way Anna May could have starred in *The Good Earth*, according to the Hays Code that prohibited interracial relationships on-screen, would be for the leading male role to be performed by an Asian actor. Hollywood wouldn't have that and gave the Wang Lung role to Jewish Austro-Hungarian Paul Muni.

If Anna May had hoped that her previous work in films like the 1932 *Shanghai Express* with Marlene Dietrich would show producers that they could cast her in lead roles and ignore the new Hays Code, *The Good Earth* would have been her breakthrough film in that respect. When she didn't get it, she rejected the offer of a supporting character—the only evil role in the film—and realized it was time to reassess her career. She didn't feel accepted in her home country of the United States and knew she wasn't well liked in China because of the stereotypical roles she had no choice but to accept if she wanted to work. She either had to take those parts or not act. Anna May Wong was born to perform and shine on the screen. She couldn't imagine a life devoid of acting.

So in early 1936, she made her first trip to China. There were two purposes for this journey. One would allow her to learn more about her ancestors' home country, and the other would show people in China that she was not the stereotypical dragon lady or wilted flower she played on-screen. She was up against a racist film industry and a country that blamed her—not the producers—for portraying Chinese unfavorably. She was determined to change that.

Anna May would record her trip in a documentary film to bring back to the US. She would certainly visit her ancestral home of Toisan in southern China. She also wanted to see the fabled city of Peking, the old capital. And then there was Shanghai. Anna May Wong only knew Bernardine from their 1934 introduction at Madame Wellington Koo's reception in London. Yet she figured she could count on Bernardine to show her around and introduce her to important people in Shanghai.

Shanghai would be her first stop in China.

Anna May sailed there at the beginning of 1936 after a tour of Japan. In an article she wrote for the *New York Herald Tribune* months later, she described her first impressions of the city on the sea. "I'll never forget my excitement when at 2 o'clock this afternoon we entered the broad mouth of the Whangpoo River. The first craft I saw there was a junk, with ribbed sails and large eyes painted on either side of the prow, so that the boat could see its way. Flat fields, dotted here and there with peasant villages and curved roof temples, stretched out to the horizon on either side of the stream."[274]

She felt taken aback when she spotted people living on boats along the Whangpoo and worried about their difficult lives and how horrible it must be to eke out an existence on the river. On closer look, Anna May noticed smiling children and babies "as fat as little laughing Buddhas." She realized there were worse ways to live than as "a nomad on the great Whangpoo."

Bernardine did not meet Anna May at the dock, as she had often done when other luminaries arrived in Shanghai. Their friendship had not yet developed, and Anna May's brother, James, had arrived in Shanghai ahead of time to arrange his sister's schedule and publicity. Plus, Anna May had a documentary to film, and her arrival in Shanghai would be recorded by a camera crew waiting for her boat to pull up to one of the many piers along the Bund.

Anna May wrote in the *New York Herald Tribune* of her reception in Shanghai and how two hundred reporters from Chinese papers across the country met her at the pier, her brother James leading the troops. "For an hour, while I doggedly maintained a pleasant expression, photographers took pictures and reporters asked questions. Some of the former even climbed into the lifeboats in their pursuit of unusual angles."[275]

Standing five feet seven inches in a fur coat with fluted sleeves, Anna May spoke a little Cantonese but couldn't understand a word of the Shanghainese or Mandarin most of the reporters spoke. "I thus had the strange experience of talking to my own people through an interpreter." She was escorted through customs by six British guards. Customs was a curious matter in Shanghai in 1936 as China didn't

---

[274] Anna May Wong, "Anna May Wong Recalls Shanghai's Enthusiastic Reception: Crowds Besieged Her On Arrival From Yokohama To Visit China 1ˢᵗ Time," *New York Herald Tribune*, May 31, 1936, page 6.

[275] "Anna May Wong Recalls Shanghai's Enthusiastic Reception: Crowds Besieged Her On Arrival From Yokohama To Visit China 1st Time," *New York Herald Tribune*, May 31, 1936, page 6.

control it. But neither did France, the UK, Japan, or the US, the other countries that administered parts of the city. Customs was instead run by a hodgepodge of all these nations. No one nation wanted to take responsibility for who entered Shanghai, lest that country's businesses be penalized. Shanghai's open border also explained how easy it was for refugees to arrive from all over the world and within China.

As much as this trip was supposed to garner publicity and good graces for Anna May, she never thought she would enjoy such a welcoming reception. After clearing customs, Anna May noticed old women, their feet bound into tiny shoes, standing amongst distinguished Chinese scholars in long robes and uniform-clad school girls, all vying for her attention. The crowd followed Anna May to a waiting car that struggled to drive away. A driver took her to the Park Hotel. "This tumultuous greeting from my own people touched me more than anything that ever has happened to me in my motion-picture career. Incidentally, I wonder how the idea got abroad that the Chinese are always stolid and without emotion."[276]

Bernardine and Anna May eventually met up at a tiffin, or lunch party. The two women got along well this time, as they both enjoyed a good laugh and found a friend in one another through their bonhomie. Lin Yutang also hosted a dinner for Anna May and invited Bernardine, Tong Ying, and Mr. and Mrs. Sun Fo, the son and daughter-in-law of Sun Yat-sen, along with several painters. "Yutang and Tong Ying were telling plots of famous Chinese novels and then Yutang like a baby began asking Anna May about all the film gossip," Bernardine wrote in a letter to Glenway.[277]

Anna May's 1936 documentary, *My China Film*, shows her stepping out of the Park Hotel in a sleeveless, ankle-length cheongsam, greeting the actor, Mei Lanfang. Anna May strolled through markets dotted with small wooden birdcages and examined the dozens of blooms on display at a flower market.

---

[276] Ibid.

[277] Letter from Bernardine to Glenway Wescott, March 30, 1936, Beinecke Library, YCAL MSS 134 Box 103 f. 1574, page 31.

By late February 1936, she left Shanghai and traveled to Hong Kong to visit her sister, Wong Ling. Anna May wrote to Bernardine from the Hong Kong Hotel, thanking her for the tiffin party and addressing her as "Mrs. Fritz."[278] Anna May was also friends with Carl Van Vechten, the photographer who took Bernardine's portraits at the end of 1934 after her mastectomy, and his wife, Fania Marinoff. Anna May wrote to Carl and Fania about meeting Bernardine in Shanghai and relayed all the great things Bernardine was doing with the IAT.

Anna May signed her first letter to Bernardine, "with kindest regards to you and Mr. Fritz."[279] The two women would never again write to each other with such formality as their friendship quickly blossomed. Yet in Anna May's articles about her trip to China, she never mentioned Bernardine, which by now must have been standard for Bernardine. She was not a household name in the US, and most of her famous friends did not think to repay her many kindnesses with public recognition, including Emily Hahn in her memoir and Anna May in her newspaper essays.

In writing about her trip, Anna May instead described a reception that Dr. and Mrs. Wellington Koo hosted for her. The timing worked out well, as the Koos were about to embark for France where Wellington would serve as ambassador of China. At this reception, men and women danced together, and Anna May became the most popular dance partner of the evening. She wrote that all the men danced well except for T. V. Soong, the former finance minister.

Bernardine made sure Anna May carried many letters of introduction for her further travels in China, including Peking and Tientsin. "I appreciate so much having all your letters and your suggestions on different subjects to discuss with the press. I will most probably touch on them upon my return to Shanghai in the near future when the usual arrival talk has been worn out."[280] Anna May ended this letter

---

[278] Letter from Anna May Wong to Bernardine, February 24, 1936, Beinecke Library, YCAL MSS 544 Box 5 f. Wong, Anna May, page 6.
[279] Ibid.
[280] Ibid.

with hopes they'd be able to meet again in Shanghai when "life will be less hectic."

During her time in Shanghai—before and after visiting Hong Kong and southern China—Anna May was whisked from party to party. She attended evening soirees where guests played pai gow, a game like baccarat, and mahjong. Sometimes Bernardine attended these gatherings, and sometimes she stayed home. But it was the Shanghai tailors Anna May marveled about the most. "Today I had my first session with a Chinese tailor. He merely hurled a few strings around me, rather as if they were lariats, and then tied a knot in each one to indicate the measurement. How, considering all his orders, he manages to remember what each stands for is something only Buddha knows."[281] She went on to describe how Shanghai tailors didn't use patterns and could simply eyeball a design to perfectly recreate it.

In Shanghai, Anna May also met Mayor Wu Te-chen and J. P. McEvoy, the cartoonist at the dinner with Lin Yutang who had sported the metal trick ring. She noted that Shanghai women enjoyed much more freedom than she had imagined. "Unlike the old-fashioned Chinese gentleman, a modern Shanghai husband does not refer to his invisible wife as 'the mean one of the inner compartments.' Instead, he takes her out to dances, restaurants and night clubs and expects her to serve as hostess of his home. The women in Shanghai actually have more freedom than many Europeans."[282] Anna May contrasted the role of Shanghai wives with the traditional custom in many cultures where wives never socialized with husbands and remained invisible, tucked away at home or confined to separate rooms when their husbands brought friends home. Anna May never wed, but she did appreciate these changing marital roles.

After Anna May left Shanghai a second time, this time for Peking, Bernardine wrote Glenway a letter that showed how close the women's

---

[281] "Anna May Wong Recalls Shanghai's Enthusiastic Reception: Crowds Besieged Her On Arrival From Yokohama To Visit China 1st Time," *New York Herald Tribune*, May 31, 1936, page 6.

[282] Anna May Wong, "Anna May Wong Finds Shanghai Life Glamorous: Speed And Noise Rival Those Of Large American Cities, She Thinks," *New York Herald Tribune*, June 14, 1936, page B2.

friendship had grown. "Anna May Wong left today, after a hectic ten days, and she said she never had been so exhausted in her life, and fell on to the deck. Shanghai is mad really. I've been trying to write about it, its gaiety, but it is too difficult."[283] Bernardine could also be referring to her own fatigue after all she had put into *Lady Precious Stream* the previous year as well as the many other events at the IAT. Shanghai itself also drained people, and Bernardine, despite her energy, was not immune to this, what with the oppressive heat and humidity, problems with Chester, tensions with Japan heating up, and bouts of dysentery and cholera all around.

In Anna May, Bernardine found a dear friend, one in whom she could confide her troubles with Chester and Rosemary. Perhaps Anna May was open to this friendship because she was single and came to rely on Bernardine's introductions during her travels in China. The two women certainly grew closer through their correspondence when Anna May traveled up to Peking. By that time, they were on a first-name basis. It's uncertain whether Anna May knew Harold Acton before her trip to China, but she wrote to Bernardine about seeing him in Peking and how they studied with the same Mandarin teacher, a Mr. Chou.[284] "Harold Acton has a magnificent new house, which is going through the various stages of being cleaned up, painted, etc., but it is simply charming in every way and I do envy him for being in it as much as I wouldn't know what to do with myself in such a large place. As soon as I get myself settled, I will present your other cards of introduction to your various friends."[285]

Vicki Baum, the Austrian Jewish author of *Shanghai '37* and *Grand Hotel*, was in Peking at the same time, and Anna May met up with her, too. "I am so sorry that she is leaving before I get into my tiny little house, as I should like to have her to tea or something," Anna May

---

[283] Letter from Bernardine to Monroe Wheeler, February 19, 1936, Beinecke Library, YCAL MSS 134 Box 103 f. 1574, page 2.

[284] Anna May Wong wrote about her Mandarin teacher, a Mr. Chou, in a letter to Bernardine, May 19, 1936, Beinecke Library, YCAL MSS 544 5 f. Wong, page 9.

[285] Letter from Anna May Wong to Bernardine, May 19, 1936, Beinecke Liibrary, YCAL MSS 544 Box 5 f. Wong, page 8.

wrote to Bernardine from Peking in May 1936.[286] She had rented a small house in a compound of traditional Chinese homes for at least a few months and urged Bernardine to visit her there. She signed this letter, "with all remembrances to Chester and much love to you."

In another letter to Bernardine, Anna May reported that she had met the educator Hu Shih at a cocktail party. Bernardine had referred to Hu Shih as her first friend in Shanghai. "One does not get very well acquainted on such occasions. I just managed to tell him that I had a card from you," Anna May wrote.[287] She asked Bernardine at one point to send some swaths of georgette, a sheer crepe fabric, to her in Peking. "Will you be good enough to get me some squares of georgette at Laou Kai Fook's? I would like a bright red, black, white and some blue. They dyed for me a yellow and jade green. I think all these colors they have dyed for me in georgette and I hope they still have some left. I tried to find georgette up here but it doesn't seem to exist except at exorbitant prices. The dust is so frightful one really needs to tie one's face up especially in rickshaw traveling."[288]

Like Bernardine, Anna May was careful with money and didn't have a lot of it. She asked Bernardine if she could front the money for the fabric and Anna May would reimburse her at once. She just didn't want to run up a large tab at Laou Kai Fook. She also wrote about this shop in her *Herald Tribune* article. "It proved to be an enormous place, heaped to the roof with shimmering bolts. I was dazzled by the richness of the colors; it seemed as if the aurora borealis had been broken into bits and distributed through the shop. Being a privileged customer, Mme. Koo had access to the 'topside' room, where they keep rare silks more than a hundred years old. I ordered several pieces to be made into Chinese gowns."[289]

---

[286] Ibid.

[287] Letter from Anna May Wong to Bernardine, June 9, 1936, Beinecke Library, YCAL MSS 544 Box 5 f. Wong, page 10.

[288] Ibid., page 11.

[289] Anna May Wong, "Anna May Wong Recalls Shanghai's Enthusiastic Reception: Crowds Besieged Her On Arrival From Yokohama To Visit China 1st Time," *New York Herald Tribune*, May 31, 1936, page 6.

Anna May fell in love with the cheongsam in Shanghai and appreciated its simple design with its high mandarin collar and ankle-length hem. She admitted to Bernardine that she was trying to rein in her spending in Peking. "Haven't bought much here because I must watch my sheckels carefully but there certainly are many beautiful things floating around these parts."[290]

Still hoping that Bernardine would visit her, Anna May reiterated her invitation. "If the family do not arrive en masse there is room in my little house here if you care to bunk with me. Think about it anyway—I would love to have you."[291] It took little convincing for Bernardine to agree to a visit. She also had friends like Harold in Peking, but Bernardine made this special trip to visit and stay with her new friend.

Aline had recently sailed back to the United States, and Bernardine missed close female companionship at a moment's notice. Plus, a visit to Anna May would mean a break from Chester. The two friends reunited in Peking before long, and Bernardine snapped a number of photos of Anna May meeting with villagers out in the countryside. Anna May, dressed in an elegant long skirt and matching coat, stood about a head taller than the villagers. In Peking, the two women spoke of the friends Bernardine had introduced Anna May to in Shanghai, including Daisy Kwok, Helene Chang, and Lee Ya-ching, the pilot.

After Bernardine returned to Shanghai, Anna May wrote with an update about their mutual friends. "Harold, I saw the night before last. He is in the throes of novels, translation and collaborations, busy as ever. I do like him so much."[292] Anna May also told Bernardine about the three Chinese stage costumes she purchased in Peking as a parting gift to herself.

At the end of that summer, Anna May returned to Hong Kong to visit her sister again. She mentioned in a letter to Bernardine that she would stay there until the end of August 1936, at which time she hoped

---

[290] Letter from Anna May Wong to Bernardine, June 9, 1936, Beinecke Library, YCAL MSS 544 5 f. Wong, page 11.

[291] Ibid.

[292] Letter from Anna May Wong to Bernardine, August 8, 1936, Beinecke Library, YCAL MSS 544 Box 5 f. Wong, page 4.

to travel back up to Shanghai for a couple of weeks before heading back to the US or Europe, "pending professional developments."[293] But Bernardine would not be in Shanghai in August 1936, so Anna May did not see her again during her travels in Asia.

After Aline left Shanghai, Bernardine felt she needed another experienced director at the IAT, but S. Y. Wong had a day job at the petroleum company so he was out for a full-time role. Bernardine sailed to Los Angeles late that summer to interview interested parties in Hollywood. The *Los Angeles Times* covered her trip. "According to Mrs. Fritz, the I.A.T. came into being as a direct response to Shanghai's demand for a center devoted to the interchange of cultural and artistic ideas." The headline of the article read, "Messenger from the Orient."[294]

On Anna May's return to Shanghai while Bernardine was away, Chester held a luncheon for her at 62 Route de Boissezon. He invited Bernardine's best friends in Shanghai, including Helene, Ya-ching, and Hilda Yen, also a pilot.[295] After a slew of farewell parties in Peking and Shanghai, Anna May sailed to Honolulu and then on to San Francisco and Los Angeles.

Bernardine would draw Anna May so far into her orbit that the actress would also become close to Rosemary. In early 1937, Bernardine wrote to Anna May from Shanghai, inviting her to Rosemary's birthday party in New York—probably hosted by one of Bernardine's relatives there—but Anna May was in Los Angeles and couldn't leave town. Anna May sent her regrets and also informed Bernardine, "I am disposing of all my European clothes and just can't imagine wearing anything else but those lovely Chinese dresses."[296] For all that Emily Hahn wrote about Mrs. Manners pushing Chinese fashions onto her Chinese friends, it seems pretty apparent that Anna May grew to love them on her own.

---

[293] Ibid., page 6.

[294] "Messenger from Orient: China Looks to Hollywood for Theater Director," *Los Angeles Times*, August 31, 1936, page A3.

[295] Anna May Wong wrote to Bernardine on January 15, 1937 about a lunch Chester hosted for her while she was still in Shanghai and Bernardine was in the United States recruiting for the IAT. Beinecke Library, YCAL MSS 544 Box 5 f. Wong, page 12.

[296] Ibid., page 13.

Bernardine and Anna May would meet up again in November 1937—this time in Hollywood—at a farewell reception for Robert Grant, the head of the Chinese mint and advisor to the Chinese government. As Grant left California to return to Shanghai, Anna May and Bernardine were invited to a small gathering by the Chinese consul, T. K. Chang. Hong Kong's *South China Morning Post* newspaper reported on this get-together and called Bernardine a "refugee."[297]

A couple years later, in 1939, Anna May reported to Bernardine that she had visited Rosemary in New York "and she is looking simply ravishing."[298] She also told Bernardine that Rosemary was actively looking for an acting job. "I do admire her perseverance and know that she'll make the grade as she is so sincere in her desire to achieve what she set out to do."[299] Just as Barbara Harrison had become a de facto mother for Rosemary, so too had Anna May.

Anna May also updated Bernardine on the goings-on of Lin Yutang and Hong, who were in New York in the late 1930s and couldn't return to Shanghai because of the war building up against Japanese aggression. She signed this letter to Bernardine in April 1939, "In the meantime, my thoughts and wishes are with you for your happiness."[300]

Anna May was referring to Bernardine's ongoing problems with Chester and wished her friend well. But Anna May would need the well wishes more. In 1951, she was the first Asian American actor to star in her own network television show, *The Gallery of Madame Liu-Tsong*, named for Anna May's given Chinese name. The series was canceled after one season. Ten years later, as she prepared to play Madame Liang in the film version of Rodgers and Hammerstein's *Flower Drum Song*, she suffered a heart attack and died in her sleep. After decades of struggling to land the roles she deserved, Anna May battled depression and turned to heavy drinking. Doctors warned her of liver failure if

---

[297] "Anna May Wong: Hostess At Studio To Head Of Chinese Mint," *South China Morning Post*, November 22, 1937, page 7.
[298] Letter from Anna May Wong to Bernardine, April 23, 1939, Beinecke Library, YCAL MSS 544 Box 5 f. Wong, Anna May, page 14.
[299] Ibid.
[300] Ibid., page 15.

she didn't stop, but her heart gave out first. Anna May Wong was only fifty-six when she died in 1961.

It doesn't appear as if Bernardine and Anna May stayed as close as they had become in Shanghai and the following few years . This could be explained, perhaps, by the way Bernardine pushed her mothering responsibilities onto her friends, including Anna May. Or perhaps the two just grew apart. In any case, Bernardine cannot be credited with Anna May's success in Hollywood. But for those months in Shanghai and Peking, Bernardine helped Anna May acclimate to China through introductions and a close friendship.

CHAPTER SIXTEEN

CHARLIE CHAPLIN COMES TO TOWN AND OTHER NOTABLE EVENTS, 1936

Charlie Chaplin escaped the United States just in time. This was a decade after his divorce from his first wife, Lita Grey, whom he married in Mexico when she was a pregnant sixteen-year-old and he thirty-five. That scandal had long blown over, and Hollywood's most renowned silent movie star was now involved with another woman: his latest co-star, the actress Paulette Goddard. When they started a relationship in 1932, Goddard was twenty-one to Chaplin's forty-three. Chaplin was at an impasse in his career by 1936 and had yet to make a film with sound, which by then were greatly outperforming silent movies. He also wasn't forthcoming to the press about his relationship with Goddard. So the two set out for Asia where they would visit with Chaplin's old acquaintance, Bernardine Szold Fritz.

Stars of Chaplin's and Goddard's caliber could cause a stir, as one could see from Anna May Wong's reception. So to alleviate the impropriety of their travels together, the couple married in Canton, a port city in southern China now called Guangzhou. The *China Press* reported their arrival in Shanghai in late March 1936. "Shanghailanders, anxious for a glimpse of the world-famous Charlie Chaplin, who will arrive here tomorrow aboard the President Coolidge may have an opportunity to meet him at a reception in the studios of the International Arts Theater, it was learned yesterday."[301] Since mid-1935, the IAT had moved its studio from 50 East Nanking Road to the top floor of the Chinese YWCA on 55 Yuen Ming Yuen Road, just off the Bund near the Cathay Hotel.

Bernardine did not enlist Chaplin and Goddard for a performance or talk at the IAT. Instead of asking them to entertain people in Shanghai, Bernardine and the IAT board arranged for a reception and viewing of a Chinese landscape painting exhibit at the IAT studio, including an introduction to the painters.[302] The IAT was protective of the Americans' privacy and opened this reception to members and their guests only. "Since its opening here, the exhibition has attracted considerable attention. Already seven of the pictures on display have been sold, one having been purchased by Mayor Wu Te-chen of Greater Shanghai," the *China Press* reported.[303]

At the reception, Chaplin and Goddard appeared more father/daughter than husband/wife. Chaplin's hair seemed as salt-and-peppery as Chester's, and his signature mustache was missing, possibly because Hitler wore his in the same style. The American actor seemed almost as if he could be a relative of Chester's. In contrast, Goddard looked like a smart young journalist with her tailored suit and inquisitive eyes. At the reception, the couple met movie star Butterfly Wu, who also got her start in silent films. Chester enjoyed the company of Chaplin and Goddard and proudly took on his role as their host. It's possible Bernardine met Chaplin in New York or Paris, but they may have even gone as far back as their Chicago days when Chaplin acted for a silent movie company there.

Bernardine and the IAT also threw a party around this time at the Cathay Hotel. With the help of Sir Victor, the IAT outfitted the Cathay

---

[301] "Charlie Chaplin Due in Shanghai Tomorrow: Reception For U.S. Film Star Planned by I.A.T.," *The China Press*, March 8, 1936, page 9.

[302] Letter from Bernardine to Glenway Wescott, March 30, 1936, Beinecke Library, YCAL MSS 134 Box 103 f. 1574, page 31.

[303] "Charlie Chaplin Due in Shanghai Tomorrow: Reception For U.S. Film Star Planned by I.A.T.," *The China Press*, March 8, 1936, page 9.

ballroom as a casino to go along with the evening's Monte Carlo theme. When Bernardine and Chester entered the party, her arm on his, she looked radiant in a long-sleeved satin dress with an A-line skirt embellished with Chinese embroidery. During the evening, Bernardine and Chester played the tables and laughed with their friends. Later they retired to a long sofa, sitting on opposite ends, with Helene Chang close to Bernardine. From their outward appearances, Bernardine and Chester seemed almost like Shanghai royalty, he a finance tycoon and she a doyenne of the arts. But trouble was always brewing under the surface when it came to Bernardine and Chester.

A year earlier, just after the success of *Lady Precious Stream*, Bernardine and Chester booked a mini-break up north. They chose this area perhaps because it was the setting of the early days of their marriage when they were starting to get to know one another just after Bernardine stepped off the train in Dairen. Even after they had settled in Shanghai, Bernardine and Chester spent short breaks in northern cities like Tientsin and Peking, usually on a yearly basis. She still appreciated Chester's love and knowledge of China and enjoyed learning from him when they traveled around the country. So this trip after *Lady Precious Stream* was something the two of them looked forward to—Bernardine because the play had consumed all of her free hours, and Chester because he wanted time alone with Bernardine, away from Aline.

But just before they were about to leave, Chester suddenly changed his mind. Instead, he decided to travel elsewhere on his own. "We see too much of each other," he claimed, not specifying where he would go.[304] Bernardine felt this made no sense, as they hadn't seen much of each other at all. Yet she really did need a rest and didn't want to cancel their reservations, so she took Aline instead.

When the two sisters returned to Shanghai after a restful break, Bernardine fell ill with a light flu, as she described it. Recovering in bed, she heard the telephone ring one day. Chester was out, and Aline

---

[304]   Letter from Bernardine to Glenway Wescott, September 5, 1935, Beinecke Library, YCAL MSS 134 Box 103 f. 1574, page 34.

was busying herself with something else in the vast apartment, so Bernardine answered the phone. As soon as she said, "Hello," an anonymous woman spoke up.

"Eediott Mrs. Freetz, the damn fool Mrs. Freetz, ask your husband," she said in a Russian accent.[305] Bernardine had no clue what this woman wanted or what she meant by her cryptic message, so she went to Chester that evening to ask what this strange phone call was all about. Why had this woman phoned her, and what did she mean about asking her husband? What in the world did she mean by "idiot"?

Chester's face fell, as if he had just been told a close relative had passed away. He slumped onto his bed and lowered his head into his hands. Without looking up, he slowly told Bernardine the story. While she and Aline were away, the young Russian maid Chester had hired to run the household crept into his room one evening without warning. He was in the process of changing into his polo clothes and, at first, paid no attention to her. Yet the maid continued to walk toward him.

Chester couldn't continue with the story and instead started to cry. "I don't know why I did it, it JUST HAPPENED. I'm a fool, please forgive me."[306] Of course, this was Chester's side of the story, and it's impossible to know what really happened because the maid's side was never told. With such a considerable power imbalance, it's difficult to believe he didn't play some role in initiating it. As to the identity of the mysterious woman on the phone, Bernardine didn't indicate in her writings if it was the maid, perhaps after Chester had let her go, or someone else who knew the maid and learned of Chester's deceitfulness.

But after all the years of suffering from Chester's breakdowns, silent treatment, and belittlement, it was only natural for Bernardine to wonder in a letter to Glenway if she were somehow at fault. "I don't make him feel important enough as a male. I admit it's possible one's maid can make one's husband feel MORE important—I detest the thought, but I can't get away from it very well."[307] She also admitted she still couldn't initiate anything romantically with Chester, going

---

[305] Ibid.
[306] Ibid.
[307] Ibid.

into great detail about her sex life and how her thoughts about sex had changed after she reached her forties.

"He refuses to take pains to be a satisfactory lover to me, and these things happen. I suppose I would mind less if I had a lover. I'd often like one, that is, the thought of being made love to has some kind of reality for me now that it never had when I was younger—but of course even if I *were* going to have a lover I'd back out because I wouldn't want anyone else to find out about the operation."[308]

Bernardine also confided to Emily Hahn and wondered how she should handle Chester. She sensed he was being nice to her only because he'd been caught. Emily listened attentively and advised Bernardine to continue her marriage and not to give up so quickly. At least Chester hadn't cheated with one of Bernardine's friends, Emily reasoned. Bernardine disagreed and felt she could have handled it better had the other woman been a friend. This was not true, though, as Bernardine felt terribly betrayed when her second husband, Hi Simons, cheated with one of her friends. So there's no reason to think she could have fixed her problems with Chester if he'd strayed with one of her close friends in Shanghai. That's not to say that Bernardine was at fault or that she even had the power to repair her broken marriages when most of the men she'd married weren't fully invested in fixing their problems.

In her heart, Bernardine believed there was nothing she could do about Chester's dalliance. This wasn't her first experience with a cheating spouse, and she seemed resigned to the fact that it could happen in any marriage. "I can't like it very much, but what in the world can I do. It seems too horrid that it should happen to ME because of all the EEDIOTICALLY romantic notions I've managed to entertain all my life about love, but if one persists in being a fool, it seems too that destiny has more than one way of turning the knife and getting you down with your nose in the dust."[309]

***

---

[308] Ibid.
[309] Ibid., page 35.

With her marriage hanging by a thread, Bernardine buried herself in IAT back-office matters, both before and after Chaplin and Goddard arrived. Ever since *Lady Precious Stream*, the IAT had enjoyed great popularity with Chinese and expat crowds. The first event to be held in the new IAT studio space at 55 Yuen Ming Yuen Road was a lecture about "Old Shanghai."[310] This topic may seem ironic since 1935, when the lecture took place, is now viewed as the epitome of Old Shanghai. The speaker was Dr. Anne Walter Fearn, an American physician from the American Deep South who had moved to China in the late 1800s and, at one time, ran her own hospital in Shanghai. Her talk coincided with a two-week exhibit at the IAT studio that showcased maps, scrapbooks, paintings, and other ephemera documenting Shanghai's previous forty-two years as a city carved into foreign concessions. Fearn was promoted as one of the most well-known of Shanghai's older foreign residents.

Bernardine also put on a Russian night, featuring some of the stepchildren of Helene Chang's sister, Georgette. Perhaps the most famous of the Chang daughters, Georgette was a Post-Impressionist painter who went on to run art schools in Singapore.[311] Married to Chinese politician Eugene Chen, Georgette became the stepmother of artist Jack Chen, writer and lawyer Percy Chen, and dancer Sylvia Chen. Eugene was born in Trinidad and Tobago and married a French Creole woman named Agatha Alphosin Ganteaume, called Aisy. Together they had four surviving children before Aisy passed away from breast cancer in the mid-1920s. Most of the Chen children spent time in the Soviet Union because of their political leanings, so Bernardine and Helene enlisted Percy's Russian wife and Jack to organize an evening of Russian dance, singing, and comedy served up with vodka and Russian tea. Jack was a cartoonist who had lived in Moscow before moving to Shanghai in the mid-1930s. His work was published in Shanghai journals before and after he settled there, including the journal, *Tien*

[310] "Dr. Fearn to Open I.A.T. Meet: 'Shanghai, In the Good Old Days' Will Be Her Subject," *The China Press*, November 20, 1935, page 11.
[311] Sonny Liew, *Warm Night, Deathless Days: The Life of Georgette Chen*. Singapore: National Gallery Singapore, 2014.

Hsia, to which Lin Yutang, Emily Hahn, and Sinmay Zau also contributed. Jack's brother, Percy, immigrated to Hong Kong a couple years before the 1949 Communist victory in China. Percy continued to hold Communist sympathies, yet lived in Hong Kong's luxurious district of Kowloon Tong and helped establish the Hong Kong Bar Association. There seemed to be no problem with the IAT celebrating Soviet culture, even though a paranoia about Communism had descended upon the Nationalist party and all around Shanghai.

Events like these fulfilled Bernardine's mission for the IAT, which called for "promoting and encouraging a fuller knowledge of the life and arts of each other by the various nationalities to be found in Shanghai. It is intended to continue this policy by means of similar programs throughout the year and by this means to achieve one of the principal aims of the IAT which is to stimulate international understanding."[312] The IAT also held Viennese and Greek evenings, and Bernardine enlisted Yone Noguchi, father of the famous American sculptor, furniture designer, and landscape architect Isamu Noguchi to speak about Japanese poetry at the Park Hotel when the poet stopped over in Shanghai on his way to India. Yone Noguchi was an expert on Edgar Allan Poe, wrote in English, and enjoyed a close friendship with the Indian poet Rabindranath Tagore.[313]

Bernardine also staged a production of *Lysistrata*, the Greek play that tells the story of women withholding sex during the Peloponnesian War to get their husbands to negotiate for peace. The *China Press* called it a "naughty, naughty play" and reported that "the premiere performance will be staged at midnight to add a touch of something or other."[314] Emily Hahn starred in the leading role of Gilbert Seldes' version of the play. The *China Press* quoted Gilbert's brother, George, a *Chicago Tribune* journalist and closeted Communist, about the play: "It

---

[312] "I.A.T. Announces Full Program For Future: Interesting Subjects Are Planned For Members," *The China Press*, January 19, 1936, page 11.

[313] "I.A.T. To Hear Famous Japanese Poet Monday," *The China Press*, October 20, 1935, page 11.

[314] "'Lysistrata' Is Next Dramatic I.A.T. Offering: Naughty, Naughty Play Will Open At Stroke Of Midnight," *The China Press*, October 26, 1935, page 9.

is a little bawdy, but by no means pornographic."[315] The *China Press* also mistakenly credited George with adapting *Lysistrata*, so this quote may have been the author's if the paper mistook one brother for the other. Regardless of which Seldes brother the *China Press* actually interviewed, the play was performed in the new IAT studio at 55 Yuen Ming Yuen Road to an audience of 250 people.

Even though these events all enjoyed large audiences, Bernardine longed for the more elaborate productions that had brought together greater numbers of Shanghai's arts aficionados. So during the summer of 1936, she turned again to Aaron Avshalomoff. *The Soul of the Ch'in* had received such critical acclaim that Bernardine hoped to recreate that aura with another ballet at the end of 1936. More than happy to accommodate Bernardine's wishes, Avshalomoff suggested his ballet score, *The Dream of Wei Lien*. The American writer and dancer Vanya Oakes assisted Avshalomoff with the libretto, and Bernardine arranged for the ballet to be staged at the Grand Theatre again, the same venue as *The Soul of the Ch'in*.[316]

Unlike the production of *The Soul of the Ch'in*, Avshalomoff conducted the Shanghai Municipal Orchestra himself for *The Dream of Wei Lien*. Yang Yu-low directed the ballet and had already enjoyed a long career in Chinese theater, beginning at the age of eight. He had studied in Russia for a time and could converse in Russian with Avshalomoff. Mrs. Ernest Tong, the wife of the counsellor of the Kwangtung Provincial Government, also helped arrange the choreography. The dancers were all Chinese, too, apart from Mrs. T. B. Dunn, the wife of the prison physician. As the *China Press* reported during rehearsals in November 1936, "It is Western music with the tinkle of pagoda bells, the evasive odor of incense and the rustle of finger-length sleeves woven delicately into long strains."[317] Mr. Zia S-man worked on the

[315] Ibid.
[316] "I.A.T. Has Heavy Fall Program: Activities Planned For All Departments and Dates Are Set," *The China Press*, November 8, 1936, page 11.
[317] W. E. Fisher Jr. "Avshalomoff Work Goes To Workshop: Comely Actresses, Bad Warriors Practice at I.A.T," *The China Press*, November 1, 1936, page 9.

score to ensure the Chinese and Western elements of the music balanced well.

The story centers around Hu Wei Lien, a young woman who lives with her father and stepmother. In order to gain more wealth, the stepmother sets out to betroth Wei Lien to an evil warrior named Ling Le Zah. Although Ling's family is very well off, Wei Lien's father worries that such a marriage will only bring sorrow to his daughter. To find strength, Wei Lien starts praying each night to the goddess Kuan Yin to help her in her marriage. She doesn't see how she can get out of it and feels she needs the support of Kuan Yin to help her survive. Yet Kuan Yin gives her different advice. The goddess tells Wei Lien not to marry Ling and rather to find a young scholar who will honor both her and her family.

The ballet was performed in three acts, the last in which the warrior Ling goes off to battle, never to be heard from again. Wei Lien meets a young scholar on his way to sit for his exams in Peking. They marry, and in honor of their wedding, the entire cast comes out on the stage for a large garden dance.

At the last minute, the ballet was moved to the Metropol Theater, another Art Deco cinema in Shanghai. In a review of *The Dream of Wei Lien*, one of Shanghai's newspapers reported it was "undoubtedly one of the finest things done in the local theatre for many months."[318] Patrons of the production included General and Madame Chang Chun. General Chang served in many roles before 1949, including mayor of Shanghai, governor of Sichuan Province, and governor of Hubei Province. For two decades after fleeing to Taiwan with the Nationalists in 1949, he served as secretary-general to Chiang Kai-shek. Also listed as patrons of the ballet were Shanghai mayor Wu Te-chen; Sun Fo, the son of Sun Yat-sen; Dr. Szeming Sze, a founder of the World Health Organization and brother of Mai-Mai Sze; Maestro Mario Paci, conductor of *The Soul of the Ch'in*; and Tsai Yuan-pei, former president of Peking University, founder of the Shanghai Conservatory of Music, and champion of education for girls. Dr. Anne Walter Fearn and Mrs.

---

[318] "IAT Ball" program, June 18, 1937, page 2.

Milton J. Helmick, the wife of the judge of the United States Court for China, also patronized the ballet. (From 1906 to 1943, the United States had a court in Shanghai that tried extraterritorial cases involving U.S. citizens in the International Settlement since they weren't held to Chinese law.)

The year 1936 had started off on a high note after the success of *Lady Precious Stream* the previous summer. Aline had returned to the US, and Anna May Wong visited Shanghai and other parts of China for the first time. The IAT was still able to schedule marionette classes, talks about Chinese theater, and stage makeup demonstrations. With another successful ballet to finish the year, Bernardine looked forward to 1937 and the many promising events planned at the IAT. Although her marriage to Chester had whittled down to almost nothing more than platonic roommates, Bernardine felt fulfilled in her work with friends and grateful for all the patrons who supported the arts in Shanghai. Together they had created a supportive community that brought joy and inspiration to hundreds. Meanwhile, war with Japan rumbled on the horizon.

CHAPTER SEVENTEEN

THE IAT BALL, 1937

The IAT Ball was not the first gala the theater company had organized, but Bernardine expected it to be the grandest yet. The gala was to raise funds for future performances, lectures, and exhibitions, and it was to be held on June 18, 1937, at the fashionable Paramount ballroom. An Art Deco building that had opened four years earlier, the Paramount was the largest dance hall in Shanghai at the time.

Bernardine was familiar with the Paramount because two years earlier the IAT had presented a pantomime there for the Pan Pacific Ball. "Columbines and Harlequins, Pierrots and Pierrets, Punchinello and Estrella and dozens of other enchanting figures will be a part of the ballet pantomime which will be given to the accompaniment of Schuman's 'CARNIVAL,'" the *China Press* reported.[319] The ball was a grand affair with a large ensemble of dancers breaking into smaller groups to create a magical fairy land.

Yet it wasn't easy to produce a pantomime. Bernardine found it to be a strenuous undertaking and shared some details about it with Glenway at the time. "We're in the midst of putting on another show,

---

[319] "P.P.A. Ball Will Be Held Soon: I.A.T. Fixing Program For Annual Party To Be At Paramount," *The China Press*, October 26, 1935.

for the annual Pan Pacific Ball. We're going to do Schuman's Carnival, with about 30 girls, and I daresay I'll die before it's over. Again, though, I'm trying to put the work on others this time. It's now 7am, and as I always am up before 6, I simply can't last out for a long day. But I can only work early in the A.M."[320]

In June 1937, the *China Press* covered preparations for the IAT Ball. The theatergoing crowd in Shanghai had been enjoying IAT productions pretty much nonstop for the past two years. It was thanks to the support of politicians and corporate leaders that Bernardine and her friends were able to continue to put on these events. Without mentioning Bernardine, the newspaper both seems to quote what she probably said frequently about the lack of cultural events and artistic community in Shanghai when she first arrived and then also applauds her success in remedying the situation. "There was once a time in Shanghai when it was considered good form and pleasantly arty for those of the left wing intelligentsia who had studied in Europe or knew their Paris, preferably the Left Bank, or had friends in Bloomsbury or had stayed a week or two in Greenwich Village, to sigh sadly in speaking of this town in which we live and murmur in pained tones, 'No soul! No artistic appreciation! O for Bohemia!' But this highbrow moan is no longer stylish and if anyone tries to trot out the old 'nobody knows how I miss the artistic coteries I've been used to' the answer is 'Don't you know the International Arts Theater?'"[321]

To celebrate the IAT's accomplishments since 1935, along with *The Soul of the Ch'in* in 1933, Bernardine and the ball committee thought it would be fun for guests to dress in costume from any of the multitude of IAT productions.[322] Choices could include any of the characters in *Lady Precious Stream*, *Lysistrata*, *The Soul of the Ch'in*, *The Dream of Wei Lien*, *Barbary Coast*, *The Dragon and the Phoenix*, the French priests at the birth control debate, and many others. On top of that, the ball

---

[320] Letter from Bernardine to Glenway Wescott, undated, Beinecke Library, YCAL MSS 134 Box 103 f. 1574, page 27.
[321] "I.A.T. Has Unusual Ball Plans: Masquerade Will Be Bohemian, Informal Entertainment," *The China Press*, June 10, 1937, page 4.
[322] Ibid.

committee required each guest to wear a mask until the clock struck midnight, at which time they could reveal their true identity. The committee would provide masks at the door for purchase if anyone were to forget one.

Dinner would be served at midnight, when participants could finally show their faces. How else could they eat before then? The ball committee arranged for Chinese and Western food on a cold buffet. Before midnight, guests would be able to enjoy a wide range of entertainment, including songs by Butterfly Wu, a dance led by Itala Chieri, and a demonstration of Chinese shadow boxing.

On the night of June 18, 1937, the guests started to gather at the Paramount. As soon as they reached the lobby, volunteer ushers handed them each a hand-stitched program with the IAT logo: a mask that was half-Western, half-Chinese, as if two sides were joined to form one face. The IAT was printed in chunky letters at the top, next to the date. The Chinese name of the IAT ran vertically on the bottom left of the program, while the English word "ball" occupied the bottom right corner.[323]

As the participants made their way to the ballroom, Bernardine couldn't tell who was whom. She, like everyone else at the ball, would have to wait until midnight for that. But she didn't have to see their faces to know that she was surrounded by the many dozens of people who had helped bring the IAT to a position she had only dreamt of when she first started her salon. She did recognize some of the friends volunteering during the early hours of the ball. Lee Ya-ching, the female pilot, helped with ticket distribution along with Percy Chen's wife and the wife of the president of Jiaotong University. Dr. R. Loewenberg, a German Jewish refugee and consultant at the Shanghai Mercy Hospital for Nervous Diseases, sold souvenir programs.

Somewhere in the masked crowd was Madame Bogomoloff, the wife of the Soviet foreign minister. Also present was Sun Fo, the son of Sun Yat-sen and a longtime supporter of the arts. Mrs. J. Hartzenbusch,

---

[323] "IAT Ball" program, June 18, 1937, page 1.

owner of a car dealership in Shanghai, was in charge of the decorations for the evening.

The Chinese foreign minister, Dr. Wang Chung-hui, and the new Shanghai mayor, O. K. Yui, sponsored the ball, as did General Yang Fu. Tony Keswick of Jardine Matheson, the Scottish opium trading company turned Hong Kong business conglomerate, also attended and served as a patron of the ball. Bernardine did not discriminate and also enlisted the help of the controversial Baron d'Auxion de Ruffe, a French aristocrat who aligned himself with the Japanese and Nazis in the mid-1930s. Others who helped with the IAT Ball included the unsavory brothel owner Dr. A. von Miorini and Chu Min-yi, the brother-in-law of Japanese collaborator and China's future puppet leader, Wang Ching-wei. Whether Bernardine was politically naïve, uninterested, uninformed, or knowingly turning a blind eye is not known.

Members of the Baghdadi Jewish community lent their name to the IAT board, including Victor Sassoon, David Sassoon, Cecil Ezra, and Denzil Ezra. In addition, Dr. Szeming Sze, Percy Chen, and Chester also appeared on the list of patrons.

A little poem—the author of which was not credited, although it sounded like something Lin Yutang would write—appeared on the program, just under the list of IAT board members and patrons:

> I much prefer among my friends
> The cheerful man, the joking guest
> Who turns his wit against himself,
> And borrows not but always lends.[324]

For those still unfamiliar with the IAT, a little write-up appeared at the beginning of the program, outlining productions like *The Soul of the Ch'in, Lady Precious Stream, Lysistrata,* and *The Dream of Wei Lien.* Daisy Kwok was also acknowledged in the program for arranging an evening program earlier in 1937 at the Lyceum Theatre in which foreigners would perform one play speaking Chinese while Chinese performers would act in another speaking only English. The enthusiastic reception

---

[324] Ibid., page 5.

of Daisy's production demonstrated yet another way in which cultures meshed in Shanghai.

For guests who were not members but wished to join, a membership form was included in the program. Membership cost ten dollars annually, which included frequently issued postcards advertising upcoming events, as well as open admission to the studio. A long list of activities and jobs was listed on the membership form for people to check if they were interested in acting, dancing, music, stagecraft, costuming, playwriting, playreading, art exhibitions, directing, amateur cinema, puppetry, shadow boxing, lectures and discussion groups, private showings of restricted films, executive work for any of the above activities, and volunteer typing.

Emily Hahn wrote a little treatise on Shanghai in the program, concluding with: "It's as good as living in Europe and Asia all rolled into one. When you read the Society news in the paper, you'll get a laugh out of all the different names you see, who've been at one party. And the practice you get in languages! My dear, it's perfectly amazing. Well now, let's see, how long have you got before you go to Peking? Three days? Oh, that's fine. Now then, there's the cocktail party at Muriel's tomorrow, and Bill afterwards, and next day Grace wants me to bring you along for bridge. We meet there every Wednesday. Of course you won't be butting in! Don't be so silly! Then Wednesday evening I have a hunch Tony'll want us to come out dancing. He always has nice parties—a darling boy, comes from Kansas City; you'll find one or two people from California there, too. And Thursday before you go, I want you to let me give a luncheon for you. I'll ask—let's see—Tony and Muriel and Bill and Grace, and Jim and Molly, and if you meet anybody else you like the looks of, just let me know. Oh yes, Shanghai's a great place. It's so interesting, what I mean."[325]

More than a few writers have portrayed Bernardine exactly like Emily's caricature of the stereotypical expat, but nothing was further from the truth. Bernardine may have been eccentric and mannered, but she had worked tirelessly since 1931, doing much more than spending

---

[325] Ibid., page 11.

her time socializing. Producing the IAT's many activities and events gave her little time for idle chit-chat.

As much as Chester rattled her cage, Bernardine was able to devote more time to the IAT after she started the production of *Lady Precious Stream*. Now looking forward to the second half of 1937, she had grand plans for more performances and programs and hoped to put on Oscar Wilde's *Salome*, experimental films, Chinese doll making courses, stage décor classes, makeup and playwriting classes, and instruction in painting, cinema acting, and I-shing pottery-making, which uses a special clay from Jiangsu Province typical in what is now known as Yixing teapots. All of these upcoming events and activities were listed in the IAT Ball program.[326]

Revelers left the Paramount in the early hours of the following day, eager for more performances, lectures, and classes from the IAT. But as history would show two months later, that was not to be. Shanghai would erupt in violence in August 1937 as the Japanese attacked. The battle was one of the bloodiest in the city's history, and some historians believe World War II started with that siege. The IAT Ball would mark the end of international theater and ballet in Shanghai for decades to come.

[326]   Ibid. page 7.

PART IV

WAR SETS IN

"Although the International Arts center [*sic*] has been forced
to close just recently due to the unparalleled havoc of the
Japanese (precipitated as they so naively announce as their
endeavor to preserve China from the invasion of the west) still
I feel now and always shall that the few years that it existed
proved definitely, for quite a number of people the worth and
validity and great reward that made its creation justified."[327]
—Bernardine Szold Fritz

---

[327] Bernardine Szold Fritz, "I Am Not a Public Speaker," unpublished manuscript courtesy of her family, page 9.

CHAPTER EIGHTEEN

MOTHER TO THE RESCUE, 1937

Just before Shanghai became inundated by Japanese artillery and gun-fire, Bernardine learned that Rosemary had taken ill in New York. She was acting at Orson Welles' Mercury Theatre and had developed a mysterious cough and debilitating fatigue. Bernardine had grown to support her daughter's acting career but felt Rosemary should find guidance from others in their family, such as Bernardine's parents, siblings, and many cousins since they were all in the US and Bernardine still lived far away in Shanghai. Bernardine was more like a distant aunt than a mother at this point. Bernardine wrote to Barbara of her family and Rosemary, "They all feel that she has turned out a lamb, and that the rest is up to God. Will she be Mary's lamb or the lamb to the slaughter? I wish I knew more about her, day by day."[328]

Yet by late summer in 1937, Bernardine, encouraged by others, prepared once again for the ill-fitting role of parent and embarked on a voyage across the Pacific to tend to Rosemary in New York. The bulk of the encouragement to do so sprang from an unlikely source: Chester. When he learned from Bernardine that Rosemary had come

---

[328] Letter from Bernardine to Barbara Harrison, undated, Beinecke Library, YCAL MSS 134 Box 126 f. 1969, page 84.

down with a mysterious affliction that had rendered her bedridden, he insisted Bernardine rush to her daughter's side. Chester had never behaved this way, always expecting Bernardine to put him first, miles ahead of Rosemary. Bernardine suspected, as anyone would, that Chester wanted her gone from Shanghai.

Chester had never recovered from the trauma of Bernardine's mastectomy, not that he had ever been an especially attentive husband before her surgery. Trying to figure out what kept Chester from being considerate was an unsolvable riddle for Bernardine, much as Bernardine's failure to be an attentive mother to Rosemary is unfathomable and unforgivable to some of her surviving relatives. Chester's troubled childhood undoubtedly played a large part, yet Bernardine still blamed herself and felt she could positively influence if not control the way Chester treated her.

For all the years Bernardine had wanted to spend time with Rosemary and felt that Chester was holding her back, she decided to go ahead and sail to New York, a bittersweet decision given her sense that Chester wanted her out of the way. She wasn't sure when she would be back but never imagined it would be the last time she would be in Shanghai. Japan was demonstrating more aggression toward China in the name of liberating it from Western powers, and the plan was for Chester to join Bernardine in the US a couple of months later before the two returned to Shanghai once Rosemary was on the mend and political tensions died down.

When they bade each other farewell, Chester turned to Bernardine. "Always remember that I trust you," he said.[329]

Bernardine had to stop herself from laughing. These were his parting words? For the first time since she had boarded the train in Paris to marry Chester in China, she was traveling alone on a long journey. As the distance between them grew with each nautical mile, Bernardine was determined not to let him try to gaslight her anymore.

Staring out at the sea, she may well have imagined Chester lining up poor Russian maids in their apartment and changing the narrative

---

[329] 'Narrative of Bernardine Szold's Life,' page 34.

so that it was the women who overcame his defenses and overwhelmed him with their unbridled passion in her absence.

And it's likely she reminisced about her 1929 solo trip to China which had set everything in motion: her life in Shanghai and her marriage to a stranger, still in many ways a stranger, who claimed then that he couldn't live without her.

When Bernardine arrived in New York, Rosemary seemed less exhausted than she'd sounded in her letters. But as soon as Bernardine heard Rosemary's cough, she knew she had made the right decision to visit. Despite her poor health, Rosemary was still staying up till all hours with friends and smoking and drinking too much. Bernardine herself smoked a couple packs a day, but she was never a heavy drinker. This wasn't true of Bert Carver, Rosemary's father, who was, by all accounts, an alcoholic. Sadly, this genetic predisposition was his legacy to Rosemary. Bernardine insisted that Rosemary give up her studio apartment and rented an apartment for the two of them at 424 East Fifty-Second Street. It was the first time they had lived together since Rosemary was a child.

A few months later, mother and daughter traveled on to Los Angeles to meet Chester, who was finally scheduled to return to the States. In Los Angeles, Rosemary could pursue acting in film as well as on the stage, and Aline and her husband, Max Sholes, lived close by in Pasadena, where he had found work as a director at the Pasadena Playhouse.

While anxiously waiting for Chester's arrival, Bernardine fell into a terrible state of limbo. She and Chester had parted on precarious terms, and her relationship with Rosemary was fragile. She wrote to Glenway, "I dare say I'll go back with him for a time, on his return. China seems like a past life now—as indeed it is really—and after all this time even Chester seems unreal, but I am impatient for him to get here. For living this one is like tightrope walking between two stars and even on earth I am always afraid of falling." [330]

By the time Chester finally arrived in Los Angeles at the beginning of 1938, he knew his business wouldn't be able to stand up for very much longer. The Cathay Hotel was bombed in August 1937, and Chester's firm had moved their office from Sassoon House to the home of his partner, Culbertson, on the outskirts of the city. The Chiang Kai-shek government retreated to the western city of Chungking as the Japanese took more territory in China, including the recent capital of Nanking in December 1937. There, the Japanese military went on a rampage, murdering two to three hundred thousand Chinese citizens and raping twenty thousand women and children. With the foreign concessions still intact in Shanghai, Chester held out hope to return there at some point to tie up loose ends, but after that, he and Bernardine would settle permanently in Los Angeles.

Initially, Bernardine rented the Harden House, part of the now Palos Verdes estate of Frank and Narcissa Vanderlip overlooking the Pacific Ocean. The Harden House attracted many notable tenants over the years, including a brief stay by writer Joan Didion and her husband John Dunne in the 1960s, and it also served as the location for the family "crossed palms" footage in the film, *It's a Mad, Mad, Mad, Mad World.*

Bernardine hosted a party for Rosemary around the time Chester reunited with them in California. The *Los Angeles Times* covered the event. "Honoring Rosemary Carver, her parents, Mr. and Mrs. Chester Fritz (Bernardine Szold Fritz), recently of Shanghai, gave a buffet supper party last Sunday at the Outpost home. Hungarian food was served."[331] The guest list included Anna May Wong.

Yet no matter how much Bernardine tried to normalize their family life, Chester could not help but reignite tensions with Rosemary. He expressed doubts that she could support herself in acting, even though she was invited to join the Pasadena Playhouse and was cast in

[330] Letter from Bernardine to Glenway Wescott, undated, Beinecke Library, YCAL MSS 134 Box 103 f. 1574, page 54.
[331] "Miss Carver Honored," *Los Angeles Times,* January 16, 1938, page 72.

a play there in the summer of 1938. And Bernardine was disturbed by Rosemary's seemingly helpless and self-centered behavior.

Nevertheless, Chester found life in Los Angeles to be exciting at first. Bernardine had quickly reconnected with old friends as well as many émigrés from Europe who were fleeing the Nazis and making Los Angeles their new home. Through Bernardine's connection with pianist Arthur Rubinstein, who had performed at the IAT some years back, she and Chester were invited to a Hollywood party on Chester's second night in California. Old acquaintances such as Charlie Chaplin were there, along with movie stars Marlene Dietrich, Errol Flynn, and Bette Davis. Victor Sassoon arrived later that week and stayed with Bernardine and Chester. In Los Angeles, they were able to reconnect with old friends like Anna May Wong and Claudette Colbert and make new friends with Hollywood royalty such as actress Janet Gaynor and her husband, costumer designer Adrian.[332]

In late 1939, Anna May hosted a tea for Lin Yutang, visiting from New York. She decorated her tables with miniature Chinese gardens, including bridges over streams. The tea delicacies were arranged around these gardens. Bernardine attended, but Chester's name did not appear on the guest list.[333]

Just as she had done in Shanghai, Bernardine hosted gatherings of artists, writers, performers, and socialites at their home, including a reception for the conductor Artur Rodziński and pianist Dalies Frantz.[334] After a concert at the Hollywood Bowl, guests like novelist Vicki Baum and the Chinese consul T. K. Chang and his wife gathered in Bernardine's and Chester's backyard for dinner.[335]

Los Angeles provided Bernardine with new and unique opportunities to become involved in the theater again. Along with actors like Joan Crawford and W. C. Fields, Bernardine joined the board of the Southern California Playgoers and planned to produce four plays,

---

[332] Chester Fritz and Dan Rylance. *Ever Westward to the Far East: The Story of Chester Fritz*, page 145.
[333] "Anna May Wong Honors Chinese Author at Tea," *Los Angeles Times*, November 26, 1939, page 64.
[334] "Bowl Artists to Be Feted at Supper," *Los Angeles Times*, August 9, 1939, page 28.
[335] Ibid.

including Henrik Ibsen's *Hedda Gabler*.[336] She had performed Ibsen plays back in Chicago at the Little Theatre, but this time she would take an organizational role, just as she had in Shanghai.

In late 1939, Bernardine helped organize a benefit concert by the Philharmonic Orchestra in Los Angeles to raise funds for the Finnish Red Cross after the Soviet invasion. Former US president Herbert Hoover was the honorary chairman of the committee, which also included Eleanor Roosevelt and Hollywood producers Louis B. Mayer and Samuel Goldwyn.[337]

This flurry of activity took a toll on Chester. Between his conflicts with Rosemary, his notable indifference toward Bernardine, and his longing to return to China, Chester had a hard time adapting to Southern California. Bernardine's salons and theater and event productions in Shanghai had seemed novel at the time, but now Chester found it all so tiresome. He made plans to close out his business in China and retire. He was only forty-eight but had amassed a fortune in Shanghai. There were accounts to settle and money to be divided amongst the three partners. Chester couldn't see doing that from afar.

As Chester prepared to sail back to Shanghai in early 1940, Bernardine purchased a house for them in Hollywood so they could be closer to the cultural and social world of Los Angeles. If Bernardine was to establish a new salon in their new life back in the States, Palos Verdes was too isolated a location. They purchased a large house at 8170 Laurel View Drive just off of Laurel Canyon Boulevard. Built in 1926, it perched like a castle on the hills above the Sunset Strip where a Schwab's Pharmacy sat across the street from the Garden of Allah hotel, and the Chateau Marmont was just a bit farther west.

Bernardine had decided to remain in Los Angeles and realized she never wanted to go back to China. There were too many painful memories from her marriage, and the US was safer than Shanghai with a war already underway and no sign of it letting up. Many of her friends, like Lin Yutang and Helene Chang, had left for the US in the late 1930s.

[336] "New Playgoer Group Will Stage Series," *Los Angeles Daily News*, August 23, 1939, page 12.
[337] "Finnish Benefit Prelude," *Los Angeles Daily News*, December 21, 1939, page 14.

Her sister Aline was in Los Angeles, so she had family close by. She also wanted to be near Rosemary.

Bernardine expressed these thoughts to Barbara. "This year with Rosemary has been such a rich one, it's been so heavenly being with her. And I want to work again, definitely get a job, and work. We don't know what will happen about China of course, and it may be that no one will go back in the end."[338]

Chester's departure did not relieve her of lost sleep and rising anxiety when it came to her thoughts about their relationship. She worried about spending "Chester's money" and even considered asking him to rent out their new house while he was in China and set her up in a smaller place.[339] Still, as she started inviting movie producers, actors, and writers to her beautiful new home, she felt better about life in Hollywood.

In April 1940, her cousin David Lilienthal visited while on a business trip for the Tennessee Valley Authority. "I can't describe this house because even now I have only seen a few rooms and the upstairs library where I am writing this. But it is beautiful beyond belief. The Chinese decorations and furniture, and the Chinese houseboys, with their long, white costumes, slippered shoes and quiet smiles simply add to a picture so remarkable, so different from anything I have ever seen before that it seems like a dream. It is somehow like being dropped onto an island, located you know not where, strange and new and quite exciting, but far, far removed from anything in your past."[340]

In September, Bernardine hosted a tea for the China Relief Council.[341] The United States had not yet entered the war—Pearl Harbor was still fifteen months away—and, in any case, most fundraising efforts in the US were for European war relief. Bernardine opened her home and gardens to the group, which hoped to raise funds for Chinese orphans

---

[338] Letter from Bernardine to Barbara Harrison, undated 1938, Beinecke Library, YCAL MSS 134 Box 126 f. 1970, page 4.

[339] Narrative of Bernardine Szold's Life," page 35.

[340] David E. Lilienthal, *The Journals of David E. Lilienthal*, Volume One, (New York, Harper and Row: 1964), page 161.

[341] "China Relief Council to Give Pickfair Party: Arrangements Made at Garden Tea on Mrs. Bernardine Fritz's Estate," *Los Angeles Times*, September 14, 1940, page 9.

and to rebuild the bombed Orthopedic Hospital in Kweiyang, China. Those in attendance included old friends Lee Ya-ching, the pilot, and the wives of cartoonist J. P. McEvoy and Hollywood producer Edwin Knopf. The Chinese consulate in Los Angeles sent a representative.

The *Los Angeles Times* reported on Ya-ching's visit and remarked on her stature—"tiny, young, and pretty enough to be a film actress"—but also gave her due credit for her aviation skills and for raising awareness for women and children plagued by war in China.[342] Ya-ching flew from New York on the same route American Airlines pilots took along the southern part of the United States. The *Times* reported, "Tonight she will address Chinese sympathizers at a Chinese colony dinner at the Soo-Chow Café. Miss Lee will be the guest of Mrs. Bernardine Fritz."[343]

With Chester back in China, Bernardine continued to think about her marriage and felt she could try to patch it up if she visited him in Shanghai. She went so far as to book passage to Shanghai and placed her trunk on the ship the night before departure that fall. At the last minute, Chester cabled for her to stay put. He would join her in the US around Christmas in 1940.[344]

Yet Chester's departure date from Shanghai dragged on again, and there was no sign he would return anytime soon. By December 1941, the Japanese had taken all of Shanghai, attacking the same day they bombed Pearl Harbor and invading a number of other Asian cities. Chester was eventually sent to an internment camp along with other foreigners from countries at war with Japan.[345]

---

[342] "China Woman Flyer Here: Declares Her Nation Will Fight on Until Japanese Driven Out," *Los Angeles Times*, April 20, 1939, page A1.

[343] Bernardine and Ya-ching continued to correspond at least through the 1950s. The Beinecke Library holds several letters from Ya-ching to Bernardine, in which she mentions Rosemary's troubles with alcoholism and arranges to send Bernardine a tailored coat from Hong Kong, where Ya-ching was living by 1957. YCAL MSS 544 Box 2 f. Lee, Ya Ching.

[344] Letter from Bernardine to Glenway Wescott, undated, Beinecke Library, YCAL MSS 134 Box 103 f. 1574, page 54.

[345] When I Skyped with Bernardine's granddaughter Wongmo while just starting this book research, she wondered if Chester could play polo in the POW camp. I had never laughed more.

While Chester was in China, Rosemary had started acting at the Del Monte Theater in Southern California.[346] At this theater, she met another young actor and, after a brief romance, married him. Bernardine worried about Rosemary rushing into this marriage just as she had done with Bert and later with Chester, but Rosemary claimed she just wanted to "find peace" and marriage seemed like a good option at the time. Though Bernardine was most certainly headed for divorce for the fourth time, she still held lofty ideas about marriage, which she wrote about in a letter to Glenway. "I don't believe in marriage that way—as the 'solution' of a woman's life. I believe so deeply in it as the best experience and unfolding for a young girl."[347] As Bernardine predicted, Rosemary's marriage ended in divorce a few years later. While still married, she had fallen in love with a young writer named John Meston who was training to fight overseas, having enlisted soon after the Japanese bombed Pearl Harbor in December 1941. She got a quick divorce in Reno, and she and John were married immediately. Rosemary followed him from training camp to training camp until he was sent overseas. She then got a job at Douglas Aircraft but was not cut out to be Rosie the Riveter, quitting after fainting from anxiety and exhaustion too often.

Bernardine made the most of her new life in Los Angeles. She found a job writing for *Script* magazine, and writers like Aldous Huxley and Henry Miller had become friends and regulars at her home.[348] She and Anna May attended a Javanese and Balinese dance performance together.[349] At other events, Bernardine socialized alongside actor Gary Cooper and director Frank Capra.[350] With her husband interned indefinitely in China, she was taking on Hollywood, just as she had taken on Shanghai and Paris before that.

---

[346] 'Narrative of Bernardine Szold's Life," page 35.
[347] Letter from Bernardine to Glenway Wescott, July 22, 1936, Beinecke Library, YCAL MSS 134 Box 103 f. 1575, page 1.
[348] Ibid.
[349] "Dutch to See Java Ballet," *Los Angeles Times*, January 17, 1940, page 25.
[350] "Other Guests," *Los Angeles Times,* January 29, 1939, page 75.

In 1944, Chester was released from the internment camp and sailed to the US. Before he left, Bernardine wrote to him about her angst over their problems.[351] She yearned for a fresh start when he returned, especially after she had worked so hard to get Rosemary back on her feet and set up a peaceful home for them in Hollywood. Chester was emotionally and physically drained from his years in the internment camp, so it's not surprising he did not address these issues in his replies to her. Bernardine traveled to New York to meet his boat, yet just as she had suspected, Chester remained as distant as ever, spending his days on Wall Street and his evenings out alone. When they returned to Los Angeles, Rosemary was there to greet them at the house. She was now living there, much to Chester's chagrin.

The tension at home was thicker than ever. Neither Bernardine nor Chester would bring up the word "divorce," but they were clearly unhappy. Chester grew more hostile with Bernardine, spending his time away every day and sometimes not returning at night. He may have even brought a "girl of his from Shanghai" and set her up in an apartment.[352]

Chester grew even more frustrated when John Meston returned and joined them on Laurel View Drive. Soon after their reunion, Rosemary and John started to spend their days and nights drinking. Bernardine was happy to share her house with the young couple, but their drinking bothered her deeply and she worried about Rosemary's health again. She also felt torn between her daughter and husband as Chester grew more incensed by Rosemary's presence in their home.

In 1945, Bernardine checked into the hospital for a hysterectomy, and Chester couldn't be bothered to accompany her, having booked himself an appointment with a dentist on the same day. This utter lack of consideration when she needed medical attention brought back vivid memories of her mastectomy for Bernardine. The same disappointment and anger rose to the surface of her mind. Given his failure once again to show any compassion, it's no surprise that Chester asked for a divorce shortly after Bernardine's operation. This was the way

---

[351] "Narrative of Bernardine Szold's Life," page 35.
[352] As relayed by Bernardine's cousin, Nancy Lilienthal.

Bernardine remembered the events that led to her fourth divorce in 1945, yet the *Los Angeles Times* noted that she had filed for divorce back in March 1944.[353]

No matter the chronology or how the decision to finally split came about, Bernardine knew divorce was the right path, as hard as it was to accept at first. Chester decided to move back to Shanghai where he thought he could resume his business.

Just before Chester sailed back to China, Bernardine wrote to him asking for a final goodbye. She hoped for a civilized conversation after everything they'd been through and after all she'd left behind when she moved to Shanghai to marry him. Yet he behaved as if Bernardine had slighted him and refused to say goodbye to her. "I had a fearful longing, when I heard he was leaving, to see him. It was, I supposed, that last vain urgency to clear up all hatefulness between us—actually I suppose I just wanted to pry at him again and try to make him SAY something—and by now I ought to know he is NOT the saying kind. He isn't even the thinking kind. So I called him and asked if he'd mind if I saw him off. Instantly—I could hear tears falling—and he said no, that I had said things he could never forget, and it had made him very unhappy and he didn't want to go through that again."[354]

Chester paid Bernardine two hundred dollars a month in alimony at first, but later gave her "a raise" to six hundred dollars a month after his friends learned of this paltry sum and pressured him into giving her more.[355] Chester also paid for Bernardine's medical bills. Yet this money wasn't enough to support Bernardine's daily living expenses. Rosemary and John Meston were still living with Bernardine, and she was in effect supporting them. To make ends meet, Bernardine sold the many Chinese artifacts she had shipped from Shanghai. The porcelains seemed especially valuable and in demand, and she received a small fortune from selling those.

[353] Divorce Suits Filed," *Los Angeles Times*, March 18, 1944, page 8. And yet according to the Fritz Library at the University of North Dakota, they separated in 1944 and divorced in 1946.

[354] Letter from Bernardine to Barbara Harrison, undated, Beinecke Library, YCAL MSS 134 Box 126 f. 1971, page 62.

[355] "Narrative of Bernardine Szold's Life," page 36.

"It's much more pleasant NOT to have to worry about the money than it is to see empty shelves where there used to be lovely objects," she wrote to Barbara.[356] Thinking about the long term, Bernardine ended up selling the house on Laurel View Drive. She used some of the money from that sale to purchase a smaller house farther east in Hollywood on North Vista Street, then moved again in 1946 to a house even farther east on North Sycamore Street on the hills just above Yamashiro's restaurant. She continued to write and sold a story to MGM Studios that she adapted from a French story, but it doesn't seem to have gone anywhere.[357]

Years later, Chester remarried. Bernardine claimed it was to a woman he had met on a ship back from China when they were still married. "His bride I now discover is a Russian woman he knew in Shanghai and met again—indeed someone thinks it's the same woman he had the affair with on the Gripsholm coming back, but I'm not sure—at any rate he met her on this long holiday abroad and they married in Zurich."[358] In Chester's memoir, *Ever Westward to the Far East*, he seemed adamant that he had not met his new wife, Vera, before he and Bernardine divorced, perhaps to address rumors to the contrary.[359] Vera had a daughter, Monique, from a previous marriage, and Chester also wanted nothing to do with her. Vera outlived Chester by two decades, and Monique went on to inherit a few million dollars, even though Chester tried his best to squeeze his second stepdaughter out of his inheritance while he was still alive.[360]

---

[356] Letter from Bernardine to Barbara Harrison, August 22, undated, Beinecke Library, YCAL MSS 134 Box 126 f. 1971, page 3.
[357] Letter from Bernardine to Barbara Harrison, undated, Beinecke Library, YCAL MSS 134 Box 126 f. 1971, page 79. Bernardine doesn't write more about this screenplay, but it's assumed since she never mentioned it in other letters that it never went anywhere. Considering that she didn't have a major work of writing published during her Hollywood years, it should be assumed the screenplay didn't go anywhere.
[358] Ibid., page 42.
[359] In a letter dated April 3, 1951 from Madame Wellington Koo to Bernardine, Madame Koo writes that she heard Chester married their friend, Flora Sun, the wife of Russell Sun, which was not true. Flora and Russell had been married at that point for thirty years and were grandparents. But it's interesting how rumors started and that Bernardine heard them.
[360] Haga, Chuck. "A footnote in the story of Chester Fritz," *Grand Forks Herald*, May 17, 2011.

CODA

LA SUNSET, 1945–1982

Bernardine spent the rest of her life in Los Angeles, hosting in her home writers, actors, and directors. Married life was a thing of the past, and she found plenty of ways to spend her days and evenings. She mixed in some of the same circles as another Jewish salon host, Salka Viertel, who immigrated to the United States from Austria around the time Bernardine first went to Shanghai. Salka's salon mostly attracted German-speaking immigrants like Greta Garbo, Thomas Mann, and director Max Reinhardt. In fact, Garbo was known as Salka's muse as Salka found regular work as a Hollywood screenwriter and wrote screenplays like *Queen Christina* and *Anna Karenina* with Garbo as the lead. Bernardine's acquaintances Charlie Chaplin and Christopher Isherwood were also regulars at Salka's, although it doesn't seem as if Bernardine attended this other salon or vice versa. Nevertheless, salons hosted by Jewish women seemed to have faded in the years following the destruction from the Holocaust because Jews were suddenly no longer viewed as outsiders and disloyal.

In the mid-1940s, Bernardine spoke about her Shanghai years at the Hollywood Chamber of Commerce's women's division along with

Professor Chen Shou-yi of Pomona College.[361] Chen was a contemporary and friend of Hu Shih and Lin Yutang, so there's a chance Bernardine knew him before both settled in California. In attendance were Dr. and Mrs. H. H. Chang, he the former assistant to Chinese finance minister T. V. Soong and later a professor of East Asian history at a number of universities in the United States.[362]

Bernardine continued to work in the theater and in 1946 helped produce *Angels Amongst Us*, a play by Jewish Czech physician and playwright František Langer. Bernardine worked on this play with her friend Jarmila Marton. During his visit in 1940, Bernardine's cousin David Lilienthal met Jarmila and her husband, director Andrew Marton. "Dee's closest friend is a young woman, Jarmila Marton, the wife of a young Hungarian, a motion picture director before he left Berlin, where she was a motion picture actress.... Her father was a leader in the Czech nationalist movement at the time of the establishment of the republic, living in Chicago, where she was born and lived until she was 14, when she went to live with her mother in Prague.... She and her husband went on to a remarkable expedition in Tibet, and shot a picture there."[363] Together, Bernardine and Jarmila adapted Langer's play for the Pasadena Playhouse.

According to the *Los Angeles Times*, Bernardine and Jarmila "made a literal translation, stressing the spiritual values with rare skill."[364] The play centered around a character named Mise, a man who had suffered intolerable hardships in a previous life and was sent back to earth as a

[361] "Talks to Be Heard by Hollywood C. of C. Women," *Los Angeles Times*, February 9, 1945, page 13.
[362] H. H. Chang's wife Rosalind and Bernardine became long-term pen pals after each left Shanghai before the Communist victory. The Beinecke Library at Yale has over seventy pages of letters from Rosalind Chang to Bernardine, mostly throughout the decade of the 1950s. Rosalind wrote long, detailed letters that often spanned three typed, single-spaced pages. Bernardine herself loved to type letters to friends and sometimes write that she hadn't heard from them in a long time. With Rosalind, it appears they enjoyed a balanced correspondence in which they reminisced about the old days in Shanghai and the newest developments in China.
[363] David E. Lilienthal, *The Journals of David E. Lilienthal*, Volume One, (New York, Harper and Row: 1964), page 161.
[364] Katherine Von Blon, "Inspirational Note Heard in 'Angels Amongst Us'," *Los Angeles Times*, May 10, 1946, page 15.

physician to ease the pain of those stricken by disease. "The premise is based upon the thought that those among us who do many good deeds and strive to lighten the burden of those passing through this world are in reality angels in disguise sent to fulfill their spiritual mission on earth."[365] Bernardine and Jarmila shared a deep interest in Asia and Eastern religions, especially Buddhism which would have a profound impact on Bernardine in the years to come.

In the late 1940s, Victor Sassoon passed through Los Angeles. China was still engulfed in civil war, and Sir V was on his way to South America to check on his business dealings there. It was looking bleak for foreign business owners in Shanghai with the Communists gaining more territory, and Sir V felt that his future could rest in Brazil. He had devoted much of the early part of World War II to helping Jewish refugees from Germany and Eastern Europe who had the great fortune to escape to Shanghai, one of the only places in the world that would take Jews without question—or papers. Now as Sir V visited LA, Bernardine and Ida Koverman, a top executive at MGM Studios, hosted a cocktail party for him at Bernardine's home. Novelist Vicki Baum was in attendance, as was Mrs. Milton Helmick, the wife of the former judge of the American courts in China.

In 1959, Sir V married his personal nurse, Evelyn "Barnsie" Barnes, a woman he'd hired several years earlier to take care of him as he became more and more immobile after a plane crash decades earlier. It was his one and only marriage. Two years after they married, Sir V passed away from heart disease at his home in the Bahamas. Barnsie and Bernardine continued a correspondence for another decade.

Another visitor in the late 1940s from her life in China was Bernardine's old collaborator, Aaron Avshalomoff, the composer of *The Soul of the Ch'in* and *The Dream of Wei Lien* who spoke at a reception in Beverly Hills.[366] Avshalomoff had been interned in Shanghai during the Japanese occupation and emigrated to the US in 1947. In Los Angeles, he spoke about the music he composed for *The Great Wall*, an

---

[365] Ibid.
[366] "China Music Group to Hear Composer," *Los Angeles Times*, January 8, 1949, page 19.

opera based on the story of Lady Meng Jiang, a woman who searched for her husband after he was sent to help build the Great Wall.

Bernardine continued to bring together the Chinese and Western arts communities. In 1951, she hosted a dinner party for Yi-Kwei Sze, a baritone born in Shanghai who went on to perform at all the grandest opera halls in the US as well as La Scala in Milan.[367]

In the early 1950s, Bernardine moved into a small house on Heather Road in Beverly Hills off of Coldwater Canyon, where she would live for the rest of her life. She kept up her correspondence with Yutang and Hong through the 1960s. Bernardine and the Lin family had both left Shanghai in 1937 just before the Japanese bombed the city. Yutang was traveling to New York to promote his book, *The Importance of Living*, which hit the *New York Times* best seller list and stayed at the top for fifty-two weeks. He and Hong never imagined they would end up stranded in New York during the Japanese invasion of Shanghai and the ensuing war. They managed to travel back to China in the early 1940s, and Yutang became president of Nanyang University in Singapore for a short period in the 1950s before returning to New York. But China and Shanghai would never again be their home. The couple split their time between New York and Taiwan, especially because their eldest daughter lived in Taipei where she worked as a novelist and an editor at the National Palace Museum while their two younger daughters lived in Hong Kong, one as the chief of pathology at the University of Hong Kong and the other as the editor of Chinese *Reader's Digest*.[368] In Taipei, Yutang worked on an ambitious, multiyear project—compiling a Chinese-English dictionary—sponsored by the Chinese University of Hong Kong.

Yutang's eldest daughter committed suicide in 1971 in Taiwan. This was the same daughter Bernardine and Hong had waited with outside the Hangchow cave when the Lins invited Bernardine to join them on vacation. After their unimaginable loss, Yutang and Hong spent

---

[367] "Other Festivities," *Los Angeles Times*, November 9, 1951, page 51.
[368] Letter to Bernardine from Hong Lin, April 15, 1965, Beinecke Library, YCAL MSS 544 Box 3 f. Lin, Yu Tang, page 6.

more time in Hong Kong with their two younger daughters. It was in Hong Kong in 1976 that Yutang succumbed to pneumonia at the age of eighty. Buried in Taipei, Yutang is memorialized there in a museum established in their home, and the Lin family's collection of poetry, painting, and calligraphy is housed at the Metropolitan Museum of Art in New York.

During her decades in Hollywood and Beverly Hills, Bernardine also stayed in close communication with Glenway, Monroe, and Barbara. George Platt Lynes passed away from lung cancer in the mid-1950s. Years before that, while Bernardine was still in Shanghai, Barbara married Glenway's brother, Lloyd. She and Lloyd had a daughter and purchased a farm in New Jersey where Glenway and Monroe also lived when they weren't at their apartment in Manhattan. Barbara died in 1977 at the age of seventy-three. Glenway passed away in 1987, and Monroe followed him a year later. Barbara, Lloyd, Glenway, and Monroe are buried at the farm along with other members of the Wescott family.

Bernardine had long given up on marriage, and after four divorces, she started to more fully understand that she wasn't the primary source of the many troubles in these relationships but that much of the conflict had stemmed from life in a patriarchal society. "This business of men wanting their own wives to be pure and true and consecrated to them—and every other woman to be a tart—it's ruining what few decent women there are left—or else they're unhappily married, or living alone."[369]

After returning to the US, Bernardine's relationship with Judaism altered a bit too. With Jews in Europe suffering genocide in the Holocaust, she could no longer make her Judaism a footnote in her life. By 1938, she was participating in Jewish causes, including something she called an "anti-Nazi luncheon," which probably referred to the Hollywood Anti-Nazi League, a group made up mainly of

---

[369] Letter from Bernardine to Glenway Wescott, undated, Beinecke Library, YCAL MSS 134 Box 103 f. 1574, page 66.

Jewish refugees from German-occupied Europe who had come to Los Angeles to work in the film industry.[370] She also donated to the American League for a Free Palestine, a nondenominational organization that supported the Hebrew Committee of National Liberation. Among their goals, the group hoped for a Jewish state and "to rebuild Palestine in its historic boundaries, with the Arab population as equal partners—as a Democratic state based on the principles of the Four Freedoms and the Atlantic Charter."[371] She helped organize a Free Palestine fundraiser at the Beverly Wilshire Hotel in the summer of 1946 in honor of Mrs. Francis J. Myers, the wife of the first Catholic senator from Pennsylvania. Bernardine's old friend Arthur Rubinstein, the pianist who performed at the IAT in Shanghai, was in attendance, along with Hollywood dignitaries like studio head Louis B. Mayer.

In February 1945, Rosemary and John Meston had a baby girl they named Feather, John's nickname for Rosemary because he liked to say she was as willowy as a feather. Rosemary continued to get small acting gigs here and there and landed a job in 1946 as Katharine Hepburn's stand-in on the film *The Sea of Grass*, but it was far from a bed of roses. In an interview with Hepburn on the set, gossip columnist Earl Wilson reported that when he asked if Rosemary was her stand-in, Hepburn replied, "Yah, that's Rosemary Carver; she has a long neck and a little face and that's all you need."[372] Unfortunately, Rosemary continued to drink heavily, and she and Bernardine often fought about it. Rosemary also frequently expressed her anger over her abandonment as a child, starting with being sent away to boarding school at such a young age.

In 1952, John cocreated the iconic hit radio and television show, *Gunsmoke*, but this success could not save their failing marriage. Rosemary and John separated when Feather was about six, and they

---

[370] Letter from Bernardine to Barbara Harrison, undated 1938, Beinecke Library, YCAL MSS 134 Box 126 f. 1970, page 3.
[371] Letter from Bernardine to Barbara Harrison, undated, Beinecke Library, YCAL MSS 134 Box 126 f. 1971, page 60. The stationery on which Bernardine wrote a letter to Barbara Harrison listed this mission statement at the top, but also a long column of supporters, including US Representatives and Senators that continued onto the back of the page.
[372] As told me to by Nancy Lilienthal.

were divorced in 1954. John had been a largely absent father and had given Rosemary custody of Feather, so Feather's life became increasingly chaotic and traumatic as Rosemary's drinking and despair led to multiple suicide attempts. Mother and daughter moved every few years from one apartment to another in the San Fernando Valley.

As a grandmother, Bernardine doted on Feather during this time of great turmoil, picking her up every Friday afternoon and spending the weekend with her, showering her with the love and attention that Rosemary never received. Bernardine treated Feather to after-school snacks, bubble baths, special outings, and stories of her travels and adventures. Perhaps most important to Feather, Bernardine introduced her to Eastern philosophy and religion. Years later, Feather recalled, "Her ear lobes had become elongated with heavy jade earrings. She would talk to me about reincarnation and karma all through my childhood, things she had learned from reading various Eastern masters. We would do yoga positions together on her Chinese rugs, and when she needed an 'answer,' she'd call up one of her eccentric friends for an *I Ching* reading. She even organized for me to go to one private school started by Krishnamurti in Ojai, California."[373]

When Feather was fourteen years old in 1959, Rosemary unsuccessfully attempted to commit suicide once again. Bernardine made arrangements for Feather to be with her father in Europe on an extended honeymoon with his new wife, Bette Ford—a model, actress, and bullfighter. Feather loved being in Europe, so John and Bette enrolled her in an international boarding school in Geneva for the next two years. Feather thrived in her new school and wrote to Bernardine, whom she called Dena.[374] She reported on her classes at school and the friends she'd made there. "The child might well have been destroyed by all of this," Bernardine wrote of Feather, "but it has done the opposite. She seems to have become direct, strong, firm, clear sighted and fear-

---

[373] As told to me by Nancy Lilienthal.

[374] Letter from Bernardine to Barbara Harrison, undated, Beinecke Library, YCAL MSS 134 Box 126 f. 1971, page 58. Bernardine wrote to Barbara that Feather called her Dena and said that no one but Barbara called her that. When I met with Bernardine's cousin, Nancy, she told me that Bernardine did not like that name. Perhaps she tolerated it only from Barbara and Feather.

less. And her letters are my greatest joy."[375] Feather returned home for her last year of high school and went on to attend Occidental College.

Rosemary felt betrayed by Bernardine. First, Bernardine had abandoned Rosemary as a child, and now, she had separated her from her own daughter. Bernardine was understandably distraught by this but would not apologize for intervening and started attending AA meetings to try to help Rosemary with her addiction.[376] But Rosemary fell into another deep depression and stayed in bed for ten months straight, enabled by a boyfriend who gladly supplied her with the alcohol she craved. Over the years, Rosemary had whittled away to nothing, emaciated and malnourished. Bernardine urged Rosemary to seek therapy, but she would not talk to a therapist and refused proper treatment for her drinking apart from the occasional detox, which did not include psychotherapy. With no other options as she saw it, Bernardine checked Rosemary into a state hospital for both detox and psychotherapy. "She said she went to bed and meant to stay there until she died to punish me for taking Feather away from her (which I did not do though it doesn't matter—it was Feather's own decision). She was dying bit by bit."[377]

These years were a time of reckoning for Bernardine. In December 1956, she and Aldous Huxley participated in the LSD experiments of UCLA's Dr. Sidney Cohen at the home of their friend, the philosopher, historian, and writer, Gerald Heard. Bernardine had five goals in undertaking the LSD experiment: to be "less evasive, less tactful"; to "realize my most creative métier"; to "understand why I never finish any work"; to "know why, having always had a religious urge, I did not, even in China, study seriously"; and to "know why I was never capable of a mature, 'emotional' relationship or good marriage."[378]

[375] Letter from Bernardine to Barbara Harrison, November 2, undated year, Beinecke Library, YCAL MSS 124 Box 126 f. 1971, page 44.
[376] Letter from Bernardine to Barbara Harrison, undated 1958, Beinecke Library, YCAL MSS 134 Box 126 f. 1970, page 11.
[377] Letter from Bernardine to Barbara Harrison, undated, Beinecke Library, YCAL MSS 134 Box 126 f. 1971, page 44.
[378] "Narrative of Bernardine Szold's Life," page 37.

Some years later, Bernardine consulted again with Dr. Sidney Cohen and asked for advice on how to handle Rosemary.[379] After these talks, Bernardine came to the conclusion that to help Rosemary and herself, she needed to establish what we now call "boundaries" and to learn to disengage from Rosemary.

In a letter to Barbara, she wrote, "It's been difficult because of Feather—that's where I've always been snared—for, by withdrawing from Rosemary, I removed myself from Feather, and perhaps the only normal contact the child has with a reasonably normal world. (It's funny perhaps to think of myself as 'normal,' but I am in comparison.)"[380] Still, Bernardine blamed herself for much of Rosemary's troubles and wondered if there was still hope for Rosemary—and herself—given all that they had endured. "I had no end of problems and disasters, due to my folly or blindness or immaturity—but I did seem to survive them all, and reasonably well.... But this time I have really cracked, and, as over the past years, pulled myself back by repeating over and over, thank god at least that Feather is safe."[381]

Rosemary's unrelenting troubles ushered in a period of great loss for Bernardine. Her younger brother, Bud, died of a heart attack in 1960 while he was in Texas directing a play. Only a decade earlier, he and his wife, Betty, had been living in Los Angeles where he had found work acting in films and coaching young actors. Their mother, Hermine, died of old age in 1961, following their father Jacob's passing in 1945, and their older sister, Olga, died of cancer in 1966. Aline and Max's only child, Terry, and her husband, Larry Van Mourick, perished in a plane crash in 1968, leaving behind two young children.

And after several more attempts, Rosemary finally succeeded in taking her own life in 1969.[382] In his journal, Bernardine's cousin David Lilienthal wrote, "When I returned yesterday afternoon Helen had read

---

[379] Letter from Bernardine to Barbara Harrison, undated 1958, Beinecke Library, YCAL MSS 134 Box 126 f. 1970, page 11.
[380] Ibid.
[381] Letter from Bernardine to Barbara Harrison, undated November 2, Beinecke Library, YCAL MSS 134 Box 126 f. 1971 page 44.
[382] Bernardine's old friend, James Feibleman, wrote a letter to Bernardine on February 4, 1971, expressing his condolences over Rosemary.

a letter from my cousin Bernardine and sadly said I should read it now. My heart has been chilled and desperately hurt ever since. Bernardine's only child, Rosemary, had killed herself. Bernardine has been a part of my life, one of its most important influences, since I was a boy of thirteen and she a rebellious young woman of eighteen (but more experienced of life's intensities and crises than most women of thirty). Poor dead Rosemary. For fifteen years or more, an alcoholic, a recluse. Her story made all the more tragic by the contrast with her gaiety as a child, and as a glamorous young woman. One of New York's most sought-after photographer's models, her head sculptured by Epstein, her swains rich playboys. And then the great love affair with John Meston, who became a most successful TV writer (*Gunsmoke* made him a millionaire). Their divorce, and then down and down. Many attempts at suicide, now a successful one."[383]

Two months before Rosemary's suicide, Feather married a young artist named Larry Greenberg in Bernardine's backyard. A small gathering of guests enjoyed a joyous reception with a hippie vibe and a bit of glamour lent by the hostess. Rosemary did not attend.

The young couple legally changed their last name to Greeneye, which they thought was more apt for their free-spirited identities, and began their travels together. First, they went to New Mexico to live in a commune. When Feather was five months pregnant, she decided it was time they go to Europe. In September 1970, while they were in Switzerland, Feather gave birth to their son, Daja. Traveling in a Volkswagen camper, they made their way to Spain where Feather received a package from Bernardine. It included the books *Our-Story My-Story Your-Story His-Story* and *Be Here Now* by the American spiritual leader and guru Baba Ram Dass, born Richard Alpert, who earlier in his career had researched and promoted the use of LSD with Timothy Leary.

These books had been recommended to Bernardine by author and musician, Laura Huxley, and deeply inspired Feather. The Greeneyes continued their travels through Morocco, Tunisia, Greece, Yugoslavia,

---

[383] David E. Lilienthal, *Journals of David E. Lilienthal, Volume Seven: Unfinished Business 1968-1981*, (New York, Harper and Row: 1983), page 156.

Turkey, Iraq, and Iran, and, in 1973, arrived in Dharamshala, India, home of the Dalai Lama. Here, Feather began her study of Buddhism in earnest, deciding to become a Buddhist nun. At the end of a retreat that both Feather and Larry were attending, Larry suffered a psychotic break, which led to his return to Los Angeles and a lifelong struggle with schizophrenia. Feather continued with her studies, becoming a nun and taking the new name of Thubten Wongmo.

Here, history began to repeat itself. To pursue her new life as a nun, Wongmo placed Daja with a large Tibetan family where he was mistreated and struggled to understand what had happened to his family. When Daja was six, Wongmo entered him into the Kopan Monastery in Nepal, where he was ordained as a monk and given the name Thubten Wangchuk. Wongmo believed she was protecting Daja from a life of temptation and dissipation, the life her mother had lived and she herself had flirted with as a fledgling alcoholic in college at Occidental. But at the monastery, young monks were poorly treated and fed, and Daja, the only non-Asian there, was taunted and teased because of the fairness of his skin and the color of his eyes. He rarely saw his mother, although she did take him to see her beloved Dena in Beverly Hills for a brief visit in 1980. Then it was back to the monastery in Nepal.

Determined to escape life as a monk, Daja pretended to have broken his vow of celibacy and was expelled from the monastery when he was seventeen years old. He fled to the US, reaching out to distant relatives, learning English, and eventually graduating from Brandeis University. He went on to become a prominent activist for Tibet and publish a memoir of his unusual life. Sadly, his fate would ultimately resemble that of his grandmother Rosemary when he took his own life in 2010 after struggling for years with issues of abandonment and depression. As of this writing, Wongmo is Bernardine's only surviving descendent.

In 1979, Bernardine was invited to be one of the thirty-two "witnesses" in Warren Beatty's 1981 film, *Reds*, an Oscar-winning story about John Reed, the journalist and Communist activist who wrote *Ten Days That*

Shook the World about Russia's 1917 October Revolution, and his wife, Louise Bryant, a journalist and suffragist. The witnesses provided their personal recollections of that historic time and historic couple. *Ten Days* had been published in 1919 by Bernardine's brother-in-law's publishing house, Boni & Liveright, and she knew of its contents early on. She also came to know Louise in the late 1920s in France. Reed had died in 1920, and Bryant went on to marry diplomat William Bullitt Jr. Although Bernardine never appeared on-screen, her voice was heard, and it is likely that her narration in the film is about Bryant. Her friends, the writers Henry Miller and Rebecca West, were two of the witnesses who did appear on-screen.

Up against stiff competition with *Chariots of Fire*, *Raiders of the Lost Ark*, *On Golden Pond*, *Arthur*, and *The French Lieutenant's Woman*, *Reds* was nominated for twelve Oscars and won three: Warren Beatty for best director, Maureen Stapleton for best supporting actress in her role as Emma Goldman, and Vittorio Storaro for best cinematography.

A month before the awards ceremony in 1982, Bernardine attended a book reading in Los Angeles. Tamara Hovey, the daughter of the editor of the *Metropolitan Magazine*, a publication featured in the movie *Reds*, spoke about the rerelease of her own biography of John Reed. Bernardine was the only "witness" from the film to attend the reading.[384] She no longer commanded the same presence as she had during her youth and middle-age years. By then, her voice could not carry well because of emphysema. Yet she enjoyed her impromptu talk in the bookstore about her participation in the film and her experiences in Chicago and New York, which intersected with many of those in the movie.

Bernardine returned home from the bookstore, took a nap, and never woke up. She was six months away from her eighty-sixth birthday.

It's easy to ask, what if? What if Bernardine had not left Rosemary in boarding schools and had provided a steady presence in her life? What

384 Sheila McHugh Simmons, "Bernardine Szold-Fritz" book proposal and "Chronology of Bernardine Szold's Life, undated in the 1980s, courtesy of Bernardine Szold Fritz's family, page 2.

if Rosemary had had a father rather than being abandoned by her biological father and three stepfathers? What if Rosemary had not succumbed to depression and alcoholism and had kept Feather by her side until she went off to college? What if Feather had had a supportive father who was engaged in her life? What if Feather had not become a Buddhist nun and Larry had not developed schizophrenia? Given all these struggles and sad outcomes, it certainly seems like Bernardine's rebellious marriage at the age of eighteen to Albert Carver unknowingly started a vicious cycle of abandonment that ended with Daja's suicide.

But that conclusion might play into a sexist trope in which the mother is blamed for everything that goes wrong with her children and descendants. Bernardine's achievements, had they been accomplished by a man, would never have been diminished by her parenting style. It's in that light that she should be remembered. After all, she broke into acting and journalism at a time when women couldn't vote. She had the courage to divorce when her marriages fell apart, even if it meant living without financial security. She was a romantic and an arts aficionado, an adventurer and a loyal friend. She felt most content bringing talented and extraordinary people together during a time of incredible innovation and accomplishment in the arts. Throughout all of this, Bernardine dared to take risks and tried her best not to care what others thought. Yet to say Bernardine was a woman ahead of her time would be to minimize the hope and free spirit of the early twentieth century in the United States, Europe, and China, and her role in all of that.

Bernardine was exactly where she belonged.

APPENDIX I

TIMELINE OF BERNARDINE'S LIFE

1896: Bernardine is born in Peoria, Illinois, on August 4 to Hermine and Jacob Szold.

1913: Bernardine moves to New York City to study at the American Academy of Dramatic Arts. On a visit home to Gary, Indiana, in November, she elopes with her boyfriend, Indiana lawyer Albert E. Carver, and drops out of school.

1915: Bernardine and Albert's daughter, Rosemary Carver, is born in Gary, Indiana.

1916: Bernardine joins Chicago's Little Theatre until it closes the following year.

1917: Bernardine and Albert Carver divorce, and after a long custody battle, Bernardine is awarded sole custody of Rosemary.

1918: Bernardine befriends a young writer named Glenway Wescott a year before he meets advertising executive Monroe Wheeler.

1919: Bernardine marries Hiram "Hi" Simons, a poet from Wisconsin. The two live in a converted garage on Huron near Rush in Chicago.

1920: Bernardine starts writing for the *Chicago Evening Post*.

1921: Bernardine and Hi Simons divorce. She moves to New York City to be closer to her friends Glenway Wescott and Monroe Wheeler. In New York, she finds work as a reporter for the *New York Daily News*, thanks to Vincent "Jimmy" Sheean, a stranger who offers to take her clippings to the city editor when she can't get past the office boy. She and Sheean become lifelong friends. She sends Rosemary to a boarding school in Upstate New York.

1923: Bernardine marries literary agent Otto Liveright and continues to write for the *New York Daily News*. Rosemary remains at her boarding school in Upstate New York.

1925: Bernardine and Otto Liveright divorce. The week their divorce is finalized, Bernardine and Rosemary move to Paris, again to be near Wescott and Wheeler. She is a guest of fashion designer Elsa Schiaparelli, whom she had known in New York. Rosemary is soon enrolled at Chateau Mont-Choisi, a boarding school in Lausanne, Switzerland. Bernardine pens a couple of letters from Paris for a new magazine called the *New Yorker*.

1927: Bernardine moves to Cambridge, England, to study literature as an "out student." She has an unconsummated affair with writer Milton Waldman, who is married to Hazel Guggenheim.

1927: Bernardine embarks on a fourteen-month trip through Europe, the Middle East, and Asia with her friend, American heiress Barbara Harrison.

1928: Bernardine and Barbara arrive in Shanghai and meet an American silver broker named Chester Fritz. Chester is captivated by Bernardine's stories of Paris and the writers and artists she's befriended there. But Bernardine doesn't think much about Chester after she and Barbara continue on to Peking and back to Paris through the Soviet Union.

1929: Bernardine is back in Paris and receives a stream of telegrams from Chester, imploring her to return to Shanghai and marry him. After encouragement from her friends in Paris, she accepts Chester's proposal and returns to China. Rosemary remains at her Swiss boarding school.

1930: Rosemary visits Bernardine and Chester in Shanghai, the only trip she will make to China.

1931: Bernardine meets Chinese intellectuals Hu Shih and Lin Yutang and starts a salon at her home at 62 Route de Boissezon in Shanghai's French Concession.

1933: Bernardine founds the International Arts Theatre when she and Russian Jewish composer Aaron Avshalomoff produce the ballet *The Soul of the Ch'in*.

1934: Bernardine and Chester spend ten months sailing to Southeast Asia, the Middle East, Europe, and the United States. Bernardine endures a breast cancer scare and has a mastectomy in Vienna. Bernardine's sister Aline Sholes sails to Shanghai with Bernardine and Chester at the end of the year.

1935: The International Arts Theatre produces plays, ballets, lectures, and fine arts exhibitions. *Lady Precious Stream* is the IAT's largest production to date. Emily Hahn and her sister Helen Asbury arrive in Shanghai.

1936: Aline returns to the United States. Anna May Wong visits China for the first time and befriends Bernardine in Shanghai. The International Arts Theatre hosts a reception for Charlie Chaplin and Paulette Goddard.

1937: The International Arts Theatre throws its first fundraising gala, which it hopes will become an annual event. Rosemary falls ill in New York and Bernardine returns to the United States to take care of her. The Japanese military bombs Shanghai in August. Bernardine settles in Los Angeles with Rosemary, never to return to Shanghai.

1938: Chester joins Bernardine and Rosemary in Los Angeles. Rosemary is cast in a play at the Pasadena Playhouse. Bernardine reconnects there with friends Arthur Rubinstein, Anna May Wong, and Victor Sassoon. Bernardine becomes involves in Jewish causes to bring attention to the Nazi atrocities in Europe and to promote a Jewish state.

1939: Bernardine's salon is back in order at her home while Chester prepares to leave for Shanghai to close up his business. Bernardine and Anna May Wong reunite with Lin Yutang when he visits Los Angeles.

1940: Chester sails back to Shanghai. Bernardine uses her salon to raise money for the China relief effort, including a reception for the female pilot Lee Ya-ching.

1941: Japan escalates World War II and takes all of Shanghai in December. Chester is soon interned in a POW camp along with other foreigners in Shanghai. Bernardine becomes a part of the Hollywood social circuit. Rosemary marries writer John Meston.

1944: Chester is released from his POW camp and is allowed to sail back to the United States. Bernardine files for divorce in California.

1945: Chester sails back to Shanghai. He later remarries a Russian divorcée and single mother and retires in Switzerland. Rosemary and her husband, John Meston, have a baby daughter they name Feather. Rosemary's drinking becomes increasingly problematic.

1946: Bernardine adapts and produces the play, *Angels Amongst Us*, with Jarmila Marton for the Pasadena Playhouse. Rosemary becomes Katharine Hepburn's stand-in for the film, *The Sea of Grass*.

1954: Rosemary and John Meston divorce.

1956: Bernardine participates in LSD experiments with Aldous Huxley at Gerald Heard's home. Rosemary's drinking increases, and her mental health continues to deteriorate with bouts of depression and suicide attempts.

1969: Feather Meston marries artist Larry Greenberg at a ceremony in Bernardine's backyard. Rosemary does not attend and commits suicide two months later.

1970: Feather and Larry travel around Europe. Feather gives birth to their son, Daja, when they are in Switzerland.

1973: Feather, Larry, and Daja arrive in Dharamshala, India, to attend a Buddhist retreat. Larry suffers a psychotic break-down, and Feather becomes an ordained Buddhist nun, changing her name to Wongmo. Larry returns to the United States and Wongmo stays in India, placing Daja with a Tibetan family while she pursues her new religion.

1976: Wongmo sends Daja to the Kopan Monastery in Nepal to become an ordained monk.

1979: Bernardine is invited to become a "witness" in the Warren Beatty film *Reds*. She doesn't appear on film, but her narration is heard.

1980: Bernardine meets her grandson, Daja, for the first and only time when Wongmo brings him to Los Angeles for a quick visit.

1981: *Reds* premiers and is nominated for twelve Academy Awards.

1982: Bernardine dies from complications of emphysema six months before her eighty-sixth birthday.

2010: Daja commits suicide.

APPENDIX II

LIST OF CHARACTERS IN ALPHABETICAL ORDER

Harold Acton: British writer and member of the Bright Young Things in 1920s London

Helen Asbury: Sister of Emily Hahn

Aaron Avshalomoff: Russian Jewish composer and Swiss-trained physician

Pearl S. Buck: American author, missionary, and daughter of missionaries in China

Albert Carver: Bernardine's first husband

Rosemary Carver: Bernardine's only child

Helene Chang: Also known as Chang Tsing-ying or Helen Chang, dress designer and daughter of Chinese stateman Chang Ching-chiang

Chang Hsueh-liang: Ruler of northeast China, also known as the Young Marshal or Peter Chang, and perhaps romantically involved with Edda Mussolini

Chiang Kai-shek: Leader of the Chinese Nationalist government, also known as the Generalissimo and the husband of Soong Mei-ling

Count Galeazzo Ciano: Husband of Edda Mussolini, son-in-law of Benito Mussolini, and the Italian consul of Shanghai

Jean Cocteau: French writer, artist, and critic who lived on the French Riviera near Barbara Harrison

Miguel Covarrubias: Mexican American illustrator whose work was often published in *Vanity Fair* and the *New Yorker*

Anne Walter Fearn: American physician who moved to China in the late 1800s

Chester Fritz: Bernardine's fourth and last husband

Emily Hahn: Nicknamed Mickey, an American author and decades-long reporter for the *New Yorker*, as well as the one-time common-law wife of Sinmay Zau

Walter Harris: British foreign correspondent of the *London Times* and travel companion of Barbara Harrison and Bernardine

Barbara Harrison: American heiress and sister-in-law of Glenway Wescott

Shih-I Hsiung: The first Chinese playwright to achieve success on London's West End with *Lady Precious Stream*

Hu Shih: One of pre-revolutionary China's most renowned educators and intellectuals

László Hudec: Hungarian architect who designed many Art Deco buildings in Shanghai, including the Park Hotel and Grand Theatre

Madame Wellington Koo: Also known as Oei Hui-lan, she was married to one of China's most distinguished diplomats in the first half of the twentieth century and was a fashion icon to young women in 1930s Shanghai

Daisy Kwok: Boutique owner with Helene Chang, actress at the International Arts Theatre, and a member of the Wing On department store family

Lee Ya-ching: China's first female pilot and a Hollywood actress

Li Ch'ing-mai: Chinese diplomat and son of late-Qing dynasty statesman Li Hung-chang

Liao Tsui-feng: Also known as Hong, cookbook author and wife of Lin Yutang

David Lilienthal: Bernardine's cousin and the chairman of the Tennessee Valley Authority and the Atomic Energy Commission

Lin Yutang: One of pre-revolutionary China's most renowned intellectuals and writers

Otto Liveright: Bernardine's third husband

George Platt Lynes: American photographer and romantic partner of Monroe Wheeler

J. P. McEvoy: American cartoonist and one-time Shanghai resident

Mei Lanfang: China's premier Peking opera star during the first half of the twentieth century

Max Mohr: German physician, friend of D. H. Lawrence, and amongst the first Jewish refugees to arrive in Shanghai from Nazi Germany

Edda Mussolini: Daughter of the Italian Generalissimo and wife of Count Geleazzo Ciano, the Italian consul in Shanghai

Virginia Armstrong Oakes: Also known as Vanya Oakes, an American writer, librarian, and dancer

Rosa Rolanda: American dancer, author, and wife of Miguel Covarrubias

Victor Sassoon: Baghdadi Jewish real estate tycoon and owner of the Cathay Hotel

George Bernard Shaw: Irish playwright who traveled to Shanghai in 1933

Sheng Peiyu: Wife of Sinmay Zau

Hi Simons: Bernardine's second husband

Soong Ai-ling: Charlie Soong's eldest daughter, the wife of Chinese finance minister H.H. Kung, and part of the famous Soong sisters, including Soong Ching-ling and Soong Mei-ling

Charlie Soong: Chinese financier and father of the Soong sisters

Soong Ching-ling: Wife of Sun Yat-sen, daughter of Charlie Soong, and part of the famous Soong sisters with Soong Ai-ling and Soong Mei-ling

Soong Mei-ling: Wife of Chiang Kai-shek, daughter of Charlie Soong, and part of the famous Soong sisters with Soong Ai-ling and Soong Ching-ling

T. F. Soong: Theater aficionado and banker, not related to the famous Soong family

Simon Harcourt-Smith: British diplomat, writer, and son of Cecil Harcourt-Smith, the director of the Victoria and Albert Museum in London

Sun Fo: A son of Sun Yat-sen and patron of the International Arts Theatre

Sun Yat-sen: Father of modern China and first president of the newly formed Republic of China in 1912, as well as the husband of Soong Ching-ling

Mai-Mai Sze: Artist, actress, and life companion of designer Irene Sharaff

Tong Ying: Shanghai actress and star of the International Art Theatre's production of *Lady Precious Stream*

Carl Van Vechten: American photographer who took Bernardine's, Rosemary's, and Anna May Wong's portraits among many others

Glenway Wescott: American author and life partner of Monroe Wheeler

Monroe Wheeler: Publisher, art curator, and life partner of Glenway Wescott, as well as one-time partner of George Platt Lynes

Anna May Wong: The most renowned Asian American actress in twentieth-century Hollywood and in Europe

S. Y. Wong: Petroleum executive and co-director of the International Arts Theatre's production of *Lady Precious Stream*

Butterfly Wu: Chinese silent movie star and patron of the International Arts Theatre

Sinmay Zau: Chinese poet and publisher, as well as husband of Sheng Peiyu and common-law husband of Emily Hahn

BIBLIOGRAPHY

Books

Acton, Harold. *Memoirs of an Aesthete*. London: Faber and Faber, 2008.

Acton, Harold. *Peonies and Ponies*. Harmondsworth: Penguin Books, 1950.

Baum, Vicki. *Shanghai '37*. New York: Oxford University Press, 1986.

Bevan, Paul. *A Modern Miscellany: Shanghai Cartoon Artists, Shao Xunmei's Circle and the Travels of Jack Chen, 1926–1938*. Leiden: Brill, 2018.

Bevan, Paul. *'Intoxicating Shanghai'—An Urban Montage: Art and Literature in Pictorial Magazines During Shanghai's Jazz Age*. Leiden: Brill, 2020.

Bien, Gloria. *Baudelaire in China: A Study in Literary Reception*. Newark, Delaware: The University of Delaware Press, 2013.

Bilski, Emily D. and Emily Braun. *Jewish Women and Their Salons: The Power of Conversation*. New Haven: Yale University Press, 2005.

Breitman, Richard and Allan J. Lichtman. *FDR and the Jews*. Cambridge, Massachusetts: Belknap Press, 2013.

Carter, James. *Champions Day: The End of Old Shanghai.* New York: W.W. Norton, 2020.

Chadourne, Marc, translated by Harry Block and illustrated by Miguel Covarrubias. *China.* New York: Covici-Friede Publishers, 1932.

Chang, Jung. *Big Sister, Little Sister, Red Sister: Three Women at the Heart of Twentieth-Century China.* New York: Alfred A. Knopf, 2019.

Chang, Nelson, Laurence Chang and Song Luxia. *The Zhangs from Nanxun: A One Hundred and Fifty Year Chronicle of a Chinese Family.* Denver: CF Press, 2010.

Chao, Isabel Sun and Claire Chao. *Remembering Shanghai: A Memoir of Socialites, Scholars and Scoundrels.* Honolulu: Plum Brook, 2017.

Ciano, Edda Mussolini and Albert Zarca, translated by Eileen Finletter. *My Truth.* New York: William Morrow, 1976.

Cuthbertson, Ken. *Nobody Said Not to Go: The Life, Loves, and Adventures of Emily Hahn.* New York: Faber and Faber, 1998.

Davies, Peter Ho. *The Fortunes.* New York: Houghton Mifflin Harcourt, 2016.

De Courcy, Anne. *Chanel's Riviera: Life, Love and the Struggle for Survival on the Côte d'Azur, 1930–1944.* London: Weidenfeld & Nicolson, 2019.

Denton, Kirk A. and Michel Hockx, eds. *Literary Societies of Republican China.* Lanham, Maryland: Lexington Books, 2008.

Dong, Stella. *Shanghai: The Rise and Fall of a Decadent City.* New York: Harper Perennial, 2001.

Earnshaw, Graham. *Tales of Old Shanghai: The Glorious Past of China's Greatest City.* Hong Kong: Earnshaw Books, 2012.

Field, Andrew David. *Shanghai's Dancing World: Cabaret Culture and Urban Politics, 1919–1954.* Hong Kong: The Chinese University Press, 2010.

Ford, Hugh. *Published in Paris: American and British Writers, Printers, and Publishers in Paris, 1920–1939.* New York: Macmillan, 1975.

Fritz, Chester and Dan Rylance. *Ever Westward to the Far East: The Story of Chester Fritz*. Grand Forks, North Dakota: Office of the President, University of North Dakota, 1982.

Goldman, Emma and Shawn P. Wilbur. *Anarchy and the Sex Question: Essays on Women and Emancipation, 1896–1926*. Oakland: PM Press, 2016.

Gonzales, Vernadette Vicuña. *Empire's Mistress, Starring Isabel Rosario Cooper*. Durham North Carolina: Duke University Press, 2021.

Gordon, Irene, Lucile M. Golson, Leon Katz, Douglas Cooper, and Ellen B. Hirschland. *Four Americans in Paris: The Collections of Gertrude Stein and Her Family*. New York: The Museum of Modern Art, 1970.

Grescoe, Taras. *Shanghai Grand: Forbidden Love and International Intrigue in a Doomed World*. New York: St. Martin's Press, 2016.

Hahn, Emily. *China to Me*. Philadelphia: Blakiston, 1944.

Hahn, Emily. *Mr. Pan*. New York: Doubleday, 1942.

Hahn, Emily. *With Naked Foot*. New York: Bantam Books, 1951.

Hemingway, Ernest. *The Torrents of Spring*. New York: Scribner, 2004.

Hibbard, Peter. *The Bund Shanghai: China Faces West*. Hong Kong: Odyssey Books, 2007.

Hsia, C.T. *The Classic Chinese Novel: A Critical Introduction*. New York: Columbia University Press, 1968.

Hsu, Tony S. *Chasing the Modern: The Twentieth-Century Life of Poet Xu Zhimo*. California: Cambridge Rivers Press, 2017.

Koe, Amanda Lee. *Delayed Rays of a Star*. London: Bloomsbury, 2019.

Kramer, Dale. *Chicago Renaissance: The Literary Life in the Midwest, 1900–1930*. New York: Appleton-Century, 1966.

Kurth, Peter. *Isadora: A Sensational Life*. New York: Back Bay Books, 2002.

Kwok, Daisy, Tess Johnston and Graham Earnshaw. *Shanghai Daisy.* Hong Kong: Earnshaw Books, 2019.

Liew, Sonny. *Warm Night, Deathless Days: The Life of Georgette Chen.* Singapore: National Gallery Singapore, 2014.

Lilienthal, David E. *The Journals of David E. Lilienthal, Volume One: The TVA Years, 1939–1945.* New York: Harper and Row, 1964.

Lilienthal, David E. *The Journals of David E. Lilienthal, Volume Seven: Unfinished Business, 1968–1981.* New York: Harper and Row, 1983.

Lim, Shirley Jennifer. *Anna May Wong: Performing the Modern.* Philadelphia: Temple University Press, 2019.

Lin, Yutang. *My Country and My People.* New York: Reynal & Hitchcock, 1935.

Marchetti, Gina. *Romance and the "Yellow Peril": Race, Sex, and Discursive Strategies in Hollywood Fiction.* Berkeley and Los Angeles: University of California Press, 1993.

Messmer, Matthias. *Jewish Wayfarers in Modern China: Tragedy and Splendor.* Lanham, Maryland: Lexington Books, 2012.

Meston, Daja Wangchuk. *Comes the Peace: My Journey to Forgiveness.* New York: Free Press, 2007.

Meyer, Maisie J. *Shanghai's Baghdadi Jews: A Collection of Biographical Reflections.* Hong Kong: Blacksmith Books, 2015.

Meyers, Jeffrey. *Hemingway: A Biography.* London: Macmillan, 1985.

Morris, Roy Jr. *Gertrude Stein Has Arrived: The Homecoming of a Literary Legend.* Baltimore: Johns Hopkins University Press, 2019.

Neuse, Steven M. *David E. Lilienthal: The Journey of an American Liberal.* Knoxville: University of Tennessee Press, 1997.

Pan, Lynn. *Shanghai Style: Art and Design Between the Wars.* South San Francisco: Long River Press, 2008.

Pohorilenko, Anatole and James Crump. *When We Were Three: The Travel Albums of George Platt Lynes, Monroe Wheeler, and Glenway Wescott, 1925–1935*. Santa Fe: Arena Editions, 1998.

Rifkind, Donna. *The Sun and Her Stars: Salka Viertel and Hitler's Exiles in the Golden Age of Hollywood*. New York: Other Press, 2020.

Rosco, Jerry. *Glenway Wescott Personally: A Biography*. Madison: The University of Wisconsin Press, 2002.

Sassoon, Joseph. *The Sassoons: The Great Global Merchants and the Making of an Empire*. New York: Pantheon Books, 2022.

Shai, Aron. *Zhang Xueliang: The General Who Never Fought*. London: Palgrave Macmillan, 2012.

Stein, Gertrude and Maira Kalman. *The Autobiography of Alice B. Toklas*. New York: Penguin Press, 2020.

Wakeman, Frederic Jr. *Policing Shanghai, 1927–1937*. Berkeley and Los Angeles: University of California Press, 1995.

Wakeman, Frederic Jr. and Wen-hsin Yeh, eds. *Shanghai Sojourners*. Berkeley: Institute of East Asian Studies, 1992.

Wei, Betty Peh-T'i. *Old Shanghai*. Hong Kong: Oxford University Press, 1993.

Weston, Edward. *The Daybooks of Edward Weston*, volume 2, edited by Nancy Newhall. Millerton, New York: Aperture Press, 1973.

Williams, Adriana. *Covarrubias*. Austin: University of Texas Press, 1994.

Williams, Adriana and Rosa Covarrubias. *The China I Knew*. San Francisco: Protean Press, 2005.

Yeh, Diana. *The Happy Hsiungs: Performing China and the Struggle for Modernity*. Hong Kong: Hong Kong University Press, 2014.

Zheng, Da. *Shih-I Hsiung: A Glorious Showman*. Vancouver: Fairleigh Dickinson University Press, 2020.

Journals, Magazines, and Newspapers

"17 Day Trial is Ended: Valparaiso Judge Refuses to Give Well Known Gary Woman Divorce of Allow Fees for Her Attorney," *The Times* (Munster, Indiana), July 18, 1917, page 6.

A Guide to Catholic Shanghai, T'ou-Se-We Press, 1937.

"A Peking Letter: A Record Number of Shanghai Visitors: The Social Whirl: Receptions, Races and Polo," *The North-China Herald*, October 5, 1932, page 39.

Along Bubbling Well Road, Historic Shanghai, World Congress on Art Deco, 2015.

"Anna May Wong Honors Chinese Author at Tea," *Los Angeles Times*, November 26, 1939, page 64.

"Anna May Wong: Hostess At Studio To Head Of Chinese Mint," *South China Morning Post*, November 22, 1937, page 7.

Argus, "From Paris," *The New Yorker*, July 11, 1925, page 24.

Around the Race Course, Historic Shanghai, World Congress on Art Deco, 2015.

Art Deco in the French Concession, Historic Shanghai, World Congress on Art Deco, 2015.

Bartlett, Maxine. "China Relief Council to Give Pickfair Party: Arrangements Made at Garden Tea on Mrs. Bernardine Fritz's Estate," *Los Angeles Times*, September 14, 1940, page 9.

"Beg Your Pardon," *Chicago Daily Tribune*, June 28, 1929, page 31.

"Bernard Szold, Former Actor is Dead at Age 66," *The Baytown Sun*, Baytown, Texas, November 16, 1960, page 16.

"Bernardine Szold Weds in China; Is Ex-Chicagoan," *Chicago Daily Tribune*, June 26, 1929, page 3.

Bevan, Paul. "The Impact of the Work of Miguel Covarrubias," *Anales del Instituto de Investigaciones Estéticas*, Universidad Nacional Autónoma de México, volumen XLII, suplemento al número 116, March 6, 2020, pages 42–43.

"Bowl Artists to Be Feted at Supper," *Los Angeles Times*, August 9, 1939, page 28.

Brent, Brandy. "Carrousel," *Los Angeles Times*, January 7, 1949, page 33.

"Charlie Chaplin Due in Shanghai Tomorrow: Reception For U.S. Film Star Planned by I.A.T.," *The China Press*, March 8, 1936, page 9.

"Chester Fritzes Leave Tuesday," *The China Press*, February 34, 1934, page 11.

"China Music Group to Hear Composer," *Los Angeles Times*, January 8, 1949, page 19.

"China Woman Flyer Here: Declares Her Nation Will Fight on Until Japanese Driven Out," *Los Angeles Times*, April 20, 1939, page A1.

"Danish Journalist Taking Theater As I.A.T. Topic," *The China Press*, November 15, 1936, page 7.

Dayton Herald, December 13, 1934, page 16.

"Divorce Suits Filed," *Los Angeles Times*, March 18, 1944, page 8.

"Dutch to See Java Ballet," *Los Angeles Times*, January 17, 1940, page 25.

"Dr. Fearn to Open I.A.T. Meet: 'Shanghai, In the Good Old Days' Will Be Her Subject," *The China Press*, November 20, 1935, page 11.

"Finnish Benefit Prelude," *Los Angeles Daily News*, December 21, 1939, page 14.

Fisher, W.E., Jr. "Avshalomoff Work Goes To Workshop: Comely Actresses, Bad Warriors Practice at I.A.T," *The China Press*, November 1, 1936, page 9.

"Former Mrs. Liveright Weds: Bernardine Szold Married in China to Chester Fritz," *New York Herald Tribune*, June 20, 1929, page 23.

Fortune Magazine, Volume XI, Number 1, January 1935.

French, Paul. "How White Russians ballet dancers sparked a revolution in China's dance scene," *South China Morning Post*, November 1, 2020.

"Fritz Declares Silver Embargo Possible Here: Local Broker Discusses Money Questions Before Rotary Club Meeting," *The China Press*, July 22, 1932, page 9.

Haden-Guest, Anthony. "In Tussle Over Will, Mistress's Family Takes a Bite Out of NYU," *Daily Beast*, April 14, 2017, https://www.thedailybeast.com/in-tussle-over-will-mistresss-family-takes-a-bite-out-of-nyu.

Haga, Chuck. "A footnote in the story of Chester Fritz," *Grand Forks Herald*, May 17, 2011.

Harpman, Julia. "Miss Ederle's Motto is 'Dover or Bust,'" *The Brooklyn Daily Eagle*, July 27, 1926, page 20.

Harpman, Julia. "Mrs. Weaver Never to Face Trial in Coburn Murder," *New York Daily News*, January 13, 1924, pages 2, 46.

Hendrix, Kathleen. "The Conversion of Feather Meston," *Los Angeles Times*, May 28, 1975, page 65.

"Here and There," *The North-China Herald*, October 11, 1933, page 79.

"Here and There," *The North-China Herald*, August 7, 1935, page 247.

"Here and There," *The North-China Herald*, October 30, 1935, page 219.

"Here and There," *The North-China Herald*, November 13, 1935, page 299.

"Here and There," *The North-China Herald*, March 18, 1936, page 511.

"Here and There," *The North-China Herald*, April 1, 1936, page 43.

"Here and There," *The North-China Herald*, July 22, 1936, page 171.

"Here and There," *The North-China Herald*, August 5, 1936, page 255.

Hutt, Jonathan. "Monstre Sacré: The Decadent World of Sinmay Zau," *China Heritage Quarterly*, The Australian National University, no. 22, June 2010.

"I.A.T. Activities Are Planned For Members," *The China Press*, March 11, 1936, page 4.

"I.A.T. Announces Concert Of Interest," *The China Press*, September 5, 1935, page 4.

"I.A.T. Announces Full Program For Future: Interesting Subjects Are Planned For Members," *The China Press*, January 19, 1936, page 11.

"I.A.T. Has Heavy Fall Program: Activities Planned For All Departments and Dates Are Set," *The China Press*, November 8, 1936, page 11.

"I.A.T. Has Summer Plans: Exhibition Of Japanese Paintings To Be Held For Two Weeks," *The China Press*, June 5, 1937, page 4.

"I.A.T. Has Unusual Ball Plans: Masquerade Will Be Bohemian, Informal Entertainment," *The China Press*, June 10, 1937, page 4.

"I.A.T. Hear Talk By Stylist: Sally Dickason Brings Review of Latest Fashions Here," *The China Press*, March 12, 1936, page 4.

"I.A.T. Housewarming Party Is Scheduled: Fortune-Telling Will Be Theme Of Meeting," *The China Press*, November 27, 1935, page 11.

"I.A.T. Opening Sunday For Art Enthusiasts," *The China Press*, March 1, 1936, page 11.

"I.A.T. Plan Russian Evening Next Week," *The China Press*, February 17, 1937, page 4.

"I.A.T. Plans To Give Shakespearean Dramas," *The China Press*, March 22, 1936, page 9.

"I.A.T. Schedules Two Events For This Week," *The China Press*, November 17, 1936, page 11.

"I.A.T. Shakespeare," *The North-China Herald*, June 3, 1936, page 409.

"I.A.T. Studio Hums With Activity Daily: New Projects Launched, Dreams Come True," *The China Press*, May 12, 1935, page 11.

"I.A.T.S. To Give Play At Carlton: 'Lady Precious Stream' To Be Produced On June 25 and 26," *The China Press*, June 8, 1935, page 11.

"I.A.T. To Hear Famous Japanese Poet Monday," *The China Press*, October 20, 1935, page 11.

"I.A.T. To Hold Reception For Two: Honorees Will Tell Of Own Experiences," *The China Press*, June 4, 1935, page 5.

"I.A.T. To Present Ballet: Patrons, Patronesses For Production Announced," *The China Daily*, December 13, 1936, page 11.

"I.A.T. To Present Ballet Based on Chinese Drama: Elaborate Interpretation of Old Stage Play Will Be Combined With Music of Shanghai Composer; To Be Presented in December," *The China Press*, August 25, 1936, page 9.

"I.A.T.S. To Sponsor Benefit: June 12 Charity Ball To Have Patronage Of Prominent Women," *The China Press*, May 18, 1935, page 11.

"I.A.T.G. To Sponsor Reception For Two: Miss White, Miss Hahn To Share Honors," *The China Press*, April 12, 1935.

Krause, Allen. Untitled, *The China Press*, June 30, 1935, page C1.

Landon, Gabrielle. "Hollywood Folk Hold Open House," *Los Angeles Times*, September 20, 1936, page 76.

Li, Ming. "Li Ming Tells How Plan For Majestic Purchase Was First Formed: Historic Tea Party At Majestic's 'Last' Fling Was Scene Of Its Origin," *The China Press*, April 16, 1931, page 13.

Lilienthal, Nancy. "Bernardine," unpublished paper written at UCLA, 1976.

Lin, Yutang. "Lady Precious Stream," *The China Critic*, Vol. X, No. 1, July 4, 1935, pages 17–18.

"Little Theater To Have First Lecture: Dr. Mohr To Be First To Speak To I.A.T. Group," *The China Press*, April 7, 1935, page 11.

"Local Passengers In Ship On Fire: All Now Safely Taken Off," *The North-China Herald*, April 8, 1936, page 60.

"'Lysistrata' Is Next Dramatic I.A.T. Offering: Naughty, Naughty Play Will Open At Stroke Of Midnight," *The China Press*, October 26, 1935, page 9.

"Many Hear Discussion At Studio: Pros and Cons Of Birth Control Viewed At I.A.T. Meeting," *The China Press*, May 7, 1935, page 11.

"Many Notables Leave On President Hoover: Lin Yutang, Mrs. Fritz, Mrs. Cheng Lin On Board," *The China Press*, August 11, 1936, page 9.

McClurg, Jocelyn. "An Experimental Life," *The Hartford Courant*, November 16, 1997.

"Men and Events," *The China Weekly Review*, July 13, 1929, page 312.

"Men and Events," *The China Weekly Review*, September 30, 1930, page 70.

"Men and Events," *The China Weekly Review*, April 25, 1931, page 280.

"Men and Events," *The China Weekly Review*, March 10, 1934, page 72.

"Messenger from Orient: China Looks to Hollywood for Theater Director," *Los Angeles Times*, August 31, 1936, page A3.

"Miss Carver Honored," *Los Angeles Times*, January 16, 1938, page 72.

"Miss Szold Wed in China," *The New York Times*, June 20, 1929, page 25.

"Mrs. Carver Loses Her Fight for Decree," *The Times* (Munster, Indiana), August 14, 1917, page 5.

"Mrs. Sholes Writes Of Sea Saga: Former Resident Tells Of Being Rescued From Tricolor," *The China Press*, May 30, 1936, page 9.

"Mrs. Sieroty to Hostess Tea in Honor of Mrs. F. J. Myers," *Los Angeles Daily News*, August 9, 1946, page 18.

"New China Tiffin Club in U.S.A.," *The North-China Herald*, August 16, 1939, page 303.

"New Playgoer Group Will Stage Series," *Los Angeles Daily News*, August 23, 1939, page 12.

"Notes and Comment, The Talk of the Town," *The New Yorker*, August 23, 1969, page 19.

"Other Festivities," *Los Angeles Times*, November 9, 1951, page 51.

"Other Guests," *Los Angeles Times*, January 29, 1939, page 75.

"Patronesses For Play Are Announced Here: I.A.T. Producing Greek Comedy Three Night," *The China Press*, December 8, 1935, page 11.

"Photographs By Weston Now Seen At IAT: Fine Exhibit Of Camera Studies Being Displayed; Collection Not Complete," *The China Press*, May 30, 1935, page 3.

"P.P.A. Ball Will Be Held Soon: I.A.T. Fixing Program For Annual Party To Be At Paramount," *The China Press*, October 26, 1935.

Provines, June. "Front Views and Profiles," *Chicago Daily Tribune*, November 9, 1934, page 21.

"Sally Dickason Will Speak At I.A.T. Soon: Date Is Postponed A Day Later For Speaker," *The China Press*, March 7, 1936, page 11.

"Shanghai's Latest Theatre: Completion of the Capitol Building: A Theatre with Five Floors of Offices Superimposed," *The North-China Herald*, February 11, 1928, page 219.

"Shijie ji 30 niandai Shanghai X xiaolong 'shendi' jintian X lai ni ting ge liu zhu shi," Xinmin wenbao, May 18, 2015.

Simmons, Sheila McHugh. "Witnesses," *Chicago Tribune*, March 25, 1982, page 36.

Slater, Jack. "A Conversation With…Social Catalyst of a Golden Era," *Los Angeles Times*, June 12, 1977, pages J1 and 8.

Soong, Stephen C., translated by Diana Yu. "My Father and Maugham," *Renditions*, Autumn, 1974, pages 81–90.

"Soundings," *Los Angeles Times*, January 5, 1943, page 33.

"Sponsors Set Date for Music Fete," *Los Angeles Times*, November 28, 1941, page 42.

St. Louis Post-Dispatch, May 25, 1938, page 36.

"Sunday Barbecue Given at Encino," *Los Angeles Evening Citizen News*, August 5, 1940, page 6.

Szold, Bernardine. "About Town," *New York Daily News*, June 29, 1924, page 69.

Szold, Bernardine. "About Town," *New York Daily News*, July 6, 1924, page 169.

Szold, Bernardine. "Carroll French Portrays 'Ultra' Setting at Drama League Course," *Chicago Evening Post*, August 19, 1920.

Szold, Bernardine. "Talons of Movie Hawks Snatch at Women in Homes and Trains," *New York Daily News*, May 18, 1923, page 3.

"Talks to Be Heard by Hollywood C. of C. Women," *Los Angeles Times*, February 9, 1945, page 13.

"Tea to Fete Concert Sponsors," *Los Angeles Times*, December 20, 1939, page 25.

"The Birth Control League," *The China Critic*, Volume 3, Number 21, May 22, 1930, page 1.

The Bund and Beyond, Historic Shanghai, World Congress on Art Deco Shanghai, 2015.

"Times Society Editor Finds World's Greatest Actress: Interviews Divine Sarah Bernhardt in Murky Gary Spot," *The Times* (Munster, Indiana), November 6, 1917, pages 1–2.

"Together Again: Rosemary Carver Greeted by Rutherford on Return," *Los Angeles Times*, September 1, 1939, page 35.

Tucson Daily Citizen, October 2, 1959, page 38.

"Viennese Cabaret To Be Featured At I.A.T: Second Part Of Program To Have Local Scenes," *The China Press*, February 9, 1936, page 11.

"Visitors Comment On Coming I.A.T. Play," *The China Press*, November 17, 1935, page 11.

Von Blon, Katherine. "Inspirational Note Heard in 'Angels Amongst Us,'" *Los Angeles Times*, May 10, 1946, page 15.

Wong, Anna May. "Anna May Wong Finds Shanghai Life Glamorous: Speed And Noise Rival Those Of Large American Cities, She Thinks," *New York Herald Tribune*, June 14, 1936, page B2.

Wong, Anna May. "Anna May Wong Recalls Shanghai's Enthusiastic Reception: Crowds Besieged Her On Arrival From Yokohama To Visit China 1st Time," *New York Herald Tribune*, May 31, 1936, pages B2, 6.

Zheng, Da. "Lady Precious Stream Returns Home," Journal of the Royal Asiatic Society China, Volume 76, Number 1, 2016, pages 19–39.

Zheng, Da. "Performing Transposition: *Lady Precious Stream* on Broadway," *New England Theatre Journal*, Volume 26, 2015, pages 83–102.

Archives

Bernardine Szold Fritz Correspondence. Yale Collection of American Literature, Beinecke Rare Book and Manuscript Library:

YCAL MSS 134 Box 52 f. 735

YCAL MSS 134 Box 103 f. 1571

YCAL MSS 134 Box 103 f. 1572

YCAL MSS 134 Box 103 f. 1573

YCAL MSS 134 Box 103 f. 1574

YCAL MSS 134 Box 103 f. 1575

YCAL MSS 134 Box 105 f. 1595

YCAL MSS 134 Box 105 f. 1597

YCAL MSS 134 Box 105 f. 1598

YCAL MSS 134 Box 125 f. 1933

YCAL MSS 134 Box 126 f. 1967

YCAL MSS 134 Box 126 f. 1968

YCAL MSS 134 Box 126 f. 1969

YCAL MSS 134 Box 126 f. 1970

YCAL MSS 134 Box 126 f. 1971

YCAL MSS 134 Box 126 f. 1972

YCAL MSS 134 Box 403 f. 4201

YCAL MSS 134 Box 405 f. 4293

YCAL MSS 134 Box 413 f. 4491

YCAL MSS 134 Box 413 f. 4492

YCAL MSS 134 Box 413 f. 4493

YCAL MSS 134 Box 413 f. 4494

YCAL MSS 544 Box 1 Buck, Pearl

YCAL MSS 544 Box 1 Chang, CC

YCAL MSS 544 Box 1 Chang, Rosalind

YCAL MSS 544 Box 1 Feibleman, James

YCAL MSS 544 Box 2 Gunther, John

YCAL MSS 544 Box 2 Hays, Aline D.

YCAL MSS 544 Box 2 Huston, John

YCAL MSS 544 Box 2 Koo, Madame Wellington

YCAL MSS 544 Box 2 Lee, Ya Ching

YCAL MSS 544 Box 3 Lin, Tsing Y.

YCAL MSS 544 Box 3 Lin, Yu Tang

YCAL MSS 544 Box 3 Liveright, Otto

YCAL MSS 544 Box 3 Lynes, George Platt

YCAL MSS 544 Box 3 Mei Lan-fang

YCAL MSS 544 Box 4 Sassoon, Lady and Sir Victor

YCAL MSS 544 Box 4 Shih Hu

YCAL MSS 544 Box 4 Smith, Helen (Hahn)

YCAL MSS 544 Box 4 Sze Mai-Mai

YCAL MSS 544 Box 4 Sze Szeming

YCAL MSS 544 Box 5 Wheeler, Monroe

YCAL MSS 544 Box 5 Wong, Anna May

YCAL MSS 544 Box 5 Woo, B.Y.

YCAL MSS 544 Box 5 Yen, Hilda

YCAL MSS 544 Box 5 Zau, Sinmay

Newbery Library

Box 13, Folder 611a, undated letter from Sherwood Anderson to Bernardine Szold Fritz, 1929.

Box 13, Folder 611a, undated letter from Sherwood Anderson to Bernardine Szold Fritz, 1929.

Box 13, Folder 611a, undated letter from Sherwood Anderson to Bernardine Szold Fritz, 1929.

Box 13, Folder 611a, undated letter from Sherwood Anderson to Bernardine Szold Fritz, 1929.

Box 13, Folder 611a, undated letter from Sherwood Anderson to Bernardine Szold Fritz, 1929.

Box 13, Folder 611a, undated letter from Sherwood Anderson to Bernardine Szold Fritz, 1927.

Box 9, Folder 394-396, letter from Sherwood Anderson to Otto Liveright, June 8, 1923.

Box 9, Folder 394-396, telegram from Sherwood and Elizabeth Anderson to Otto Liveright, December 25, 1922.

Box 23, Folder 1179-1180, letter from Otto Liveright to Sherwood Anderson, October 30, 1923.

Box 23, Folder 1179-1180, letter from Otto Liveright to Sherwood Anderson, September 18, 1923.

Box 23, Folder 1179-1180, letter from Otto Liveright to Sherwood Anderson, July 24, 1923.

Box 23, Folder 1179-1180, letter from Otto Liveright to Sherwood Anderson, July 6, 1923.

Box 23, Folder 1179-1180, letter from Otto Liveright to Sherwood Anderson, January 23, 1924.

Box 23, Folder 1179-1180, letter from Otto Liveright to Sherwood Anderson, December 12, 1923.

Box 23, Folder 1179-1180, letter from Otto Liveright to Sherwood Anderson, November 27, 1923.

Box 23, Folder 1179-1180, letter from Otto Liveright to Sherwood Anderson, November 17, 1923.

Box 23, Folder 1179-1180, letter from Otto Liveright to Sherwood Anderson, May 26, 1924.

Box 23, Folder 1179-1180, letter from Otto Liveright to Sherwood Anderson, March 18, 1924.

Box 23, Folder 1179-1180, letter from Otto Liveright to Sherwood Anderson, October 22, 1924.

Box 23, Folder 1179-1180, letter from Otto Liveright to Sherwood Anderson, July 14, 1924.

Box 23, Folder 1179-1180, letter from Otto Liveright to Sherwood Anderson, November 20, 1924.

Box 23, Folder 1179-1180, letter from Otto Liveright to Sherwood Anderson, undated.

Box 23, Folder 1179-1180, letter from Otto Liveright to Sherwood Anderson, November 12, 1924.

Box 23, Folder 1179-1180, letter from Otto Liveright to Sherwood Anderson, March 19, 1925.

Box 23, Folder 1179-1180, letter from Otto Liveright to Sherwood Anderson, March 4, 1925.

Box 23, Folder 1179-1180, letter from Otto Liveright to Sherwood Anderson, February 20, 1925.

Box 23, Folder 1179-1180, letter from Otto Liveright to Sherwood Anderson, November 29, 1924.

Box 23, Folder 1179-1180, letter from Otto Liveright to Sherwood Anderson, June 15, 1925.

Box 23, Folder 1179-1180, letter from Otto Liveright to Sherwood Anderson, June 4, 1925.

Box 23, Folder 1179-1180, letter from Otto Liveright to Sherwood Anderson, April 29, 1925.

Box 23, Folder 1179-1180, letter from Otto Liveright to Sherwood Anderson, April 6, 1925.

Box 29, Folder 1516, letter from Bernardine Szold Fritz to Sherwood Anderson, undated, 1929.

Box 29, Folder 1516, notes from Bernardine Szold Fritz, undated.

Southern Methodist University Archives

Sassoon, Victor. Personal Diary, April 25, 1935.

Sassoon, Victor. Personal Diary, May 4, 1935.

Sassoon, Victor. Personal Diary, May 5, 1935.

University of Arizona

Collection of the Edward Western Archive, Center for Creative Photography, Scrapbook A.

Public records

Carver, Rosemary Catharine. Birth Certificate, Indiana State Board of Health, January 26, 1915.

Fritz, Bernardine Szold and Chester William Fritz. Certificate of Marriage, American Consular Service, Dairen, Manchuria, June 18, 1929.

Fritz, Bernardine Szold. SS Conte de Savoia, List of United States Citizens, from Villefranche, France to New York, arriving August 29, 1934.

Fritz, Bernardine Szold. SS Mariposa Voyage, List of Manifest In-Bound Passengers for Immigration Officials at Port of Arrival, from Los Angeles to Honolulu, December 13, 1934.

Fritz, Bernardine Szold. SS Empress of Japan, List of Manifest of Outward-Bound Passengers for Immigration Officials at Point of Departure, Honolulu Bound for Manila, Philippine Islands, December 21, 1934.

Fritz, Bernardine Szold. Dollar Steam Lines, SS President Hoover, Oath to Inward Passenger List, August 1936.

Unpublished articles, letters, and documents

Fritz, Bernardine Szold. "A Certain Client," unpublished manuscript courtesy of her family.

Fritz, Bernardine Szold. "Across Siberia," unpublished manuscript courtesy of her family.

Fritz, Bernardine Szold. "At a Chinese Restaurant One Night," unpublished manuscript courtesy of her family.

Fritz, Bernardine Szold. "Baroness de Pidol," unpublished manuscript courtesy of her family.

Fritz, Bernardine Szold. "Bernardine to Chester," unpublished and unsent letter courtesy of her family.

Fritz, Bernardine Szold. "Bernhardt," unpublished manuscript courtesy of her family.

Fritz, Bernardine Szold. "Fania Marinoff and Carl Van Vechten," unpublished manuscript courtesy of her family.

Fritz, Bernardine Szold. "I Am Not a Public Speaker," unpublished manuscript courtesy of her family.

Fritz, Bernardine Szold. "It Seems Like Yesterday," unpublished manuscript courtesy of her family.

Fritz, Bernardine Szold. Letter to her parents from Shanghai, undated 1932, courtesy of her family.

Fritz, Bernardine Szold. Letter to Rosemary from Shanghai, undated, courtesy of her family.

Fritz, Bernardine Szold. Letter to the Consul General of the USSR pertaining to her inquiries about Jack Chen, January 29, 1973, courtesy of her family.

Fritz, Bernardine Szold. "Marriage in Dairen," unpublished manuscript courtesy of her family.

Fritz, Bernardine Szold. "Pidol Stories," unpublished manuscript courtesy of her family.

Fritz, Bernardine Szold. "Shanghai," unpublished manuscript courtesy of her family.

Fritz, Bernardine Szold. "The Trans-Siberian Railroad to Marriage in Dairen," unpublished manuscript courtesy of her family.

Fritz, Bernardine Szold. "Tsingyi," unpublished manuscript courtesy of her family.

International Arts Center. "IAT Ball" program, June 18, 1937.

Levin, Lawrence. Transcription of interviews with Bernardine Szold Fritz, September 25, 1976, courtesy of Bernardine Szold Fritz's family.

Lin, Yutang and family Christmas card, undated, courtesy of Bernardine Szold Fritz's family.

"Narrative of Bernardine Szold's Life," courtesy of David Szanton.

Simmons, Sheila McHugh. "Bernardine Szold-Fritz" book proposal and "Chronology of Bernardine Szold's Life," undated in the 1980s, courtesy of Bernardine Szold Fritz's family.

Simons, Hiram Austin. "Maybe the Dead, too, Grieve," unpublished poem, Union Pier, Michigan, September 17, 1922, courtesy of Bernardine Szold Fritz's family.

"Special Chinese Programme," Shanghai Municipal Orchestra, Grand Theatre, May 21, 1933.

Szold, Bernardine. "Less About Hemingway," unpublished manuscript courtesy of her family.

Szold, Bernardine. "Lin Yu-tang," unpublished manuscript courtesy of her family.

Szold, Bernardine. "Lin Yu Tang. Shanghai 1935," unpublished manuscript courtesy of her family.

Szold, Bernardine. "Trouble in China," unpublished manuscript courtesy of her family.

Szold, Bernardine. "Why Britannia Rules the Wave," unpublished manuscript courtesy of her family.

ACKNOWLEDGMENTS

My first thank you goes to Christine Tan for giving me the idea in the first place. Some people have pen pals; Christine sends books. Over the years, she has sent me a number of non-fiction narratives that all pointed to Bernardine in one way or another. I wanted to know more.

Bernardine's granddaughter, Wongmo, graciously answered my questions, sent memories of Bernardine and fabulous photos, and gave me the names of her cousins, Nancy Lilienthal and David Szanton.

Nancy and David, this book is for you. I feel that ten thousand thank yous can never encompass the warmth, generosity, friendship, and trust you have given and placed in me to tell Bernardine's story. It seems like decades ago when you each opened your homes and showed me the hundreds of pages Bernardine had written over the decades. Nancy, I have so enjoyed our phone conversations and our many laughs over the years. I could talk to you forever! Thank you also for fact-checking and editing the manuscript. And for the lebkuchen!

Also, thank you, Jan Gilden, Dorrie Iten, and Liza McKee.

And not in any special order: Erica Lyons, Christina Matula, Peter Gordon, Wendy Nelson Tokunaga, Jennifer Barron, Xixuan Collins, Xu Xi, Spencer Wise, Brittany Drehobl, Christine Stone, Tiffany Hawk, Yi Shun Lai, Heather Diamond, Nicki Chen, Dorie Jones Yang, Jocelyn Eikenburg, Kara Tatelbaum, Scott Spacek, Cheryl Postrozny, Jyl

Bonaguro, Jean Iversen, Yelena Lembersky, Gloria Chao, Leslie Lindsay, Karen Fang, Yunxiang Gao, Sunny Stalter-Pace, and Elizabeth Rynecki.

Robin Hemley, thank you for mentoring me through this book project. I am truly honored!

Carrie Pestritto, thank you for your enthusiasm from the very start and for paving the way for Bernardine to glitter on the page. I will always be grateful!

Claire Chao, thank you for whipping my elevator pitch into shape and for all of your support. Tina Kanagaratnam, thank you for your countless e-mails and fact-checking on a moment's notice. Patrick Cranley, thank you for the blueprint of Bernardine's Shanghai apartment. Katya Knyazeva, Paul Bevan, and Paul French, thank you for answering my many questions and sharing your immense knowledge of Old Shanghai.

Librarians are crucial to any book research, and Jessica Tubis at the Beinecke Rare Book and Manuscript Library at Yale patiently took my many orders for digital scans of material in a number of different archives. Also to Emily Grover at Indiana University's Lilly Library. Thank you to the librarians at Chicago's Newberry Library. And at the Hinsdale Public Library, Martha Kennedy, Karen Kleckner Keefe, and Cynthia Dieden.

Rocky May, Ruben Pena, and the D181 teachers who chose to teach remotely the first full year of the pandemic: thank you for doing such a fabulous job and keeping my kids fully engaged and eager to learn each day. I accomplished what would have taken five years to write in just the 2020–21 school year, all thanks to you!

Katie Gee Salisbury, thank you for sharing letters, photos, and publishing stories. I'm so glad Bernardine, Anna May, Fania, and Carl brought us together!

A huge thanks to Roxy Szal at *Ms.* magazine and Boris Dralyuk, formerly at the *Los Angeles Review of Books*, for publishing essays taken from this book. To Jordan Blumetti and Zibby Media for publishing an essay about Bernardine in *Moms Don't Have Time to Write*.

Alicia Brooks, I will always remember the day I queried you and when you phoned me—all within a matter of hours! I couldn't have written a more exciting ending to this story. Your excitement about Bernardine and your faith in my writing have made this five-year journey seem easy! I am so honored to be represented by you and to be a part of the JVNLA family.

Debra Englander, you have been a dream editor. If Bernardine were around today, I am certain she would ask you and Alicia to lunch. It has also been an honor and privilege to work with so many others at Post Hill Press. Heather King, Caitlyn Limbaugh, Alana Mills, and Ashlyn Inman, thank you for all your help with marketing, the cover art, and the production schedule. Madeline Sturgeon, thank you for your wonderful copyedits and fact-checking. Olivia Brothers and Sara Stickney, thank you for starting the publicity process so early and for all your help. Morgan Simpson, thank you for a wonderful proofread. And thank you Conroy Accord for the stunning cover.

To Mary Emerson, thank you for taking me to Shanghai in the first place.

And last but not least, my family! Thanks to my mom for driving me to and from the Phoenix airport for my daytrips to visit Nancy and David in California. Thank you to my kids, Martin, Rachel, and Jake for letting me be your mom. Lots of love to Theresa. And to Tom, for this life as a writer, for being my best book promoter, and the most loving partner ever.